P9-DGV-272

The Reluctant Economist

Perspectives on Economics, Economic History, and Demography

Where is rapid economic growth taking us? Why has its spread throughout the world been so limited? What are the causes of the great twentieth-century advance in life expectancy and of the revolution in childbearing that is bringing fertility worldwide to near replacement levels? Have free markets been the source of human improvement?

Economics provides a start on these questions, but only a start, argues economist Richard A. Easterlin. To answer them calls for merging economics with concepts and data from other social sciences and with quantitative and qualitative history. Easterlin demonstrates this approach in seeking answers to these and other questions about world or American experience in the last two centuries, drawing on economics, demography, sociology, history, and psychology. The opening chapter gives an autobiographical account of the evolution of this approach and why Easterlin is a "reluctant economist."

Richard A. Easterlin is University Professor and Professor of Economics in the Department of Economics at the University of Southern California. He is a member of the National Academy of Sciences, past president of the Population Association of America and Economic History Association, a Fellow of the American Academy of Arts and Sciences, and a former Guggenheim Fellow. He is editor of *Happiness in Economics* (2002) and author or coauthor of *Growth Triumphant: The 21st Century in Historical Perspective* (1996), *The Fertility Revolution* (1985), *Birth and Fortune: The Impact of Numbers on Personal Welfare* (1980, 2nd ed. 1987), and *Population, Labor Force, and Long Swings in Economic Growth: The American Experience* (1968).

The Reluctant Economist

Perspectives on Economics, Economic History, and Demography

RICHARD A. EASTERLIN
University of Southern California

CAMBRIDGE UNIVERSITY PRESS
Cambridge, New York, Melbourne, Madrid, Cape Town, Singapore, São Paulo

Cambridge University Press
40 West 20th Street, New York, NY 10011-4211, USA

www.cambridge.org
Information on this title: www.cambridge.org/9780521829748

First published 2004
Reprinted 2005

Printed in the United States of America

A catalog record for this publication is available from the British Library.

Library of Congress Cataloging in Publication Data

Easterlin, Richard A., 1926–
The reluctant economist : perspectives on economics,
economic history and demography /
Richard A. Easterlin. – 1st ed.
p. cm.
Includes bibliographical references and index.
ISBN 0-521-82974-7 (cloth)
1. Economic history. 2. Demography
3. United States – Economics conditions. I. Title.
HC26.E17 2004
330 – dc21 2003055136

ISBN-13 978-0-521-82974-8 hardback
ISBN-10 0-521-82974-7 hardback

For

my mentors

in economics, Moses Abramovitz and Simon Kuznets
in economic history, Daniel Thorner
in demography, John D. Durand and Dorothy Swaine Thomas
in social psychology, Elliot Aronson

Contents

List of Tables and Figures

TABLES

FIGURES

Preface

Everyday life for most Europeans and Americans today is a world apart from human experience throughout most of history. Our predecessors worried about having enough food to get through winter; we lose sleep over putting children through college. In the past, scarcely one child in two lived to be an adult; today almost all do. Families formerly had as many children as they could; now they intentionally limit their childbearing. At one time people lived almost entirely in the countryside; these days they are mainly concentrated in cities and their environs.

This book is my attempt to make sense of these and other striking changes in human experience – some of them worldwide in scope, others largely or wholly American. The first substantive chapter (Chapter 3) reviews the recent history of modern economic growth, which is a phenomenon that in the past two centuries has totally transformed material living levels in such areas as food, clothing, and shelter. The unabated rate of advance raises the question of where economic growth is taking us. Some would answer in terms of a happy postmaterialistic society; others would stress presumed adverse effects such as environmental deterioration or globalization. I suggest that there is no movement toward higher nonmaterialistic ends, nor are the "bads" commonly attributed to economic growth the principal concern. Rather, the fundamental problem is systemic: that we are caught up in a process of unending economic growth. This process drives us onward toward ends that are not rationally considered, but instilled by economic growth itself.

The improvement in our material lives is the result of potent new production technologies that have been developed and adopted over the last two centuries. The limited spread of the new technologies in the world before 1950 leads to the problem addressed next, Why Isn't the Whole World Developed? (Chapter 4). The answer, I suggest, is the enormous diversity in the capabilities of societies worldwide to master the new production methods when they first came into use – a diversity in cultural heritage that is proxied in the chapter by international disparities in schooling. The root of such differences must be sought in the markedly different histories of the various cultural areas of the world in the centuries preceding the appearance of the new techniques.

Where they were adopted, the new techniques transformed material living levels, the work people did, and where they lived. The forces underlying the new concentration of population in and around cities, and the tendency for urbanization in free market economies to occur in wavelike movements is the subject of Chapter 5. Though the possible relevance of these wavelike movements to contemporary experience is frequently overlooked or dismissed, I suggest that today's developing world may replicate the longer-term fluctuations common to the historical experience of the developed countries.

What of the modern improvement in survival prospects that has so greatly lengthened life expectancy? Is it simply a byproduct of economic growth? My answer is no, that this "Mortality Revolution" was a development analogous to, but largely independent from, the "Industrial Revolution," building on an evolving technology of disease control due to advancing biomedical knowledge. This growth in biomedical knowledge lagged the breakthroughs in physical knowledge underlying the onset of modern economic growth; hence, the Mortality Revolution occurred later than the Industrial Revolution (Chapter 6). Free market institutions, which are much credited these days for promoting economic growth, were of dubious help in fostering the marked advance in life expectancy. Instead, governmental intervention was essential. Such intervention has successfully raised life expectancy noticeably even in the absence of economic growth. A view of human improvement that weights life expectancy equally with economic advance leads to a more noncommittal view of the benevolence of free markets than currently prevails among economists and economic historians (Chapter 7). The free market bias of these disciplines, I believe, reflects their preoccupation with "industrial" revolutions and ignorance of the "mortality" revolutions whose significance for human improvement deserves much greater recognition.

There has been a "fertility revolution," too. In the past most parents throughout the world had as many children as they could. Now in many places the number of offspring per household is approaching two or less as parents deliberately limit family size. To understand the radical change in childbearing behavior requires more than the version of the "economics of fertility" that has become standard in the economics literature. In Chapter 8, I try to expand this theory to encompass a much broader range of fertility behavior in time and space. Chapter 9 applies this expanded version specifically to two less developed areas to find out why, after centuries of unregulated fertility, parents began to control family size deliberately. The single most important reason suggested by the analysis is the unprecedented improvement in the survival prospects of infants and children brought about by the Mortality Revolution.

In the remainder of the book, the geographic scope narrows to American experience. Two centuries ago, Thomas Malthus speculated that the rapid population growth engendered by America's plentiful supply of land would eventually be brought to an end by higher mortality as diminishing returns to labor set in. Malthus was wrong; the adjustment of population to farming opportunities in the United States was largely accomplished by farm parents' voluntarily reducing childbearing. This was brought about by their concern for giving their children a "proper" start in life. The adjustment of family fertility to the environment, and the interplay between economic and population change in the settlement of farming areas of the United States, are the subjects of Chapter 10.

Chapter 11 turns to the most vivid feature of America's post–World War II demographic history: the remarkable baby boom and subsequent baby bust characterized by economist Bert Hickman as "perhaps the most unexpected and remarkable social feature of the time" (Hickman 1960, 161–2). This fertility swing was the result of a sharp break after 1940 with the labor supply and demand conditions that had prevailed throughout most of U.S. history. The pronounced twists in age structure caused by the fertility swing have had widespread ramifications affecting women's labor market entry; divorce, crime, and suicide rates among the young; and political alienation (Chapter 11).

College enrollments in business rose dramatically in the 1970s and 1980s. Why? The usual explanation offered by economists of career decisions, changes in relative wages, does not fit. Rather, young people's preferences changed. They started to place greater importance on money as a life goal and saw business training as a means to that end. The relation between prices and preferences in choice of career and the causes of preference change are taken up in Chapter 12. This essay illustrates especially the possibilities of using subjective data on motives, attitudes, and expectations in economic research.

Chapters 3 through 12 exemplify my approach to research. A common element of these chapters is an attempt to understand historical experience, whether in the large, or more narrowly focused in time and place. Quantitative time series help define the problem and test hypotheses. In the absence of such data, the historical record is prone to loose and dubious interpretation. But quantitative time series must be supplemented by qualitative history. The analyses here turn most often to economic history and demographic history, my particular areas of specialization, but, according to the dictates of the topic, they draw also on the literatures of the history of education, history of science, social history, history of public health, and American colonial history. Such work provides qualitative facts, insights into cause and effect, and suggestions as to motives and feelings of the agents. As indicated in Chapter 2, I deplore the mainstream economics paradigm that rejects subjective testimony, whether qualitative, as in historical documents, or quantitative, as in social science surveys. It seems to me that an economics model is fundamentally flawed if its presumed cause–effect relations are belied by the subjective testimony of the agents. Psychologists listen carefully to what people say about their motives, feelings, and expectations and learn from such information. Perhaps it is time for economists to do the same.

I stress here the importance of an historical approach because it is so rare in economics these days. Prodigious efforts by national and international agencies have generated an enormous and valuable body of quantitative data in recent decades that provides a basis for international point-of-time (cross-sectional) comparisons on topics such as those examined here. But to my mind, such cross-sectional work can be used as a basis for inferring historical change if, and only if, the cross-sectional relationships among countries are consistent with individual countries' historical experience. I am puzzled by the lack of a disciplinary stricture to this effect. On many of the topics studied here, the simple cross-sectional relations currently observed among countries – for example, between economic growth, on the one hand, and life expectancy, fertility, and school enrollment, on the other – are not replicated in historical experience (Easterlin 2000).

The evolution of my approach to research is described in the autobiographical essay of Chapter 1. I have already mentioned as elements the use of history, quantitative measurement, and subjective testimony. Reference by an economist to the central role of economic theory is perhaps superfluous. Economic theory is important in providing basic concepts and a framework suggesting possible cause–effect relations. Economic theory often needs to be supplemented, however, by conceptual and empirical work in other disciplines, and several of the present chapters draw substantially on work in demography, sociology, and psychology – disciplines I have found especially relevant to the subjects covered here.

Chapters 2 and 3 are previously unpublished. Chapter 7 has been expanded to include material on less developed countries deleted as irrelevant by the editors of the economic history journal in which it first appeared. The other published articles were originally prepared for specialized audiences and appeared in journals in economics, economic development, economic history, and demography – half since 1995; the rest, in the 1970s and 1980s. I have shortened and reworked many of them to focus on the substantive analysis and results and to make them more accessible to the nonspecialist. Those interested in technical details should consult the originals. The chapters are grouped into three parts – economics, economic history, and demography – but the reader will find that there is considerable overlap among the divisions.

Research is much like solving a mystery, that is, assembling and sifting through various clues and speculating on how they might fit together to explain the problem posed. I have enjoyed working on the mysteries investigated here and learned something along the way. I hope the reader shares some of my enjoyment and learns a little, too.

Richard A. Easterlin
Pasadena, California
May 2002

Acknowledgments

This work has benefited from the ideas and help of many, especially my wife, Eileen M. Crimmins. Other family members have contributed in numerous ways – Andy, Barb, Carolyn, Dan, Matt, Molly, Nancy, Peter, and Sue. I owe much to my mentors to whom this volume is dedicated.

Dennis Ahlburg, Lance E. Davis, Diane J. Macunovich, Christine M. Schaeffer, and Morton O. Schapiro have invariably contributed both ideas and encouragement. As always, the technical assistance of Donna Hokoda Ebata has been invaluable. I have been fortunate, too, to have had many excellent research assistants over the years such as, most recently, Paul Rivera, Pouyan Mashayekh-Ahangarani, and John Worth.

Colleagues or former colleagues at the University of Southern California who have been especially helpful are Nauro B. Campos, Richard H. Day, David Heer, Timur Kuran, Bentley MacLeod, Vai-Lam Mui, Jeffrey B. Nugent, James Robinson, and Yasuhiko Saito; at the University of Pennsylvania, George Alter, Gretchen A. Condran, James C. Davis, Vartan C. Gregorian, Alan Heston, Frank R. Lichtenberg, Almarin Phillips, Robert A. Pollak, Samuel H. Preston, Robert Summers, Etienne van de Walle, Michael L. Wachter, and Michael Waldman. Individual chapters here have especially benefited from suggestions by Lee J. Alston, Tommy Bengtsson, Ed Diener, William Easterly, Stanley Engerman, Robert E. Gallman, Robert Higgs, Alex Inkeles, Dean T. Jamison, Dirk van de Kaa, Arie Kapteyn, Allen C. Kelley, Kenneth Land, Ronald D. Lee, Joel Mokyr, Larry Neal, Douglass C. North, Warren Sanderson, Roger S. Schofield, and E. A. Wrigley.

I am grateful for permission to publish the following articles in revised form:

"The Story of a Reluctant Economist," *The American Economist* 41:2 (Fall 1997), 1–11; "Why Isn't the Whole World Developed?" *Journal of Economic History*, XLI:1 (March 1981), 1–19; "Locational Restructuring and Financial Crisis," *Structural Change and Economic Dynamics* 11 (2000), 129–38; "Industrial Revolution and Mortality Revolution: Two of a Kind?" *Journal of Evolutionary Economics* 5:4 (1995), 393–408; "How Beneficent Is the Market? A Look at the Modern History of Mortality," *European Review of Economic History* 3:3 (December 1999), 257–94; "An Economic Framework for Fertility Analysis," *Studies in Family Planning* 6:3 (March 1975), 54–63; "New Perspectives on the Demographic Transition: A Theoretical and Empirical Analysis of an Indian State, 1951–1975," (with Eileen M. Crimmins, Shireen J. Jejeebhoy, and K. Srinivasan), *Economic Development and Cultural Change* 32:2 (January 1984), 227–53; "Population Change and Farm Settlement in the Northern United States," *Journal of Economic History* 36:1 (March 1976), 45–75; "What Will 1984 Be Like? Socioeconomic Implications of the Recent Twists in Age Structure," *Demography* 15:4 (November 1978), 397–432; "Preferences and Prices in Choice of Career: The Switch to Business, 1972–87," *Journal of Economic Behavior and Organization* 27:1 (June 1995), 1–34.

PART ONE

ECONOMICS

1

The Reluctant Economist

At the start, I was not a reluctant economist. In the beginning, economics opened up a new and exciting world. The Keynesian Revolution was in full swing, and, like other graduate students, I was caught up in it. The message of the revolution was new and straightforward: major depressions and staggering unemployment were not an inevitable evil of industrialization. Societies had the power, through public policy, to prevent and correct serious depressions.

Today, disillusionment with this message prevails among economists. But it is not the supposed failures of the Keynesian Revolution that have made me into a reluctant economist. As a teacher of introductory macroeconomics, I am still more Keynesian than many of my colleagues. Rather, my reluctance stems at bottom from a research philosophy forged at the hands of my mentor, Simon Kuznets, the third Nobel laureate in economics. In a field in which theory was and is the be-all and end-all of intellectual accomplishment, Kuznets taught that the touchstone of achievement is insight into empirical reality. Moreover, other social sciences might, along with economic theory, contribute to one's understanding. But it was some years before firsthand experience was to make me a true believer in this philosophy.

STUMBLING INTO ECONOMICS

Most young people today have a good idea of their prospective work, for only about 6 percent of high school seniors respond "don't know" when

Reprinted with permission in revised form from "The Story of a Reluctant Economist," *The American Economist* 41, 2 (1997): 1–11.

asked about the kind of work they think they will be doing at age 30 (Bachman, Johnston, and O'Malley 1988). My problem was that I liked almost everything I studied – English, math, history, foreign languages – perhaps natural sciences least, but even that was not bad. I loved to read. Throughout my high school years, I was one of today's 6 percent "don't knows." What followed was a trial-and-error period that led me eventually to economics. The path to economics was shaped partly by my own choices but even more by factors beyond my control.

The economist's simple model of occupational choice puts the expected rate of return in the forefront of job choice. To my generation, reared in the shadow of the Great Depression, income, along with job security, was certainly very important. In my personal experience, however, this factor operated largely to rule out certain choices – most notably, a youthful ambition to be a writer. But it left open a wide array of options that appeared to my limited knowledge to have quite acceptable returns.

In fact, it was events beyond my control, along with personal preferences, that led me eventually to economics. The external events were World War II and the veterans' policies associated therewith plus an extremely strong post–World War II labor market for young adults. Eventually, I was to realize that these forces had greatly influenced not only my personal experience but also that of my entire generation. This revelation provided powerful confirmation for me of the insights that economics could provide into the forces shaping our lives and led eventually to a research monograph on population and labor force that put the post–World War II boom in the perspective of past long-term swings in the economy (Easterlin 1968b).

In retrospect, these exogenous forces provided a succession of opportunities for me to explore my interests, and personal preferences determined where I ended up. I tried engineering and didn't like it. I served as a deck officer on a U.S. Navy cruiser and didn't like it – although such a career had, in fact, been a serious aspiration when I was young. I tried farming and didn't like it. I studied for an M.B.A. degree (the combination of business and engineering was said to reap a rich material harvest) and didn't like it. But, incidental to the M.B.A. program, I was required to take economics. Finally, I discovered what I liked.

Why did economics appeal? The analytical requirements suited my abilities, but this also was true of engineering and business. In the case of economics, however, these analytical abilities were being applied to the solution of urgent social problems. My interest in these problems had been nurtured by outstanding history and English teachers in a large New York City public high school. Though I didn't realize it at the time, these teachers were forming interests that would help shape my future.

Should economic models of occupational choice give more attention to preferences? Some may say no, that individual differences in tastes are irrelevant or tend to cancel out and economics is interested only in group behavior. But this argument ignores factors that systematically affect group preferences as a whole. It seems likely that more systematic attention to the study of preference formation might enhance the economic modeling of occupational choice – a point to which I will return later.

One lesson from my own job search process may be noted, namely, failed choices sometimes turn out well. The romantic aspirations of my youth to go to the Naval Academy were frustrated by my having failed a physical exam. A subsequent opportunity to experience Navy life, thanks to participation in the Naval Reserve Officers Training Program, demonstrated that it was not for me. Moreover, if I had had my way, when I did go into the Navy, I would have been an aircraft carrier pilot. My father, however, forced me to opt for engineering. If I'd had free choice, I probably wouldn't be writing this now. Similarly, when I decided to study for an M.B.A. degree, my first choice was Harvard. Had I gone there instead of being turned down, I would probably never have made it into economics. At the University of Pennsylvania, where the economics department was in the business school, the switch from an M.B.A. to economics was easy. I'm not sure what this means for the theory of revealed preference, but it certainly seems that *ex post* outcomes can be much different from those envisaged *ex ante*. On the basis of my personal labor market experience, the knowledge on which choices are based is highly imperfect, and much "learning-by-doing" goes into finding the niche where one's abilities and interests match job requirements.

SOCIALIZATION IN ECONOMICS

Economic theory, as taught to undergraduate and graduate students, starts from the assumption that preferences are given and unchanging. Yet a little reflection by economists on their graduate school experience should disabuse them of this notion. Graduate school not only teaches subject matter but also the *values* of the economics profession – what are the important subjects of economic research, what is the status hierarchy of the profession, which individuals are the proper role models. Graduate training *is* indoctrination (Klamer and Colander 1990; Reder 1999).

But I will consider subject matter first because that is what sold me on economics. I have already noted the heady atmosphere when I was a graduate student at Penn. There were the superb theoretical synopses and extensions of Keynes in Lawrence Klein's *Keynesian Revolution*, J.R. Hicks's LM-IS analysis, and Paul Samuelson's multiplier–accelerator interactions. There were the insights into the Great Depression in Alvin Hansen's *Fiscal Policy and Business Cycles*, the classic statement of the secular stagnation thesis. Moreover, as an economics instructor, I had the opportunity to choose and use Paul Samuelson's brilliant introductory text when it first appeared. By comparison with the other texts then available, it was a quantum advance. It brought the Keynesian Revolution into the classroom. And it was written in a way that conveyed persuasively to students the new power of economics to work for human betterment.

I was much taken with economic theory – micro as well as macro – partly by the pure pleasure of theory for theory's sake and partly by the new conception it provided of the world about me. I was lucky to be taught by two excellent microeconomic theorists of the time, Sidney Weintraub and Melvin Reder (the latter regrettably moved on from Penn after only one year).

Two major methodological innovations in economics were under way at this time: the development of mathematical economics and econometrics. Penn, however, was then a backwater of graduate economics study, and my exposure to these subjects was limited. Moreover, I had had a full dose of math in undergraduate engineering, and though I liked it and did well, its novelty had worn off. So the mathematical feature of these developments did not appeal to me as it did to some from nonengineering backgrounds.

Penn's graduate program included some courses not usually offered in graduate economics. One such course, of which I was a beneficiary, was in central banking and was offered by a gifted teacher and practitioner, Karl Bopp. This course helped teach me respect for historical perspective (it traced the evolution of central banking in Western Europe and the

United States). Bopp was a vice president at the Federal Reserve Bank of Philadelphia, and the course also provided his insider's knowledge of contemporary monetary policy, complementing my understanding of fiscal policy developed in Keynesian analysis.

And then there was my education in the values of the economics profession. I learned that economics is the queen of the social sciences. I learned that theory is the capstone of the status hierarchy in economics. I learned the brand names whose research I was to revere and respect. I learned that tastes are unobservable and never change. I learned that subjective testimony and survey research responses are not admissible evidence in economic research. I learned that what was then called "institutional economics" (Commons, Veblen, etc.) was beyond the pale, as were other social sciences more generally. I learned that there is a mere handful of economics journals really worth publishing in, and that articles in inter- or extradisciplinary journals count for naught. I learned that economic measurement as then practiced by the National Bureau of Economic Research (NBER) was to be denigrated as "measurement without theory."

It was years before I could shake off some of the tastes that graduate economics education had inculcated and begin to think for myself. Some I have never overcome; thus, I still pay disproportionate attention to economists' judgments of my work.

SCHOOLING BEYOND ECONOMICS

At Penn, Simon Kuznets was a remote figure. He came in one afternoon a week to teach a graduate class and meet with his few thesis students. The courses he offered were in economic development, business cycles, and statistics; curiously, there were none that related to his pioneering research on national income. Kuznets's appointment was not in the economics department but in the even weaker statistics department, and he participated hardly at all in the affairs of either or in those of the university. Most of his time was spent on research off-campus at his home with occasional visits to the NBER in New York.

I took two courses from Kuznets, one in statistics, which chiefly conveyed a strong skepticism toward the field and urged the use of simple, understandable methods, and one in economic development, which was essentially a course in general economic history. This development course, too, transmitted a strong sense of skepticism, not, however, toward economic history but toward economic theory. Kuznets's basic point was simple: the "givens" of economics – technology, tastes, and institutions – are the key actors in historical change, and hence most economic theory has, at best, only limited relevance to understanding long-term change. In Kuznets's view, what was then called "development theory" – even the widely hailed work of Schumpeter – lacked concrete empirical reference.

I was impressed by Kuznets's intellect, as were graduate economics students generally, but these courses did not make me into a Kuznetsian. Rather, it was chiefly what Kuznets wrote. As a graduate student, I collaborated on several studies of national income with Raymond T. Bowman, the economics department chairman and a great admirer of Kuznets. Thanks largely to Bowman's urging, I also did a thesis under Kuznets's direction on conceptual aspects of the measurement of economic growth. As a result of these two lines of work, I read virtually everything Kuznets had written on national income and economic growth. It was this reading that demonstrated for me the scope, depth, and brilliance of Kuznets's mind.

Kuznets believed that insight into other times and places started not from economic theory but from knowledge of the facts – especially quantitative facts. It is typical of Kuznets that one of his rare speculative pieces, "Towards a Theory of Economic Growth," is mostly devoted to summarizing the facts that growth theory must explain. In the present age of endogenous technical change and the "new" growth theory, this article remains well worth reading (Kuznets 1955, see also Kuznets 1966).

Kuznets also believed that it is important to know the scholarly literature of specialists in the study of other times and places. As work on my dissertation led to a growing interest in economic development and away from macroeconomic policy, Kuznets channeled me into an interdisciplinary seminar on South Asia, where I came into contact with scholars doing humanistic and social science research on India and came to know some leading Indian scholars such as N. V. Sovani. Kuznets also encouraged my tutelage in the literature of economic history by Daniel Thorner, who was himself an eminent scholar of Indian economic history.

It was my good fortune that Kuznets and sociology professor Dorothy S. Thomas, a renowned demographer and the first woman president of the American Sociological Association, were starting a collaborative research project just as I was finishing graduate school. Thomas's period of graduate work in sociology at Columbia University had overlapped Kuznets's in economics, and like Kuznets she had been strongly influenced by Wesley C. Mitchell. Mitchell, an institutional economist at Columbia, was head of the recently founded, privately financed NBER. The Kuznets–Thomas project reflected this heritage. It aimed to use the U.S. decennial censuses from 1870 to 1950 to develop estimates of internal migration, labor force, and income by state (Kuznets and Thomas 1957, 1960, 1964). I was invited by Kuznets to do the income estimates as well as estimates of manufacturing activity.

This three-year project affected my development in two ways. For one thing, it gave me my first practical experience in economic measurement. I learned firsthand what had already been clear from Kuznets's writings: that there is no measurement without theory (Kuznets 1948a,b). I also came to respect the mission of the NBER as originally conceived by Mitchell. This was to build a broad quantitative base of economic measures that would further the "cumulation of economic knowledge" (Burns 1948; Kuznets 1947, 33–4). In my personal experience, the value of this philosophy is demonstrated by the fact that, in economic history, the most often cited work of mine is still my estimates of state income done in the 1950s as part of the Kuznets–Thomas project.

But these notions about the importance of economic measurement ran strongly against the tide of mainstream economics. I can still remember the shock and sense of betrayal I felt one day when economic theorist George Stigler, himself an NBER staff member and eventual Nobel laureate, opined that a doctoral dissertation providing historical estimates of the U.S. balance of payments was not appropriate for a Columbia University Ph.D. in economics.

The other effect of the Kuznets–Thomas project was to introduce me to the field of demography. My mentor here (with Kuznets's encouragement) was Dorothy Thomas, who in numerous coffee klatches during the project expounded on the field of demography and its practitioners and forced me to attend meetings of the Population Association of America and observe and meet real demographers. Thanks largely to her influence, I acquired an education in a field outside of economics – one with quite different values. In demography, careful measurement is extolled, and those who develop techniques for making something out of fragmentary data are highly regarded. In graduate study in demography, a course in techniques of measurement is the core of the requirements. In economics, there has never been a methodology of measurement, and it is doubtful that a course in measurement could even make it into the graduate economics curriculum as an elective if there were anyone with the temerity to propose it.

Demographers also place high value on establishing the factual record, which was exemplified for me at the time by several now classic studies associated with Princeton's Office of Population Research (Davis 1951; Durand 1948; Kirk 1946; Taeuber 1958). Such work is customarily dismissed by economists as purely descriptive. To me, however, the demographer's respect for facts resonated with the goals of Wesley Mitchell's NBER.

I do not wish to imply that my appreciation of demography was an overnight thing. The first draft of my paper analyzing the causes of the American baby boom (Easterlin 1968b, Chap. 4; see also Chapter 11 herein) was replete with the usual arrogant economist's jibes at demographic research. On reading this, Dorothy Thomas took me aside and said, "Look, Dick, this paper would not have been possible without all the prior demographic research that it builds on – why not be more charitable?" I was shamed into remembering a characteristically pertinent maxim of J. M. Keynes': "If economists could manage to get themselves thought of as humble, competent people, on a level with dentists, that would be splendid" (Keynes 1932, 373). The outcome was that I changed the tone completely. One benefit, beyond my personal training, was that the paper, when published, attracted favorable attention from demographers and established my credentials in the field.

In addition to demography, I became increasingly involved in the discipline of economic history, a field that at the time was dominated by historians. The welcome extended by historians and demographers to the incursion of economists in their fields has always been a source of wonder to me because my own discipline of economics has hardly reciprocated.

The situation in economic history, however, was different from that in demography. The field was astir with the potentials of the "new" economic history whereby economists aspired to rewrite history through the application of economic theory and econometrics to historical problems. I am regarded as a member of this school, and I do feel that these tools contribute to historical study. But I also believe that the traditional approach of historians was of great value, and I regret very much that they have now largely been driven from the field. Indeed, I have long felt that my early work on state income estimates would have been better if I had known more traditional American economic history. It sometimes seems these days as if the new economic history is more interested in using historical data to test economic hypotheses than in using economics to understand history. To my mind, the field would have been richer if it had followed Kuznets's agenda for a comparative worldwide study of the economic growth of nations based on measurement and *multi*disciplinary theory (Kuznets 1949).

In any event, my experiences in both demography and economic history did much to further my education beyond economics. Training in economics has always been chock-full of requirements that leave little time to gain an appreciation of other disciplines. This is bad enough, but most aspiring economists are indoctrinated in the view, as I was, that such knowledge is not even necessary and are taught to look on other disciplines with contempt. I was lucky that the period of my dissertation training and my early postgraduate years provided a serious counter to this. I wish that such opportunities were more generally available to young economists today.

THE MAKING OF A RESEARCH PHILOSOPHY

Several years ago I was the chair at the University of Southern California of the economics department's recruitment committee for newly minted Ph.D.s. In this capacity, I had the opportunity to read abstracts of dissertations from many students from the nation's leading graduate economics departments, which was an experience that revealed a great deal about the discipline.

Model building is the name of the game. Empirical reality enters, if at all, chiefly in the form of "stylized facts." Econometrics, though a formal course requirement everywhere, plays a surprisingly small part in economic research – showing up in perhaps one dissertation in five. There is no such thing as descriptive dissertations or theses devoted to the measurement of economic magnitudes. Although topics in disciplines other than economics are not uncommon, there is little use or knowledge of the work done in other disciplines.

From what has gone before, it will be clear that this is a philosophy that makes me uncomfortable. I see the point of departure of research as some empirical problem such as the post–World War II American baby boom and bust. One is likely to have some theoretical preconceptions about causation, but the first step is to establish facts, both quantitative and qualitative, drawing, as needed, on relevant work not only in economics but in other social sciences as well. These facts will inform the investigator more fully about what needs to be explained and may also suggest new possibilities regarding causation. Economic theory enters by providing a systematic framework for theorizing, but other disciplines may suggest relevant causal factors that need to be brought into the theoretical analysis and also supply pertinent facts. Simple empirical methods provide an initial check on the consistency of theory and data; more rigorous methods are used subsequently to formally test one's conclusions. Qualitative evidence, such as subjective statements of the actors as found in social science surveys or the materials of historical research (diaries, letters, etc.), should be consistent with the model.

This is not the usual approach to economic research, nor do I have any illusions that it will become more common. And it was not the approach that I started with. But it is one that has helped me to understand a little about the world in which I live.

There is hypothesis testing in this approach, but a finding of support for a hypothesis is not the end of research. The goal is to explain reality, and typically this involves more than one hypothesized causal factor. For example, I referred earlier to the substantial economics literature hypothesizing that occupational choice is determined by prospective returns. The goal of this literature is largely to establish the validity of this hypothesis. If, however, one's research goal is to explain observed job choices in a particular place in a particular period of time, it is likely that expected returns will prove to be only one factor at work and not necessarily the most important. Thus, although expected returns have demonstrably played a part in the changing occupational choices of American college students, one of the most dramatic occupational developments – the shift toward business careers in the 1970s and 1980s – was driven chiefly by a marked change in preferences as evidenced by life goals of the young (see Chapter 12).

I have already emphasized the importance of instruction by data and the interaction between empirical study and hypothesis formulation and testing. Let me illustrate from my early experience in the study of long swings or "Kuznets cycles" in population and the economy. Then, as now, there was the issue of whether such fluctuations were real or simply a statistical artifact. To study these swings, I assembled a vast number of time series from widely differing sources: population and its components, commodity output of various types, capital stock, labor force and employment, building permits, patents, land sales and prices, financial series, new incorporations, and international trade and payments. Some series were annual, and many were confined to the intermittent dates of the population and industrial censuses. The time spans differed widely. I also knew (or learned about) possible causal relationships among various subsets of these series from work by others, not only on long swings, but also on building cycles, urban growth, immigration, and the like. Ultimately it was the consistency in movements among a wide variety of series, many of which were fragmentary, and the consistency of these movements with theoretical expectations that convinced me of the reality of long swings and led to the formulation of a broad model of economic–demographic interactions during long swings (Easterlin 1968b; see also Chapter 5 herein). Perhaps someone else might have more quickly conceived such a model a priori and tested it with the few, long annual time series available. For me, it took several years of working through data and exploring various causal speculations before I arrived at what seemed a satisfactory understanding of this empirical problem.

The notion of "instruction by the data" has its pitfalls. The biggest is that the pursuit of data becomes an end in itself and an excuse for postponing theoretical analysis. To avoid this, data collection and analysis must proceed in tandem, not sequentially.

LETTING GO OF ECONOMIC THEORY (MAINSTREAM VERSION)

It is hard to overcome the preconceptions indoctrinated by graduate economics training. In the early years of my career, I sought faithfully to explain childbearing behavior on the basis of income and prices and to eschew appeal to preferences. I was also a devoted follower of the doctrine that behavior is always the result of deliberate choice. Reality led me to retreat from both views.

Fixed preferences went first. The empirical problem was the American baby boom and bust from the end of World War II through the 1970s. If children are a "normal good," how does one explain the marked rise and subsequent fall in childbearing in a period when income moves sharply upward? "Prices" won't do it, for the opportunity cost of young women, the factor stressed most in current economic literature, was demonstrably higher during the baby boom than the subsequent baby bust.

The answer came ultimately from sociology via the concept of economic socialization. One's notions of a desirable living level are initially formed from one's personal experience while growing up. The parents of the baby boom came from the economically deprived environment of the Great Depression and World War II; the parents of the baby bust came from the economically affluent post–World War II period. Even with incomes and prices the same for the two sets of parents, one would expect them to differ in their willingness to have children because of disparities in the material aspirations they had formed as they grew up. The parents of the baby boom with low material aspirations and good income prospects felt relatively affluent; their children, the parents of the baby bust, with much higher material aspirations relative to income, felt poorer and less able to have children. By recognizing the role of changing material aspirations (preferences) along with growth of income, I was able to arrive at a plausible interpretation of the baby boom and bust – one consistent with the evidence (Easterlin 1980; Chapter 11 herein).

Another empirical problem undermined my conviction that behavior could always be explained as being deliberate choice. In this case, the problem was the shift from large to small family size that occurs in the course of what demographers call the "demographic transition." Like most economic demographers today, I had assumed that, throughout history, fertility behavior was the result of conscious choice (cf. Schultz 1981). I had already been made uncomfortable when chided by my colleague and friend at the University of Pennsylvania, demographer John Durand, about the irrelevance of a deliberate choice model to the observed fertility of permanently or partially sterile women, but I thought

I could get by on the grounds that this was not very important quantitatively. Matters became much worse, however, when I encountered a large body of survey research data in the demographic literature indicating that, before the demographic transition, most couples in developing countries said that they did not deliberately limit family size. This implied that observed fertility behavior in these societies was what demographers call "natural" or unregulated fertility. Moreover, demographers Ansley Coale and James Trussell (1974a, 1975), by the use of an ingenious and innovative technique, had made a persuasive case that natural fertility was also the common condition in the historical experience of the developed countries before the shift to low fertility. Eventually, in collaboration with others, I arrived at an explanation of natural fertility consistent with economic theory and rational behavior (Easterlin 1978; Easterlin, Pollak, and Wachter 1980; Easterlin and Crimmins 1985). The result led me to recognize that the mechanisms underlying the observed relation of fertility to income in pretransition societies might have little to do with deliberate household decisions about family size and might reflect, instead, social norms or physiological relationships. Variations in fertility in pretransition societies might result, for example, from variations in breastfeeding behavior that arose not from interest in, or even awareness of the effect of breastfeeding on family size, but simply from different societal conceptions of the link between breastfeeding and the health of mother and child. In such circumstances, fertility was being influenced not by conscious choice but inadvertently by household decisions directed toward other objectives (see Chapters 8 and 9).

In recent decades, some economists have sought to bring the subject of mortality as well as fertility under the dominion of the theory of household choice [see, for example, Schultz (1981) and the survey by Behrman and Deolalikar (1988)]. The leading empirical problem with regard to mortality is the amazing decline that has occurred in both developed and developing areas over the past century (this decline is the other component of the demographers' demographic transition). The suggested explanation is straightforward: health is the product of conscious household decisions. Growth in income associated with economic development induces an improvement in the quantity and quality consumed of food, clothing, shelter, medical care, and so on, and this, in time, improves health and reduces mortality.

I cannot plead innocence of this view; at one time, I used it explicitly to infer, in the absence of direct measures of mortality, the probable course of American mortality in the nineteenth century (Easterlin 1977). As in the case of fertility, however, the more I studied the literature outside of economics, the more I was led to question such a simple economic model. Before the latter part of the nineteenth century, households, governments, and those in the healing arts had little knowledge of how to prevent or treat disease, which is a situation that prevails even today in parts of the Third World (Caldwell et al. 1988, 1990). In such circumstances, actions by households or others to prevent or treat disease – however well-intentioned – were largely ineffective or even counterproductive, as in the case of bloodletting. It was not until the growth of epidemiological knowledge and then validation of the germ theory of disease in the middle and latter part of the nineteenth century that truly effective action started to become possible (see Chapters 6 and 7). The leadership in implementing this knowledge was provided not by households but by public entrepreneurs, the leaders of the new public health movement. Initially, in the middle and latter part of the nineteenth century, the focus of the public health movement was on water and sanitation measures to clean up the environment. These actions significantly reduced mortality independently of household decisions. As time went on and knowledge continued to grow, the emphasis of public health officials shifted toward measures to ensure a purer food supply and education of the public in personal hygiene, maternal and childcare practices, good nutrition, and the importance of immunization. This new knowledge made it possible *for the first time* for households generally to make informed decisions to prevent disease. Eventually, as the continuing advance in knowledge led to the development of chemotherapy in the 1930s and thereafter, the medical profession became equipped with antimicrobial drugs that made possible *for the first time* an effective response to household demands for the cure of disease.

Thus, as knowledge has advanced, the determination of health and mortality has been brought increasingly within the province of human control. Today, in developed societies, deliberate household decisions, along with those of medical practitioners and governments, can improve health and reduce mortality. Viewed in historical perspective, however, this is a very new development and has not yet reached parts of the Third World even today.

Letting go of the preconceptions of economic theory did not come easily. It was brought about chiefly by two fundamental beliefs instilled in me by Kuznets. One was taking an empirical problem as the point of departure for research. The other was respect for the evidence accumulated by specialists on the subject. In the case of fertility and mortality, this evidence came chiefly from demographers, public health specialists, historians, and anthropologists. Survey evidence that demonstrated the widespread absence in time and space of deliberate control of family size had to be accepted as reflecting empirical reality, and a plausible model had to explain such behavior. Regrettably, many economists define such observations away by dismissing subjective testimony as inadmissible (Easterlin 1986 and Chapter 2 herein). Had I not had the benefit of schooling in demography, I would have missed out on an opportunity to better understand observed behavior. Similarly, in regard to mortality, evidence had to be recognized of the immense breakthrough in knowledge of the control of communicable disease and the key role of public entrepreneurship in implementing this new knowledge. Economists' insistence on starting with household choice put the cart before the horse.

One reason why most economists start with the theory of household choice is that its relevance to behavior in contemporary developed societies has been well demonstrated. As mentioned at the beginning of this section, my own model of the American baby boom and bust employs the theory of household choice expanded to allow for systematic variation in preferences. Similarly, in the low-mortality regime of the United States today, understanding household choices regarding lifestyle and health care utilization helps provide insights into differentials and trends in American health and mortality. In recent decades, a substantial economic literature has amassed on fertility and mortality in the developed countries, especially the United States, in which the theory of household choice plays a central role. Unfortunately, this literature has become the point of departure for economic research on fertility and mortality in other times and places, and a theoretical model applicable to developed countries has become the starting point of research on less developed nations rather than empirical study of those societies. Such empirical work is readily available in social sciences other than economics, as well as by geographic area specialists, but economists have been taught to dismiss such work and trust in the wisdom of economic theory. As a result, economics approaches the study of other times and places through glasses tinted by preoccupation with the study of contemporary developed countries – especially the United States. This is not the way Simon Kuznets would have had it. By word and example, Kuznets taught a respect for facts and for research in other social sciences and by area specialists.

As I have indicated, making the break with the assumption of given preferences wasn't easy. But once it was made, the effects ramified. The model I used to explain the baby boom and bust was based on the recognition that one's material aspirations are shaped in important part by one's material upbringing. Previously, I had confidently assumed that higher income and greater subjective welfare go hand in hand. But the relative income model implied that a generation raised under more affluent circumstances would, as a result, have higher material aspirations – in short, that as society's income increases, people's views of the goods they "need" increase correspondingly. Thus, the positive effect of higher income on well-being predicted by the economist's model of household choice could be negated by the adverse effect of increased material aspirations. Subjective testimony on personal happiness provides striking confirmation of this expectation: as per capita income increases, subjective welfare remains unchanged despite a marked growth in material living levels (Easterlin 1974, 2002 and Chapters 2 and 3 herein). Again, mainstream economics has spared itself confrontation with the evidence by its dogmatic rejection of subjective testimony on well-being – this, despite a large research literature in psychology and sociology pointing to the meaningfulness of such measures.

In the study of subjective well-being, as in my work on demographic topics, I again learned the value of research in disciplines outside of economics. My work on subjective well-being was initiated in 1970–1 while I was a Fellow at the Center for Advanced Study in the Behavioral Sciences. This fellowship provided an opportunity for extended contact with scholars in psychology and sociology who introduced me to relevant work in these fields. I was especially fortunate to enjoy the friendly and patient tutelage in social psychology of Elliot Aronson. Thus, during my career, I have been fortunate to have had the opportunity for serious contact with scholars and work outside of economics – first in demography and history and then in sociology and psychology – that taught me firsthand the value of Kuznets's stress on the relevance to reality of social science generally, not just economic theory.

A HISTORICAL PERSPECTIVE

We live today in the midst of two great revolutions that are sweeping the world and have changed human life forever (see Chapter 6). The Industrial Revolution of the late eighteenth century marked the onset of modern economic growth, a phenomenon that has raised material living levels by tenfold or more among the leaders in the process. The Mortality Revolution that started in the late nineteenth century has already more than doubled life expectancy at birth in many parts of the world. Together, these revolutions portend, perhaps as early as a half-century hence, a world largely freed from hunger and starvation and from the enormously high rates of infant and child mortality that have plagued humankind throughout history (Easterlin 1996).

The origins of these revolutions lie in the development and growth of natural science since the late seventeenth century. Scientific knowledge grew earliest in the fields of mechanics, astronomy, chemistry, and electricity and had its payoff in widespread and continuing improvements in methods of production that raised productivity and per capita income. Scientific knowledge came later in the biological and medical fields, and because of this, the Mortality Revolution, based on new methods of disease control, started later than modern economic growth. The factor input and institutional requirements of the Mortality Revolution are less than those for modern economic growth, and because of this the Mortality Revolution has spread more rapidly.

Thus, a new world is being erected on the advances in natural science. This world is richer and healthier, but it is also much more complex and highly interdependent. It is a world of staggering new problems – abrupt shifts in political power as modern technology spreads, new environmental concerns arising from the side effects of this technology, and conflict within and among nations between gainers and losers in economic growth.

Ultimately, the solution to such problems depends on the social sciences. I am an economist because I believe that economics is essential to understanding the world and that the framework of economic theory enables one to think systematically about many interrelationships. Indeed, the first major payoff to the advance of social science knowledge was, as I have noted, the insights of the Keynesian Revolution into one of the major new problems of economic growth: mass unemployment. It is unfortunate that the profession of economics has retreated from this belief in the ability of economic science to help us control our destiny because the need for policy-relevant research is greater today than ever before.

But economics alone is not enough, and this is why I am a reluctant economist. We cannot comprehend the world around us without knowledge of the facts and insights provided by the other social sciences. Economics is a valuable starting point, but only a starting point, in the application of social science to the world's problems. As I reflect on my own philosophy, instilled by Kuznets and molded by experience, it boils down to a few words: it is good to be an economist; it is better to be a social scientist.

2

Economics and the Use of Subjective Testimony

There is a long and respected history in the social sciences of survey research that elicits subjective testimony (i.e., self-reports) on feelings, beliefs, values, expectations, plans, attitudes, and behavior, including intensive inquiry into possible shortcomings of such data. This extensive body of evidence is unfortunately largely excluded from economic analysis even though economic theory almost invariably includes reference to motivations, expectations, well-being, and the like. The typical economist's view, encapsulated in the concept "behaviorism," was put succinctly as follows by Victor Fuchs, president of the American Economic Association in 1995: "Economists, as a rule, are not concerned with the internal thought processes of the decision maker or in the rationalizations that the decision maker offers to explain his or her behavior. Economists believe that what people *do* is more relevant than what they say" (Fuchs 1983, 14, italics in original). As this statement suggests, economists are not apologetic about this dismissal of subjective testimony (note the use of the perjorative "rationalizations" rather than "reasons" in the quotation). On the contrary, they consider it a feather in the discipline's methodological cap (Reder 1999, 294–6). Economic historian Deirdre McCloskey puts the attitude of economists in the following way:

> Unlike other social scientists, economists are extremely hostile toward questionnaires and other self-descriptions.... One can literally get an audience of economists to laugh out loud by proposing ironically to send out a questionnaire on some disputed economic point. Economists ... are unthinkingly committed to the notion that only the externally observable behavior of actors is admissible evidence in arguments concerning economics. (McCloskey 1983, 514)

This disciplinary stricture against listening to what people say is unfortunate, I believe, because it excludes from study by economists a large body of evidence that provides insight into economic behavior and personal well-being.[1] In what follows, three cases are noted from my own research in which I've found that subjective testimony contributes to better understanding of a problem than a methodological approach that excludes such data.

INCOME AND SUBJECTIVE WELL-BEING

In welfare economics and among economists generally, it is commonly assumed that higher real income increases individual well-being; that is, with more goods at their disposal, people will feel better off. Indeed, it is this assumption that drives economists' advocacy of economic growth as a public goal (Abramovitz 1959). Of course, economists recognize that well-being does not depend on income alone, but where a very large increase in income occurs of the magnitude brought about by economic growth, one would expect, as A. C. Pigou (1932) argued many years ago, that overall well-being would increase, though not necessarily to the same extent.

Before the 1940s there were no data to test the proposition that feelings of well-being increase when real income grows substantially. True, in developed countries the measured per capita amounts of food, clothing, shelter, and other goods had been rising for a century or more. But these "objective" indicators provide no test of the proposition because any welfare inference based on them depends on an outside observer's personal judgment that when people have more, then they must feel better off. Such an inference does not tell us whether people actually do feel better off. This is a question that, in the end, only they themselves can answer.

Fortunately, after World War II, surveys began to be conducted that asked people about their feelings of well-being, that is, how happy they are or how satisfied they are with their lives. The simplest Gallup

[1] There are exceptions. In the United States, the Institute for Social Research of the University of Michigan has the longest record of the use of subjective data in economic research. Cf. Juster and Stafford (1985); Katona (1960); Strumpel, Morgan, and Zahn (1972).

poll–type question offers the respondent three options for an answer (e.g., "very happy," "pretty happy," "not very happy"), but some survey instruments go as high as eleven categories (Cantril 1965). Whether the survey question is simple or elaborate, the results are highly consistent.

These surveys have been accumulating steadily in the past half-century and have been a gold mine to scholars in disciplines other than economics; a research bibliography compiled by Veenhoven (1993) reports nearly 2,500 contributions. Indeed, in psychology, a new subfield of "hedonic psychology" has started to emerge (Kahneman, Diener, and Schwarz 1999). As with any data – subjective or objective – there are shortcomings, but these have been carefully studied for several decades now, and there is a substantial consensus that these self-reports of happiness or life satisfaction are meaningful and reasonably comparable among sizable groups in the population (Easterlin 2002; Frey and Stutzer 2002; Kahneman et al. 1999).

What, then, do these surveys tell us about how well-being changes when real income increases greatly? The answer is startling. In the United States, since the 1940s there has been, on average, no significant change in subjective well-being despite a more than doubling of real per capita income.

True, the United States is a rich country, and maybe what we are finding is that well-being does not increase once a country passes some minimum real income threshold. Perhaps in a poorer country, one below that threshold, well-being does rise as economic growth substantially raises the amount of goods consumed by the average person.

Consider, then, the case of Japan in the period from the late 1950s to the late 1980s. In 1958, Japan's real per capita income was below that of many of today's developing countries (Easterlin 1995). From 1958 to 1987, real per capita income in Japan increased a staggering fivefold. Consumer durables such as electric washing machines, electric refrigerators, and television sets, which were found in few homes at the start of the period, became well-nigh universal, and car ownership soared from 1 to about 60 percent of households. What happened to subjective well-being? The answer is, no change (Easterlin 1995).

As it turns out, there is a plausible explanation for the constancy of subjective well-being as real income rises. This explanation turns on a type of "deflation" mechanism similar to that by which economists adjust income in the prices current in each year to obtain "real" income. In this case, however, the deflator is not the level of prices but people's material aspirations – how much they feel they need to live comfortably. As real income rises over time, material aspirations grow commensurately with income (Easterlin 2001). Although people have more, they feel they need more to live comfortably. In effect, in people's minds the positive effect on well-being of having more goods is being "deflated" by a corresponding increase in what they perceive as their "needs." The result is a constant level of subjective well-being over the long term. A specific indicator of this growth in "needs" comes from a survey question that asks respondents how much income is needed by a family of four to get along. An analysis of how "get along" income changes with actual income yields an "elasticity" of one; that is, a 1-percent change in actual income generates, on average, a 1-percent change in what people think is needed to "get along" (Rainwater 1994; see also Chapter 3 herein).

THE SWITCH TO BUSINESS CAREERS

Let me shift to the subject of occupational choice. Most economists are aware that, between 1972 and 1987, American college business school enrollments soared as a proportion of total undergraduate enrollment with profound consequences for the labor market not to mention the relative position within academia of business schools. Why? Although one can readily find numerous articles on occupational choice in the economics literature, there is virtual silence on the shift to business even though it is the most striking occupational change of the period. The reason is clear: the favorite explanatory variable in economics, the relative rate of return (price), cannot adequately explain this trend.

If subjective testimony were admitted, however, one would find that the biggest part of the explanation is that a major redirection in life goals of the young occurred, a shift toward making money, and that this altered their occupational preferences significantly in favor of business. Evidence of the change in life goals comes from two surveys, one of high school seniors and one of college freshmen. The data on high school seniors are from Monitoring the Future, a nationally representative survey conducted annually since 1975 by the University of Michigan's Survey Research Center (see, e.g., Bachman, Johnston, and O'Malley 1987). This survey has been the leading source of knowledge about attitudes toward, and use of, drugs among American youth, but it includes as well many questions about the values, expectations, and experiences of high school seniors. The data on college freshmen are from a survey of around 200,000 entering college students conducted annually since 1965. This survey is under the auspices of the Higher Education Research Institute of the University of California, Los Angeles (Astin, Green, and Korn 1987). The survey responses are weighted to provide a nationally representative sample of all first-time, full-time college students entering in the fall of each year. Both the high school senior and college freshmen surveys include, among other things, quite similar questions about the importance to respondents of various life goals ranging from material well-being (making money) and marriage and family formation to the "public interest" (helping others, contributing to society) and personal self-fulfillment. The principal finding on life goals in the period since the mid-1970s (when the two surveys overlap) is the same: there is a big increase in the importance of making money. This occurs among both those who plan to go to college and those who do not and is about equal in magnitude for the two groups (Easterlin and Crimmins 1991).

Some economists may assume that the increased importance of making money is simply a reflection of an adverse change in macroeconomic conditions during the period that created increased economic insecurity among the young and led them to put more emphasis on money as a goal. Again, subjective testimony enables one to test this proposition. If data on youth expectations from the Monitoring the Future survey are examined, one finds that they do not fit this hypothesis. When asked about job expectations at age 30, young adults in 1987, compared with those in 1972, not only expected to hold better jobs but felt more certain of getting such jobs. Other self-report data from the Monitoring the Future survey show that, in general, young people at the end of the period were more confident about themselves and their future than were young people at the beginning of the period. Thus, young people were becoming more, not less, positive about their future prospects at the same time that the switch to business occurred. The idea that adverse market conditions created economic insecurity among the young, and thus caused the shift in their life goals, is belied by self-reports.

What *is* consistent with the evidence is that adverse macroeconomic conditions led older adults to place greater emphasis on making money. The evidence on older adults' attitudes comes from yet another survey source: Roper surveys that probe individuals' conceptions of "the good life" (Roper Organization 1989). In this case respondents are offered a list of twenty-four items relating to material living levels, family concerns, and job circumstances and asked whether they consider each to be part of "the good life," "the life you'd like to have." The responses reveal a strong shift among adults of all ages in the direction of private materialism toward things like "a lot of money" as part of the good life. This shift in adults' attitudes occurs in conjunction with a general deterioration in macroeconomic conditions and precedes by several years the shift in life goals of the young. Thus, subjective data on older adults' attitudes and young persons' life goals, together with "objective" macroeconomic indicators, suggest a complex but plausible scenario – that deteriorating macroeconomic conditions led older adults to place more emphasis on money making, and this increased emphasis on money was gradually transmitted to the young as they were raised. Hence, macroeconomic conditions did affect the values of the young, but indirectly rather than directly, and with a lag via their socialization experience. Subjective evidence of several types thus yields new insight into the mechanisms underlying an important area of economic behavior, occupational choice, and also helps reject alternative hypotheses about the mechanisms underlying this behavior such as increased insecurity among the young. (For more on this, see Chapter 12.)

CHILDBEARING AND CONTRACEPTIVE USE

Let me turn to my third example of how subjective testimony provides insights into behavior. In economics the prevailing model of fertility determination assumes that in all times and places households have consciously decided about the size of their families based on income, prices, and tastes. But because children are the product of sexual intercourse – an activity pursued for the pleasure it yields in its own right – decisions about family size typically require conscious action to limit fertility such as the use of abstinence, contraception, or induced abortion. If the prevailing model based on deliberate choice is correct, then one would expect a fair proportion of households of reproductive age to report the use of such practices.

To determine the actual extent of deliberate family size limitation there is, again, a large body of self-report data. Since the 1930s, demographers have been asking people about their reproductive attitudes and behavior. Of relevance here are surveys, commonly called "KAP surveys," that ask people about their knowledge of, attitudes toward, and practice of fertility control. In these surveys, individuals are asked, among other things, whether they know about each of a lengthy list of family size limitation practices, both "traditional" practices (e.g., abstinence, withdrawal, condom) and, in surveys from the 1960s onward, "modern" practices (e.g., oral pill, IUD, sterilization). Then respondents are asked, first, a general question about whether they have ever tried to limit their family size, and, following this, whether they have ever used any of the specific practices previously mentioned or any others. These KAP surveys were initially conducted in the United States and other developed countries, but since World War II a large number have been done in developing countries worldwide.

In developed countries, households do, indeed, report widespread use of such family size limitation practices and have done so since these surveys were instituted (Easterlin, Pollak, and Wachter 1980, 107).[2] But in developing countries the picture – up through the 1960s and 1970s – is much different. Despite the large number of practices named by the interviewer, and even though some respondents know of some of these practices, a large proportion of the reproductive age population – often as much as 90 percent or more – report never having attempted to limit family size (Easterlin et al. 1980, 107).

What, then, is one to make of the standard economic model of fertility determination implying a type of household behavior that is contradicted by subjective testimony? If one accepts the evidence I have mentioned, then a model is needed explaining the absence of deliberate control in many times and places. Here, again, the KAP surveys are helpful – in this case via responses to questions on desired family size. These data imply that, in developing countries, parents have typically had difficulty having as many children as they desired, and, because of this, have had as many as they could. In modern times, as infant and child mortality has come down sharply, parents have come to realize that unregulated fertility yields more children than they want and have, in consequence, been pushed into limiting their fertility via the practices

[2] There is, however, behavioral evidence that many households in developed countries did not deliberately limit family size in the nineteenth century or earlier (Easterlin et al. 1980, 108).

cited earlier in this section (Bulatao and Lee 1983; Easterlin and Crimmins 1985; Chapters 8 and 9 herein).

Clearly, as long as economists reject subjective testimony, there is no need to confront survey evidence that contradicts the standard economic model. If, however, such self-report data are recognized as evidence with which an economic model must be consistent, then we must either assume that respondents in developing countries are untruthful while those in developed countries are not – a most unlikely situation – or we must expand our model so that it can explain the new evidence.

HARD AND SOFT DATA

Some economists may object that subjective data are "squishy" compared with the "hard" numbers used in economics. But how many economists, I wonder, are prepared to defend such "hard" numbers as the inflation rate, about which there has been sufficient question to set up governmental review committees? These hard numbers of economics also include unemployment, which regularly generates critiques of undercount and overcount. In response to such concerns, the Bureau of Labor Statistics in 1994 revised its measurement procedures in a way that raised the unemployment rate by about 0.6 percentage points. When the profession marveled in 2000 as the annual unemployment rate fell to 4 percent, no one mentioned that, if prior procedures had been used (those in effect when the common assumption was that 6 percent or higher was the nonaccelerating inflation rate of full unemployment), the reported unemployment rate would have been below 3.5 percent. To my knowledge, discussions of the "natural rate of unemployment" have also totally ignored this measurement change.

In Chapter 7, an article by Lant Pritchett and Lawrence H. Summers is cited that uses international cross-sectional data to generalize about the relation of life expectancy to real gross domestic product (GDP). Their article offers some appropriate cautions on the reliability of the life expectancy data, but not a word is said about real GDP (Pritchett and Summers 1996, 848–9). There are, however, serious issues about the omission of home production in GDP, which is a problem especially relevant when studying countries at widely disparate levels of income such as those in the Pritchett–Summers article. There is also the difficulty of adjusting nominal to real income. The contributions toward the solution of this problem by Allan Heston and Robert Summers, following the pioneering work of Irving Kravis and Milton Gilbert, earned them well-deserved recognition as Fellows of the American Economic Association. But the great majority of real GDP estimates do not employ the sophisticated Summers–Heston procedures, which are by no means infallible. Need one mention too that, in regard to U.S. GDP itself, there are serious reservations about the output estimates for service industries that comprise substantial parts of the total – the government sector, finance, health, education, and so on?

Or, take the "full income" concept that is generally recognized as a preferable income measure for analyzing a variety of behaviors (see, e.g., Chapter 8). Are years of schooling (husband's? wife's? some combination? adjusted for quality?) an accurate empirical counterpart of this concept?

In the discipline of economics we have for so long come to live with imperfect data that we disregard the possible biases in these data or even forget about them. But when less familiar data such as subjective testimony are presented, we are quick to note the shortcomings and dismiss the data as meaningless. A recent article by two economists on subjective survey data, for example, states as its "primary objective" to turn economists' "vague implicit distrust" of subjective testimony "into an explicit position grounded in facts" (Bertrand and Mullainathan 2001, 67). Aside from the staggering hubris that such a sweeping objective can be accomplished in a mere six pages, this strikes me as a rearguard action. The use of subjective testimony in economics is growing.[3] Its use outside of economics has expanded to the point that serious challenges are being made to the efficacy of economic policy (see the discussion

[3] See, for example, Darity and Goldsmith (1996); Frey and Stutzer (2002). Contemporary research at the National Bureau of Economic Research makes considerable use of subjective testimony (see the research summaries published regularly in National Bureau of Economic Research, various dates). Dominitz and Manski (1999) advocate the use of subjective testimony on expectations, particularly the "probalistic elicitation of expectations," that they feel "might improve on the traditional qualitative approaches of attitudinal research" (p. 23). This work is a good example of more open-mindedness about a certain type of subjective testimony and of how economists may contribute to the conceptual refinement of survey questions. However, in arguing for their specific approach, the authors implicitly downplay the potential usefulness of traditional categorical survey questions and thus tend to discourage the use by economists of a substantial body of data that has accumulated over the years such as the categorical questions in the General Social Survey.

in Easterlin 2002, Introduction). When asked by nonspecialists about such challenges, economists will not be able to hide for long behind the defense that subjective testimony is no good.

The fact is that no data conform to the conceptual ideal. The operative research question is whether the biases in the data at hand are likely to distort the conclusions seriously. We do not know what *the* unemployment rate is, but numerous variants rise in recession and fall in expansion, and the movement over time is what interests many analysts. The Bureau of Labor Statistics has identified several poverty measures. Although they signify different levels of poverty at a point in time, they all move in quite similar fashion from year to year. In my own work, I have used the reports on personal happiness in the General Social Survey since 1972. The question wording and placement have been constant over time. I do not know whether happiness is correctly measured at a point in time, but I have confidence in what the answers tell us about change over time.

No large body of data, hard or soft, I believe, should be dismissed out of hand. It is the task of specialists in a given area, such as labor economics or economic history, to study and evaluate each piece of data potentially relevant to the problem at hand. The parent disciplines responsible for subjective testimony – demography, sociology, psychology – have produced a substantial methodological literature on data problems and their solutions. This literature can be read either with a view to finding excuses to dismiss these data (Bertrand and Mullainathan 2001) or for helpful guidance on how the data may be intelligently used. I hope the more positive attitude will, in time, prevail.

CONCLUSION

I have cited three cases in which self-report data contribute to understanding human behavior and feelings – cases that are not adequately explained by standard economic models precluding the use of such data. One body of data relates to self-reports on subjective well-being. Another is on life goals, expectations, and self-confidence of the young. A third relates to self-reports on deliberate family size limitation and desired family size. In each case, underlying mechanisms are suggested that are not envisaged in the usual economic models.

The data I have used are but a sample of a broader range of subjective testimony compiled in other disciplines relating to motives, expectations, plans, beliefs, feelings, and actions that could be used to make economists' models of behavior more complete. Unfortunately, for many economists the use of these data is precluded not by uncertainty as to their robustness but by the disciplinary paradigm of behaviorism. At its most extreme, this doctrine takes the form that a scientific theory is none the worse if its premises are unrealistic so long as the theory's predictions are usefully true.[4] The cost of accepting this doctrine has been cogently put by Nobel laureate Paul Samuelson (1992, 242): "Such a dogma will be self-indulging, permitting its practitioners to ignore or play down inconvenient departures of their theories from the observable real world." I believe the examples I have noted demonstrate Samuelson's point. Currently, in mainstream economics it is accepted practice to admit collateral data such as prices and wages in testing hypotheses. One may, perhaps, hope that a time will come when subjective testimony will be admitted to this charmed circle.

[4] The genesis of this methodological stance in economics is discussed by Lewin (1996). This article also notes recent signs that the discipline may be gradually turning away from behaviorism.

3

Is Economic Growth Creating a New Postmaterialistic Society?

We are currently in the midst of a revolution in the human condition that is sweeping the world. Most people today are better fed, clothed, and housed than their predecessors two centuries ago. They are healthier, live longer, and are better educated. Women's lives are less centered on reproduction, and political democracy has gained a foothold. Western Europe and its offshoots have been the leaders of this advance, but in the twentieth century most of the less developed countries have joined, including most recently the newly emerging nations of sub-Saharan Africa. The picture is not one of unmitigated universal progress, but it is unquestionably the greatest advance in the condition of the world's population ever achieved in such a brief span of time. Indeed, it is so great that some analysts see today's leaders in human development as on the verge of a new postmaterialistic world.

Most people are only dimly aware of this transformation in the human condition because economic and social revolutions, unlike political ones, are not abrupt upheavals and become apparent only over long periods of often a half-century or more. Moreover, the popular media, to which we are daily exposed, inevitably highlight short-term and negative changes such as famine, financial crisis, and epidemic rather than dwelling on gradual, longer-term achievements, such as the worldwide eradication of smallpox, the successful immunization of 80 percent of the world's children against the six major vaccine-preventable childhood diseases, or the remarkable establishment and preservation of political democracy in India – a nation accounting for a sixth of the world's population. Our perspective is additionally distorted by the disproportionate effect of our own experience and that of those around us in the Western world. When we visit the less developed world we are struck by the current disparity between living conditions there and in the West and fail to appreciate how great the changes there have been in recent decades.

In what follows I first review briefly the progress since 1950 in today's less developed countries (LDCs) and assess some of the principal obstacles to further progress. The question posed in this chapter's title is then addressed: If one assumes the obstacles are successfully overcome, is economic growth transporting us to a new postindustrial, postmaterialistic society?

ACCOMPLISHMENTS

Let me briefly cite a few of the changes that have taken place in the last half-century in today's LDCs, which collectively account for four-fifths of the world's population.

1. The material living level of the average person has multiplied since the early 1950s by threefold. By material living level, I mean the economic goods consumed per capita – food, shelter, clothing, appliances, transportation, educational, medical, recreational services, and so forth. The rate at which improvement has been occurring in today's LDCs, as indexed by the annual growth rate of gross domestic product (GDP) per capita from 1952 to 1995, is 2.5 percent, which is about twice as large as that of the more developed countries (MDCs) in the nineteenth century when they were at a similar early stage of rapid economic growth.
2. Life expectancy at birth in the less developed world has risen by 21 years, from an average of 41 years in the early 1950s to over 62 today (Table 3.1, line 1). In some LDCs, life expectancy currently is similar to that in the developed world. As in the case of GDP per capita, the rate of improvement in LDCs has been much more rapid than in the historical experience of the West.
3. The high level of fertility that previously prevailed in the LDCs – so widely deplored by many in the developed world – has been cut by almost half from an average of over six births per woman in the early

Table 3.1. Life expectancy, fertility, and literacy, less developed countries, 1950–5 to 1990–5

	(1) 1950–5	(2) 1990–5	(3) Change, (2)–(1)
1. Life expectancy at birth, years	40.9	61.9	21.0
2. Total fertility rate, births per woman	6.2	3.3	–2.9
3. Adult literacy rate, percent	40	70	30

Note: The United Nations geographic classification of less developed countries is used here and in subsequent tables. More developed areas comprise Europe, the United States, Canada, Japan, Australia, and New Zealand; less developed, all others. In computing averages for geographic areas, as in Table 3.2, countries are weighted by their shares in the region's population.

Source: Lines 1 and 2, United Nations Department of Economic and Social Affairs (1998), pp. 12, 516, 518, 546–66. Line 3, UNESCO (1957), World Bank (1999).

1950s to close to three at the present time (Table 3.1, line 2). Again the rapidity of change in LDCs far exceeds that of the MDCs at a comparable stage.

4. With the rapid decline in fertility, the average rate of population growth in developing areas has been cut by four-tenths in the last four decades – from over 2.5 percent per year to about 1.5 percent – confirming that the post–World War II "population explosion" was a transient phenomenon as originally envisaged in the concept of the demographic transition.
5. In 1950, about four adults out of ten in the less developed world were literate; today the corresponding figure is over seven out of ten (Table 3.1, line 3). This is a much more rapid rate of advance in literacy than took place in the developed countries in the past.

Although there are exceptions, the typical pattern in LDCs is one of improved living conditions throughout the population. The advances in average condition just cited have been fairly evenly shared or are more equally distributed than they were a half-century ago. The evidence on income distribution in LDCs – for forty-five countries since the 1960s – shows no trend in inequality either for better or worse. Poverty, measured as the proportion of persons living below some absolute level of subsistence, has been considerably reduced. Differences within national populations in both literacy and life expectancy have declined.

Improvements such as these do not occur at a uniform rate from year to year. This is especially true of economic growth, which historically is marked by intermittent periods of slow growth or stagnation; the Great Depression of the 1930s and the East Asia Crisis of the late 1990s are cases in point. Too often, analysts seek to project the future on the basis of ongoing or very recent experience and make unduly optimistic or pessimistic predictions because shorter term rates of change may be substantially higher or lower than the long-term average. To minimize the effect of such shorter-term movements, the focus here is on time spans of nearly a half-century or more.

The figures cited are averages for the world's less developed countries as a whole. Although the picture varies from one place to another, all major regions of the world have participated significantly in this advance. Asia, which accounts for about six-tenths of the world population, has had the most notable rates of improvement (Table 3.2, lines 1–3). Within Asia, India is something of a laggard relative to East Asia, but India has nevertheless improved at about the LDC average on all measures used here. Only in sub-Saharan Africa, which accounts for about a tenth of the world population, is the picture mixed. Economic advance has been small, for average living levels in the 1990s were only about one-fifth greater than in the 1950s. However, life expectancy has improved by about twelve years since 1950, which is a substantial increase (Table 3.2, line 6). This gain is projected by the United Nations to be largely sustained, despite the serious problem of HIV in some countries there, before a marked upward trend resumes around 2010. Important strides have also been made in sub-Saharan Africa with regard to the reduction of illiteracy, and there are also signs of incipient fertility decline (Table 3.2, line 6).

I have pointed out that the rate of advance in economic and social conditions in today's LDCs has, on average, been greater than in the MDCs when they were at a comparable stage. If one compares LDCs' with MDCs' performance in the same time period – since the 1950s – the picture is somewhat different. With regard to GDP per capita, the MDCs' annual growth rate of 2.7 percent since 1950 has slightly exceeded the 2.5 percent of the LDCs, and the income gap, the ratio of MDC to LDC GDP per capita, has consequently grown from 5.1 to 5.5 (Table 3.3, line 1). In contrast, the gaps with regard to life expectancy,

Table 3.2. Major less developed regions: Share of world population in 2000 and indicators of change in economic and social conditions, 1950s to 1990s

Geographic area[a]	(1) Percentage share of world population in 2000	(2) Ratio of GDP per capita in 1995 to that in 1952	(3) Increase in life expectancy, years	(4) Decline in fertility rate, births per woman	(5) Increase in adult literacy rate, percentage points
			ca. 1950 to ca. 1995		
1. China	21	5.0	27.6	4.3	34
2. Asia other than China and India	21	4.6	22.6	2.7	48
3. India	17	2.5	21.6	2.4	33
4. Northern Africa	2	2.4	20.4	2.8	41
5. Latin America	9	1.9	16.7	2.9	29
6. Sub-Saharan Africa	11	1.2	11.7	0.6	39

[a] Ranked by column 2.

Source: Column 1 is the medium variant projection in United Nations Department of Economic and Social Affairs, 1998. In column 2, China and India are from Maddison (1998), p. 40; other areas from Maddison (1995), appendixes A, C, and D. Northern Africa is a weighted average of Egypt and Morocco, which together account for over half of the region's population; sub-Saharan Africa is a weighted average of the rates for seven countries, accounting for about half of the region's population (see Maddison, p. 206). Columns 3–5, same as Table 3.1.

Table 3.3. Gap between more developed countries (MDCs) and less developed countries (LDCs), various indicators of economic and social conditions, ca. 1950 and ca. 1995

	(1) ca. 1950	(2) ca. 1995
1. Real GDP per capita: Ratio of MDCs to LDCs	5.1	5.5
2. Years of life expectancy at birth: MDCs minus LDCs	15.7	12.2
3. Total fertility rate: LDCs minus MDCs	3.4	1.6
4. Percentage of adults literate: MDCs minus LDCs	53	28

Source: See Tables 3.1 and 3.2.

fertility, and literacy have all narrowed (lines 2–4). Thus, although the gap in economic conditions has widened a little, that in social conditions has noticeably lessened.

The measures so far do not take account of political conditions, and here the picture is less positive. The shift from colonial rule to independence in several countries must be recognized as an important advance in the political realm. But if one considers the prevalence of political democracy in LDCs, there is little evidence of improvement over the last half century (Table 3.4, line 2). Most striking, perhaps, is the achievement of sustained democracy in India (line 2c). Against the background of limited political democracy in most of the less developed world today, India stands out as a sharp exception. The contrast with China is notable. When human rights are added to the human development comparison, China's relative success in economic growth, health, and fertility reduction (Table 3.2, lines 1 and 3) must be weighed against India's remarkable record of political democracy. India's feat has been accomplished with a population much more heterogeneous linguistically than in most countries and with income and literacy levels markedly lower than those of the United Kingdom and the United States in the first half of the nineteenth century, when those countries' democratic attainments were less than India's today.

Although there is ambiguity regarding political conditions, the pieces of evidence presented demonstrate that the world is embarked on a sweeping transformation of economic and social conditions. This process is irreversible because it is rooted in the application of unprecedented

Table 3.4. Indicators of political democracy, major areas of the world, 1950–9 and 1990–4 (from minimum of 0 to maximum of 1.0)

	(1)	(2) Executive branch	(3)	(4)	(5) Legislative branch	(6)
	1950–9[a]	1990–4	Change, (2)–(1)	1950–9[a]	1990–4	Change, (5)–(4)
1. More developed areas	.72	.92	.20	.81	.85	.04
2. Less developed areas	.33	.34	.01	.52	.56	.04
a. China	0	0	0	.20	.33	.13
b. Asia other than China and India	.32	.34	.02	.53	.50	−.03
c. India	.90	.80	−.10	1.00	1.00	0
d. Northern Africa	.08	.04	−.04	.27	.32	.05
e. Latin America	.32	.69	.37	.70	.73	.03
f. Sub-Saharan Africa	.25	.14	−.11	.46	.35	−.11

[a] For Northern and sub-Saharan Africa, data are for 1960–9 or years in that decade for which a country's data are available.

Note: The measure for the executive branch is that of "institutionalized democracy," as reported in Jaggers and Gurr (1996). This measure is the sum of four component measures and varies from 0 to 1.0 in 0.1 increments. The components are measures of the competitiveness of political participation (ranging from 0 to 0.3), competitiveness of executive recruitment (0 to 0.2), openness of executive recruitment (0 to 0.1), and constraints on the chief executive (0 to 0.4). See Gurr, Jaggers, and Moore (1991) for further discussion.

The measure for the legislative branch is that of "legislative effectiveness" as given in Banks (1971, 1992, updated 1995). The measure is scaled here as follows: 0 = no legislature exists; 0.3 = ineffective legislature; 0.7 = partially effective legislature; 1.0 = effective legislature. See Banks (1971, xvii) for discussion.

breakthroughs in human knowledge about the natural and social world, and, short of global catastrophe, this knowledge will not be lost. As substantive evidence of this immense acceleration in the growth of knowledge, let me note a few indicators:

1. Discoveries in West European physics from 1650 to 1700, the time now hailed as the "Scientific Revolution," were occurring at an average rate of less than two per year. Two centuries later the rate was over thirty per year (see Chapter 6).
2. A medical historian writing in 1983 of the progress of biomedical knowledge following the validation of the germ theory in the late nineteenth century, says, "In a single century the understanding of disease increased more than in the previous *forty* centuries combined" (Hudson 1983, 121, italics added).
3. In the social realm, for dealing with the problem of unemployment – once viewed as an "act of God" or as punishment for individual failings – new governmental tools of monetary and fiscal policy exist today that largely reflect the twentieth-century progress of economic science. In addition, there are now institutions for international cooperation on economic policy, which, though imperfect, were nonexistent a century ago.

OBSTACLES

A look at experience over the past half-century demonstrates that the world is embarked on an unprecedented transformation in living conditions. This transformation can be projected to continue throughout the twenty-first century as scientific and technological knowledge, natural and social, continue to grow and diffuse throughout the world, bringing the world's population generally to a level of human development never before known. But the lessons of the past also suggest that this future will not easily be achieved, for there are serious obstacles along the way – some more serious and some less.

A favorite obstacle for some is population growth, which is thought to inhibit economic advance because of the pressures it creates on limited natural resources and capital formation. This reasoning, however, overlooks major counterarguments. The most important is that reduced mortality, the source of high population growth, has been brought about by a great reduction in the prevalence of infectious disease. This reduction in disease has not only lowered mortality but also increased health, and an improvement in health means that workers are able to work more hours per week and with greater vigor. This health effect has a positive impact on economic productivity, tending to offset any negative effects due to increased population numbers. The post-1950 upsurge in population growth rates in LDCs has typically been accompanied not by a slowing of growth of per capita income but by an unprecedented increase in growth rates of per capita income. These per capita income growth rates substantially exceed those of the developed countries in the nineteenth century even though the population growth rates of today's LDCs are also much greater than those of the developed countries in the past. Moreover, it is now clear that the population explosion in LDCs is a transient condition as historical research on the "demographic transition" suggested over a half-century ago. As mentioned, rates of childbearing in most LDCs have been falling sharply, and the rate of population growth in LDCs since its late-1960s peak of 2.5 percent has declined steadily to a current value of 1.5 percent. The LDCs' population growth rate is projected by 2025 to be less than 1 percent, which is about the same as in the MDCs only three decades ago.

As the threat of excessive population growth has waned, warnings of ecological disaster brought on by rapid economic growth have come to the forefront. Some argue, for example, that energy resources are insufficient to sustain rapid economic growth on a worldwide scale. Such "expert" forecasts are not new; consider these excerpts from past U.S. agency forecasts on the outlook for oil in this country (Simon 1996):

1885 U.S. Geological Survey: Little or no chance for oil in California.
1891 U.S. Geological Survey: Same prophecy for Texas and Kansas as in 1885 for California.
1914 U.S. Bureau of Mines: Total future production limit of 5.7 billion barrels, perhaps ten-year supply.
1939 Department of the Interior: Reserves to last only thirteen years.
1951 Department of the Interior, Oil and Gas Division: Reserves to last thirteen years.

Similar forecasts about the rising real costs of energy and of total mineral resources have also proven to be mistaken. The basic reason these forecasts have been wrong is that they failed to allow for the critical role that technological progress plays in enhancing the stock of energy and mineral resources via discovery and invention (Simon 1996, Chap. 1).

Concern about environmental degradation has also increased as recognition has grown that economic growth carries with it adverse consequences in the form of air pollution, water pollution, and depletion of soil and forest resources. It is not possible here to deal in detail with such concerns, but, again, a look at historical experience is helpful. A description of the "Great Stench" arising from the accumulation of sewage in London's Thames River in the summer of 1858 is apropos:

> For the first time in the history of man, the sewage of nearly three millions of people had been brought to seethe and ferment under a burning sun, in one vast open cloaca [sewer] lying in their midst.... Stench so foul, we may well believe, had never before ascended to pollute this lower air.... The river steamers lost their accustomed traffic, and travellers, pressed for time, often made a circuit of many miles rather than cross one of the city bridges. (as quoted in Winslow 1943, 288)

Such conditions, common in the nineteenth-century experience of MDCs, engendered concerns much like those voiced today about environmental pollution. These earlier concerns were in time successfully addressed by advances in the technology of urban water supply and sewage disposal and the establishment of a public health organization (see Chapter 7 herein). Today's new environmental problems are being similarly addressed by the development of new technologies and institutions. An assessment only a few years ago of the future outlook by the president of the nonprofit research organization, Resources for the Future, is worth noting. It stated, first, that "it is virtually inconceivable that ambient environmental conditions in the United States, as well as in other Western democracies, will not continue to improve in the decades to come," and that "this favorable environmental experience in developed economies represents a triumph of technology – some required by regulation, some the result of market forces" (Portney 2000, 203). The assessment then suggests that conditions in today's LDCs are following the historical environmental pattern of the MDCs:

> [E]nvironmental quality may deteriorate during a period in which developing countries begin to industrialize, but at some point this deterioration is stopped and reversed as incomes rise....The principal environmental challenge for the

developed world today is to help the developing countries increase their standards of living in ways that help them skirt, to as great an extent as possible, the pollution-intensive period through which the developed countries passed. (Portney 2000, 204)

Reasoning along similar lines, a 1992 World Bank study focusing on environmental problems of the LDCs concluded that "continued, and even accelerated, economic and human development *is* sustainable and can be consistent with *improving* environmental conditions..." (World Bank 1992, iii, italics in original).

The environmental problem for which projection is most difficult is that of climate change due to the accumulation of greenhouse gases in the atmosphere. It is difficult to assess the seriousness of this problem and the urgency of the need for action because of many uncertainties about cause and effect, but the general line of solution is clear: international cooperation on policies to slow the growth rate of carbon dioxide emissions (Portney 2000).

By far, the most worrisome obstacle to continued human improvement is a quite different problem: the international political repercussions of the further spread of modern economic growth. There is first the problem of reactions against modern economic growth, such as that of fundamentalist Islam today, spawned by the growing dominance everywhere of the materialist culture of modern economic growth itself. Such reactions are not themselves new. The nineteenth century witnessed the rise of a significant romantic movement in Western Europe, and China's twentieth-century Cultural Revolution may be seen as a similar type of reaction. What is new is the recent transposition of this type of movement to the international arena – with the leader in modern economic growth, the United States, taken as the symbol of cultural decay – plus systematic resort to terrorist attack as the weapon of reaction. Historically, such reactions have been unavailing against the rising material aspirations engendered by economic growth. But today the danger is greatly increased by the growing availability of means of mass destruction, and the question remains open whether containment and elimination of such threats via international cooperation will ultimately prevail.

The second concern is the disturbance to the balance of political power brought about by the spread of modern economic growth itself. Although economic growth is not the only source of political conflict, it has been the most pervasive and powerful factor in the last two centuries (Kennedy 1987). This is because the rate of economic growth has become so great, and the technology underlying such growth bestows on a populous nation a vast increase in military potential and thus in political power. Since 1800, the differential occurrence of modern economic growth in a world of competing nation-states has created vast disturbances in the international balance of power. It has led to a temporary extension of political sovereignty by MDCs over LDCs and to repeated challenges to the leaders in development by newcomers to the scene, erupting in world wars. The leadership of Great Britain throughout much of the nineteenth century and the subsequent appearance of rivals such as Germany and the United States, followed by Japan and the former Soviet Union, correspond to the timing and spread of modern economic growth.

The foundation of the current world power structure, with the West at the top, is the economic gap between rich and poor nations. As this gap is narrowed – as more and more populous, LDCs become members of the developed set – power must shift to the newer members as it has in the past. The rise of Japan to membership is but a harbinger of what is to come. The major countries of the East Asian "miracle" – Indonesia, Thailand, Korea, Taiwan, and Malaysia – which collectively number over 320 million people, are not far behind. Behind them are China and India, which together account for more than one-third of the world's population. It is hard to see how the West can maintain the political dominance of the world that it has enjoyed in the last two centuries as economic strength once again becomes more evenly distributed.

It is commonly assumed in the United States today that this country can and should maintain its position as the world's dominant political power. But economic growth in the twenty-first century will inevitably require, as it has in the past, continued redistribution of political power to newly developing large nations. The further redistribution of political power in the world in the twenty-first century can gradually be accomplished through the leadership of the United States and other developed countries, but if a peaceable solution to this problem cannot be found, there is the danger that it will erupt in disastrous military conflict much as it did in the nineteenth and twentieth centuries. One can hardly be sanguine that this redistribution of world political power will be successfully accomplished because the solution to this problem, in contrast to that of environmental degradation, rests even more on social than natural science and because both awareness of, and concern for, the problem remain so limited.

ARE WE ENTERING A NEW POSTMATERIALISTIC ERA?

Let us suppose, however, that catastrophic international upheaval is averted and the transition to worldwide human development is successfully achieved. If this comes to pass, what will the world be like? Will "the economic problem" have been put to rest and will humanity have turned to more meaningful pursuits?

Ever since psychologist Abraham Maslow's 1950s formulation of a "hierarchy of needs," it has been widely assumed that the satisfaction of material wants is but one lower stage in human evolution and that economic growth brings with it a movement toward higher nonmaterialistic ends (Cox and Alm 1999, Chap. 9; Maslow 1954; van de Kaa 1999, 29 ff.). According to Maslow, humans have a variety of needs, and they satisfy them in a certain order. For a person on the margin of existence, food is everything. Physical safety comes next; its priority is almost as high as that of sustenance, but a starving man will risk his life to get food. Once an individual has satisfied material needs – those for physical and economic security – "*at once other (and higher) needs emerge* and these, rather than physiological hungers, dominate the organism"(Maslow 1954, 83, italics in original). These higher needs are, first, needs for love, belonging, and esteem. Later, intellectual and aesthetic goals, which Maslow calls "self-actualization needs," become important. Thus, he offers a vision of human progress from a struggle for physical survival to total personal fulfillment.

A similar refrain has been sounded in the economics literature. In the mid-nineteenth century, political economist John Stuart Mill saw England, by virtue of its recent progress, as being on the verge of a stationary state, one in which growth of population and output would come to a halt. Mill viewed this prospect with equanimity because, to him

> a stationary condition implies no stationary state of human improvement. There would be as much scope as ever for all kinds of mental culture, and moral and social progress, as much room for improving the Art of Living, and much more

likelihood of it being improved, when minds ceased to be engrossed by the art of getting on. (Mill [1850] 1965, 756)

Writing in 1931, John Maynard Keynes, the most eminent economist of the twentieth century, looked forward to

the day . . . not far off when the Economic Problem will take the back seat where it belongs, and . . . the arena of the heart and head will be occupied . . . by our real problems – the problems of life and of human relations, of creation and behavior and religion. (Keynes 1932, vii)

Keynes once offered a toast that put it even more succinctly: "To economists, who are the trustees, not of civilization, but of the possibility of civilization" (Harrod 1982, 194).

More recently, in an article published in 1997, Nobel laureate Robert W. Fogel asserted:

[I]n the future luxury will be defined increasingly in terms of spiritual rather than material resources. The touchstone of well-being in the future for both young and old will be measured increasingly in terms of the quality of health and the opportunity for self-realization. (Fogel 1997, 1905)

In economics, such views, even today, have remained no more than casual suppositions. But supposed empirical support for the emergence of a postmaterialistic society in the last few decades has recently been advanced by a prominent American political scientist, Ronald Inglehart, based on the results of numerous surveys conducted here and in Europe (Inglehart 1977, 1988, 1997). Since World War II, the West has enjoyed a half-century of unprecedented peace and prosperity. With the satisfaction of material needs in this period, Inglehart claims – as do some American and European colleagues – that these surveys demonstrate that a new generation of individuals has emerged characterized by higher "postmaterialist" values: social and self-actualization goals. To judge from Inglehart's work, humankind is seemingly becoming less engrossed with "the art of getting on" and is, at last, turning to "the Art of Living."

But is it? I think the facts are to the contrary. An instructive starting point is the evidence on human happiness previously mentioned. Since World War II, many representative national surveys have been conducted in various countries in which respondents are asked a simple question about how happy they are: very happy, fairly happy, or not very happy. In these surveys each person is free to define happiness in his or her own terms. Hence, one might suppose that no useful comparisons of persons could be made. As it turns out, however, the factors affecting happiness are fairly similar for most persons. Happiness everywhere is governed by the things that take up most of one's personal everyday life: making a living and raising and maintaining a healthy family. Hence, scholars studying these data have concluded that meaningful comparisons can be made at least among sizable groups of people.

The critical importance of economic conditions is indicated by the fact that in every national survey ever conducted the rich are, on average, happier than the poor. This does not mean, of course, that every rich person is happy and every poor person unhappy – as I said, I am talking here about comparisons among groups of people.

This finding of a positive *point-of-time* relation between happiness and income would lead one to expect that the vastly higher levels of real income that economic growth brings would lead to advances in happiness in the same – positive – direction. And this is where the "catch" comes – the paradox of happiness. Over time, happiness does *not* rise with income, and this is true even with very large increases in income. Let me cite a few examples, some of which were touched on in Chapter 2:

1. In the United States since World War II, real per capita income has more than doubled. The average level of happiness, however, is the same today as it was in the late 1940s.
2. The story is similar for Europe. There are nine European countries for which happiness-type measures go back at least two decades. Between the 1970s and 1990s, real income per capita rose substantially in all of these countries by amounts ranging from 25 to 50 percent. In five of the nine countries, happiness was unchanged; in two it went up, and in two it went down. Net change in happiness for all nine countries: zero.
3. The experience of Japan is of special interest because of its relevance to today's poor countries. The happiness data for Japan go back to the late 1950s when it had an income level below that of many of today's LDCs. Between the 1950s and late 1980s, Japan had the most phenomenal economic growth ever witnessed. Real income per capita multiplied by an incredible fivefold. What happened to

happiness during this period of unparalleled income growth? The answer is, no change.

4. Finally, let me shift from the country as the unit of analysis to a birth cohort, that is, a group of persons born in the same span of years such as 1946 to 1950. In following an American birth cohort, or "generation," over their adult life cycle, one finds that average income rises steadily and substantially throughout the working years and then levels off. Does this growth in income mean that people, on average, get happier as they progress through the life cycle? The answer is no. For the typical cohort, happiness is, on average, remarkably stable throughout the *entire* adult life cycle (Easterlin 2001).

One may reasonably ask, What does all this have to do with Maslow's and Inglehart's progression up the hierarchy of needs? The answer is, a great deal. For in resolving the paradox of happiness, we are led to understand the way that economic growth is preparing our future.

At a point in time happiness and income are positively related; yet, over time there is no relation. Why this paradoxical pattern? A simple thought experiment suggests the basic reason. Imagine that your income increases substantially while everyone else's stays the same. Would you feel better off? The answer most people would give is yes. But now suppose that your income stays the same, whereas everyone else's increases substantially. How would you feel? Most people would say that they feel less well off even though no change has actually occurred in their real income or living level.

Now what this thought experiment is demonstrating is that judgments of personal well-being ("happiness") are made by comparing one's *objective* situation with a *subjective* (or internalized) living level norm, and this internal norm is significantly influenced by the average level of living of the society as a whole. If the average living level in society increases, a rise in subjective living level norms results – the measure of how people feel they *ought* to live. In a situation in which incomes increase generally, an individual whose income is unchanged will feel poorer even though his or her *objective* circumstances are the same as before. Karl Marx put it this way: "A house may be large or small; as long as the surrounding houses are equally small it satisfies all social demands for a dwelling. But if a palace rises beside the little house, the little house shrinks into a hut" (as quoted by Lipset 1960, 63).

Hence, although happiness, or subjective well-being, varies positively with one's own income, it also varies negatively with the incomes of others. At any given time, the incomes of others are fixed, and those who are more affluent feel happier, on average. This is the point-of-time relationship. However, raising the incomes of *all* does *not* increase the happiness of *all* because the positive effect on one's well-being of higher income for oneself is offset by the negative effect of a higher living level *norm* brought about by the growth in incomes generally.

Stated simply, material aspirations – how we feel we *ought* to live – depend on a society's state of affluence. In times and places where incomes are lower, aspirations are lower. As incomes rise, aspirations rise.

Let me give some specific evidence that aspirations vary with the level of real per capita income.

1. A point-of-time comparison of aspirations in rich and poor countries comes from a very comprehensive survey done by social psychologist Hadley Cantril several decades ago. Cantril's interviewers asked people an open-ended question on what they would need to be "perfectly happy." Here are some answers from respondents in India (Cantril 1965, 205–6):

A 35-year-old agricultural laborer says:

I want a son and a piece of land… I would like to construct a house of my own and have a cow for milk and ghee. I would also like to buy some better clothing for my wife. If I could do this then I would be happy.

A 30-year-old sweeper says:

I wish for an increase in my wages because with my meager salary I cannot afford to buy decent food for my family. If the food and clothing problems were solved, then I would feel at home and be satisfied. Also if my wife were able to work the two of us could then feed the family and I am sure we would have a happy life and our worries would be over.

A 45-year-old housewife says:

I should like to have a water tap and a water supply in my house. It would also be nice to have electricity. My husband's wages must be increased if our children are to get an education and our daughter is to be married.

Finally, here is the response of a 40-year-old skilled worker:

I hope in the future I will not get any disease. Now I am coughing. I also hope I can purchase a bicycle. I hope my children will study well and that I can provide them with an education. I also would sometime like to own a fan and maybe a radio.

Now compare what Americans at that time said *they* would need to be perfectly happy (Cantril 1965, 222):

Here is a 27-year-old skilled worker:

If I could earn more money I would then be able to buy our own home and have more luxury around us, like better furniture, a new car, and more vacations.

A laboratory technician, 34-years-old, says:

I would like a reasonable enough income to maintain a house, have a new car, have a boat, and send my four children to private schools.

Here is a 24-year-old bus driver:

I would like a new car. I wish all my bills were paid and I had more money for myself. I would like to play more golf and to hunt more than I do. I would like to have more time to do the things I want to and to entertain my friends.

And, finally, a 28-year-old lawyer:

Materially speaking, I would like to provide my family with an income to allow them to live well – to have the proper recreation, to go camping, to have music and dancing lessons for the children, and to have family trips. I wish we could belong to a country club and do more entertaining. We just bought a new home and expect to be perfectly satisfied with it for a number of years.

These responses illustrate that the aspirations one acquires are a product of the society in which one lives and that, the more affluent the society, the higher the material aspirations.

2. That is how material aspirations differ between a rich and poor country at a point in time. Next, let me indicate how aspirations change over time within the same country. Since 1975, Americans have been asked the following question: "We often hear people talk about what they want out of life.... When you think of the good life – the life you'd like to have – which of the things on the [following] list [of 24 items], if

any, are part of that good life as far as you personally are concerned?" (Roper Starch Organization, 1979, 1995.)

Ten of the listed "good life" items relate specifically to "big ticket" consumer goods: "a home you own," "a car," "a color TV," and so forth. For every one of the ten consumer goods listed, there is an increase between 1975 and 1994 in the percentage identifying it as "part of the good life." For consumer goods to which a high proportion of the population aspired at the start of the period, such as "a home you own," the increase is necessarily modest. But for items that were initially low on the "good life" list, the increase is sizable. In 1975, the proportion of Americans saying "a vacation home" was part of the good life was 19 percent; two decades later it was 44 percent. In 1975, the proportion identifying a swimming pool as part of the good life was 14 percent; in 1994, 37 percent.

These data are at sharp variance with Ronald Inglehart's claim that since World War II postmaterialist values have emerged that have, in his words, "tended to neutralize the emphasis on economic accumulation" (Inglehart 1988, 1203). The basis for Inglehart's claim is the responses to survey questions about what the aims of a nation should be for the next ten years. Such questions, however, do not tap the personal aspirations of individuals, the goals that chiefly motivate their behavior; rather the questions relate to what people want for their country. As Hadley Cantril demonstrated over 40 years ago, there is a great difference between people's responses when asked about their concerns for their country and those they give regarding their personal concerns (Cantril 1965; cf. also Clark and Rempel 1997, Chaps. 1–4).

In contrast to Inglehart's questions relating to national goals, the good life data just cited ask *specifically* about one's personal interests – "the life *you'd* like to have," "the things [that] are part of [the] good life as far as you *personally* are concerned (Roper Starch Organization, 1979, 1995; emphasis added)." Let me cite two other of these "good life" responses that bear on the purported emergence of "postmaterialist" values. Besides specific consumer goods, the good life list includes items relating to job characteristics that people view as forming part of the good life. Two are of special interest here: one, "a job that pays much more than the average" and the other, "a job that contributes to the welfare of society." We may, I think, take the former (pays much more than the average) as relating chiefly to materialist values, and the latter (contributes to society), to postmaterialist values. Both in 1975 and 1994, the percentage of people naming the materialist response as part of the good life exceeded that of people giving the nonmaterialist response. But even more important, if we look at the trend in responses reflecting materialist concerns relative to those reflecting social concerns, the excess of those with materialist concerns rose between 1975 and 1994 from 7 to 21 percentage points. This suggests a shift toward materialist values, not away from them, which is a development consistent with the increased aspirations for big ticket consumer goods. This shift may eventually prove to be a longer-term fluctuation, rather than a secular trend, but it is clearly at variance with Inglehart's assertion that there has been a movement away from materialist values in the last several decades.

WHERE IS ECONOMIC GROWTH TAKING US?

It is time now to consider the implications of this evidence for the future. As I have noted, a common theme of Maslow and disciples of his such as Inglehart is the liberating effect of economic progress – that as material wants become satisfied, people will increasingly turn to higher-order pursuits.

But suppose that material needs are *never* satisfied because each step up on the ladder of material abundance brings with it a new set of "necessaries" – a swimming pool, a tennis court, an exercise room, a vacation home, a private security system, and so on – desires, we tell ourselves, that would make us perfectly happy if only they were satisfied.

Indeed, the evidence is that this is the human condition. When asked, people invariably say that higher income will increase their happiness. Yet, when they actually do get more income, their happiness does not increase, and they find themselves in the same state of still striving for more. The explanation of this paradox is that, when people project into the future the likely effect on their happiness of higher income, they are basing the projection on their *current* subjective level of material aspirations. What they do not realize is that, as incomes in society rise generally, so too will their views on their own needs – the material content of the "good life" – and the effect of this increase on their subjective needs will be to negate the expected growth in happiness due to having more goods to enjoy.

Thus, the evidence suggests that economic growth is not a mere stage in human development that frees humankind from the burden of physiological needs and thereby fosters the attainment of higher cultural needs. Instead, economic growth is a carrier of a material culture of its own that ensures that humankind is forever ensnared in the pursuit of more and more economic goods.

The world today is in the midst of a great revolution brought about by the spread of economic growth. Country after country, culture after culture, including the ancient cultures of Japan, China, India, and Persia, are falling before the juggernaut of economic growth. A new universal religion is sweeping the world: the worship of economic goods. Just consider today's middle-class youth. Throughout the world they hail the same music groups, follow the same sporting events, and aspire to similar Nike-like lifestyles. Language is no barrier; historical culture is no barrier. The mass media, the messengers of economic growth, have brought the word to every corner of the earth that money is the key to happiness – not a great deal of money, of course but just enough to live "happily." But what the public does not know is the elastic nature of "just enough" – that its magnitude will always be rising from one generation to the next – the proverbial carrot on a stick. Americans today, while building ever-bigger and better furnished homes, complain about providing for others: the burden of decent schools for children, health care for all, support of the elderly, and, more generally, of help for those throughout the world who are disadvantaged. Europeans, richer than ever before, are dismantling the welfare state. These Western societies are the leaders in economic growth; their present is the future to which economic growth is leading the world so long as we allow it to.

But is this the future to which we want the enormous productivity of modern economic growth to be put? Is this the form the world's wealth *must* assume in the twenty-first century? It does not take much imagination to think of alternatives. We could devote more resources to caring for others at home and abroad or to creating a more aesthetic environment with gardens, parks, and the like. We could take more of the benefits of higher productivity in the form of increased leisure and use that time to enjoy family, friends, and relatives; to get to know our neighbors; to participate in community affairs; to engage in music and the arts, philosophical contemplation, or religious pursuits; to pursue athletic activities; to develop our learning through continuing education;

or simply to commune with nature. Economists, the most influential of the social scientists, under the illusion that they are value-free scientists, take as sacrosanct the preferences of individuals. These preferences lie behind the choices that currently determine the uses to which the fruits of economic growth are put. But these preferences are themselves a direct result of economic growth – of the immersion of young people as they grow up in the materialistic and individualistic culture that economic growth creates. Ultimately, we must face the issue of whether we take individual preferences as inviolable and remain the servants of economic growth or address openly and fully what we mean by the good life and become the masters of growth.

PART TWO

ECONOMIC HISTORY

4

Why Isn't the Whole World Developed?

It is now over two centuries since the coming of modern economic growth was signaled by James Watt's invention of the single-acting steam engine. In this period, output per capita and per unit of labor input have risen at long-term rates never seen before in human history – first in northern and western Europe and North America; then, in the period up to 1950, in Japan, southern and eastern Europe, Oceania, and parts of Latin America; and, finally, since World War II, in much of the rest of the world. The great disparity among regions in the timing of the onset of modern economic growth has produced the current immense gap in living levels between the more and less developed countries of the world (Chapter 3, Table 3.3, line 1).

The primary task of the discipline of economic history is to describe and explain economic change in the past. Given the unprecedented geographic contrasts in economic growth over the last two centuries, an objective look at historical experience would not, I think, place the questions that have so long dominated the study of economic history in the foreground. The preoccupation of Western scholars with American and European – largely northwestern European – economic history can only seem provincial, for the striking feature about these areas is the fundamental similarity in their experience. Rather, the foremost issue of modern economic history, the one that challenges explanation, is why the spread of economic growth was so limited in the period up to 1950; why isn't the whole world developed today? No one can pretend to know the answer to this question, but it is worth speculating about it if only to build a case for a redirection of research in economic history.[1]

TECHNOLOGICAL CHANGE AND ECONOMIC GROWTH

Let us imagine, to start with, a world not unlike that of the late eighteenth century – a world of low and roughly similar levels of economic productivity everywhere and with fairly limited international contacts through trade, migration, and investment. Suppose now that in one nation economic productivity starts rising rapidly and steadily because of an unprecedented rate of technological progress. Before long, a second nation sets off on a similar course as technological change also accelerates dramatically, and, then, a third. After a century or so, the total number of nations so embarked remains – on a worldwide scale – small, though increasing.

Consider now a few implications of this development. Eventually, large and growing disparities would emerge between income levels in those nations enjoying the fruits of rapid technological progress and those that are not. International trade and investment would expand greatly as a result of sharp shifts in comparative advantage caused by differential technological progress and also the unprecedented growth of per capita income in some areas. Trade would also be promoted because international transfer costs would fall substantially as those nations benefiting from new technology applied it to problems of international as well as domestic transport. The resulting increased flow of goods and resources internationally would have some beneficial effect on world income levels generally, but such effects would be relatively small compared with the dominating effect on income levels of major differences among countries in productivity growth due to technological change.

[1] A beautifully written book by evolutionary biologist Jared Diamond (1998) proposes a geographic explanation. Differential development of the various parts of the world stems from differences among them in the availability of wild plants and animals adaptable to domestication and the east–west or north–south orientation of the continents' axes (cf. p. 29, in Diamond's book).

These factors seem relevant to explaining geographic differences in the transition from hunter-gatherer societies to settled agriculture, although even in this regard, these factors cannot explain the timing of this transition. Today's great worldwide differences in living levels, however, stem from the much later shift from settled agriculture to industrial societies.

This, I suggest, is the essence of what occurred in the century and a half through 1950. During this period, international income differences grew at unprecedented rates, as did foreign trade and investment. The prime mover in this drama was the sharp acceleration in the rate of technological change in a relatively small number of nations.

If this view is correct, then it follows that explaining why modern economic growth has spread so slowly becomes a matter of explaining why rapid technological change was limited for so long to so few nations.

To answer this, one must first consider whether rapid technological change, when it occurred in a country, was based on a new technology that was indigenous or stemmed from a borrowed technology. The widely accepted view is that a common technology basically diffused from one country to the next (Henderson 1972; Landes 1969; Saxonhouse 1974; Strassman 1959; Tuge 1961). This is evidenced by the striking likeness of modern industrial and transportation technology among the various high-productivity nations. In the case of agriculture, in which local environmental conditions play an important part in production, perhaps one might hesitate to stress the borrowed over indigenous elements in modern technological change. But even in agriculture, one finds that many of the principles of modern technology (irrigation, seed selection, livestock breeding, fertilizer, and, more recently, development of hybrids and use of pesticides) exhibit quite similar features among nations. Thus, it seems reasonable to conclude that the question of explaining differential technological change among nations in the modern period is a matter chiefly of accounting for the limited diffusion of a common technology.

A central conclusion of research on technological diffusion is that the transfer of technology is primarily a person-to-person process (Rosenberg 1970; see also Teece 1976). As Nathan Rosenberg points out, "the [economist's] notion of a production function as a 'set of blueprints' comes off very badly... if it is taken to mean a body of techniques which is available *independently* of the human inputs who utilize it" (Rosenberg 1970, emphasis added). Ingvar Svennilson states, "much of the detailed knowledge that is born in the course of industrial operations can more easily and in part *exclusively* be transferred by demonstration and training in actual operations" (Svennilson 1964, emphasis added). To Kenneth Arrow, "it seems to be personal contact that is most relevant in leading to . . . adoption [of an innovation]" (Arrow 1969; see also Spencer 1970).

This emphasis on the personal element in the diffusion of technology suggests that understanding this transfer might usefully be approached by viewing it as an educational process in which a new and difficult subject, "modern" technology, must be taught and learned. From this point of view, explanation of the limited spread of modern economic growth turns into a matter of identifying the factors that have constrained the dissemination of a new type of knowledge – that of modern production methods.

TECHNOLOGICAL CHANGE AND FORMAL SCHOOLING

Viewing the transfer of technology as an educational process leads naturally to questions about teachers and students. If new technological knowledge spread slowly, did the fault lie on the teachers' side or the students'?

One reason for minimizing the teachers' responsibility is that, when entrepreneurs or governments in have-not nations wanted the new technology, they seem to have been able to beg, borrow, buy, or steal teachers as well as to send their nationals to the technologically advanced nations for instruction. After the Meiji Restoration, for example, Japan imported numerous foreign scholars and technological experts and sent students to study at Western universities and institutes (Henderson 1972; Schairer 1927; Tuge 1961).

The more important question thus lies on the side of the students. What is it that makes for effective learning? The answer is that learning is partly a matter of inherent intelligence, partly of aptitudes, and partly of incentives. What all teachers seek are bright, well-trained, and highly motivated students.

I think we can safely dismiss the view that the failure of modern technological knowledge to spread rapidly was due to significant differences among nations in the native intelligence of their populations. A more persuasive case might be made concerning incentives for learning; institutional differences among countries undoubtedly created variations in the incentives for mastering the new technology. But it is important to recognize that the new technology itself created incentives for learning via the competitive pressures exerted through international trade.

Thus, the rapid response by producers in parts of Continental Europe and the United States to the British Industrial Revolution was partly induced by the growing flood of imported British manufactures into their markets. The new technology also created pressures for its more widespread adoption by endowing its possessors with superior military capability. The threat to political sovereignty thus posed was a strong incentive for governments in low-productivity countries to initiate and promote programs of technological modernization, as in Japan. Eventually, such economic and political pressures were felt in many nations throughout the world; yet often the new technology failed to be taken up. The question is, Why?

The answer, I suggest, has to do in part with differences among countries in the extent of their population's formal schooling: the more schooling of appropriate content that a nation's population had, the easier it was to master the new technological knowledge becoming available. Moreover, substantial increases in formal schooling tend to be accompanied by significant improvement in the incentive structure and the opportunities open to the population. Hence, increased motivation provided by new opportunities often accompanies increased aptitudes for learning new technology.

Were there significant international differences in formal schooling when modern technology first came on the scene in the late eighteenth century? The answer is an emphatic yes. As a step toward establishing the facts, Figure 4.1 presents historical data for twenty-five of the largest countries of the world (in 1960 they accounted for over three-fourths of the world's population) on a very crude indicator of educational development, the primary school enrollment rate, and the percentage of a country's total population enrolled in primary school.[2] This measure is subject to conceptual and measurement biases, most notably to variations in the proportion of school age population to the total, but it is a reasonable indicator of significant differences among nations and trends over time in their population's exposure to formal schooling.[3] If none

[2] The countries chosen were those with 1960 populations greater than 18 million. Because of insufficient historical data, Poland, Pakistan, and Vietnam are omitted.

[3] Among other comparability problems are the occasional use of attendance rather than enrollment data, variations in the time of year for which enrollment is reported, differences in the length of the school day and school year, and differences in schools included in the "primary" category (e.g., kindergartens).

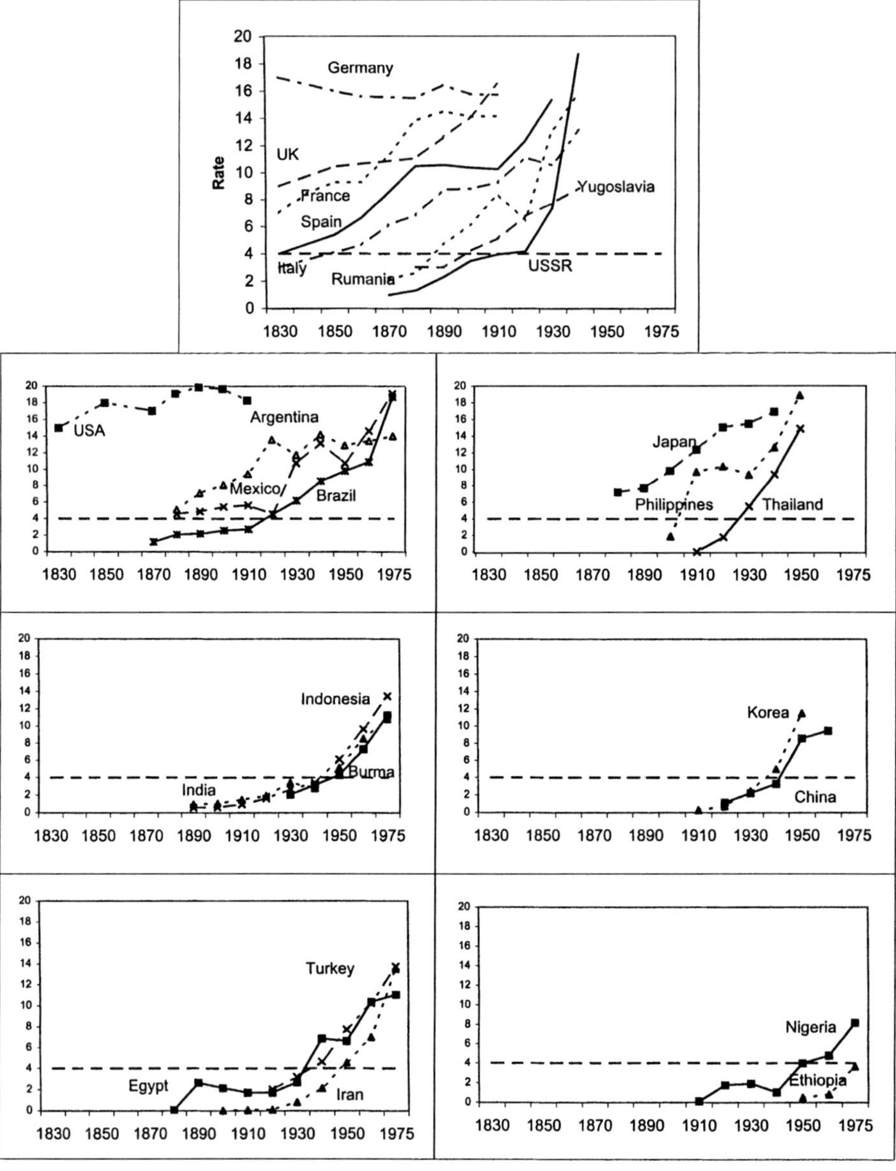

Figure 4.1. Primary school enrollment rate, by country, 1830–1975 (percent of total population).
Source: Table 4.1.

Table 4.1. Estimated primary school enrollment rate, by country, 1830–1975 (percent of total population)

	Year														
Country	1830	1840	1850	1860	1870	1882	1890	1900	1910	1920	1930	1939	1950	1960	1970
USA	15.0		18.0		17.0	19.1	19.9	19.7	18.3						
UK	9.0		10.4			11.1	12.6	14.1	16.5						
France	7.0	8.5	9.3	9.3	11.3	13.8	14.5	14.1	14.1						
Germany	17.0		16.0	15.6		15.5	16.4	15.8	15.7						
Italy	3.0			4.6	6.1	6.8	8.7	8.8	9.3	11.1	10.6	13.1			
Spain	4.0		5.4	6.6	8.5	10.5	10.6	10.4	10.3	12.3	15.4				
Rumania					2.1	2.6	4.7	6.2	8.4	6.4	13.1	15.8			
Yugoslavia						3.0	3.0	4.2	5.1	6.7	7.7	8.9			
USSR					1.0	1.3	2.3	3.5	4.0	4.2	7.3	18.7			
Argentina						5.1	7.1	8.1	9.4	13.6	11.7	14.2	12.9	13.4	14.0
Mexico						4.6	4.9	5.4	5.6	4.6	10.7	13.1	10.7	14.6	19.3
Brazil					1.2	2.1	2.2	2.6	2.7	4.6	6.2	8.5	9.8	10.9	18.7
Burma											2.1	3.2	4.3	7.3	11.3
India							0.9	1.1	1.5	1.9	3.4	2.8	5.1	8.5	10.8
Indonesia							0.6	0.6	1.0	1.6	2.7	3.4	6.1	9.6	13.5
Japan						7.2	7.7	9.8	12.4	15.1	15.5	17.0			
Philippines								1.9	9.7	10.4	9.4	12.7	18.9		

(continued)

Table 4.1. (continued)

Country	Year														
	1830	1840	1850	1860	1870	1882	1890	1900	1910	1920	1930	1939	1950	1960	1970
Thailand									0.1	1.8	5.5	9.4	14.9		
Egypt						[a]	2.6	2.2	1.7	1.7	2.7	6.9	6.6	10.4	11.0
Iran								[a]	0.1	0.1	0.8	2.1	4.6	7.0	13.5
Turkey										2.0	3.2	4.6	7.8	10.3	13.2
China										1.2	2.2	3.3	8.6	9.5	
Korea									0.3	0.7	2.5	5.0	11.5		
Nigeria									0.1	1.8	1.9	1.0	4.0	4.8	8.2
Ethiopia													0.5	0.8	3.7

[a] Less than 0.05.

Source: A: Arthur S. Banks. *Cross-Polity Time Series Data* (Cambridge, 1971); B: *The Statesman's Yearbook 1883–1960* (London, 1883–1960); C: E. Levasseur, *L'Enseignment primaire dans les pays civilizes* (Paris, 1897); D: Richard A. Easterlin, "A Note on the Evidence of History," in C. Arnold Anderson and Mary Jean Bowman, eds., *Education and Economic Development* (Chicago, 1965), pp. 422–9; E: Andrew J. Grajdaznev, *Modern Korea* (New York, 1944); F: UNESCO, *Statistical Yearbook 1977* (Paris, 1978) and United Nations, *Demographic Yearbook 1977* (New York, 1978). Source of data for 1975 is F; for all other dates A, except as follows: USA 1830, 1850–D; UK 1830, 1850–D; France 1830–D; 1840–60–C; Germany 1830, 1850–D, 1860–C; Italy 1830–D, 1860, 1870–C; Spain 1830–D, 1850–C; Rumania 1870, 1890–C; USSR 1890–C; Argentina 1882–C; Burma 1930–50–B; India 1890–1930–B; Indonesia 1890–1939–B; Philippines 1900–39–B; Thailand 1910–39–B; Egypt 1882–1939–B; Iran 1900–39–B; Korea 1910–39–E; Nigeria 1910–50–B.

of a country's school age population were enrolled in school, the measure would be zero. If all of the school age population were enrolled, the measure in the periods of concern would be in the vicinity of 15 to 20 percent, which is the typical share of those of school age in a country's total population. Roughly speaking, a school enrollment rate less than 4 percent signifies relatively little exposure of a nation's population to formal education. If, for example, the school age population accounted for 16 percent of the country's population, a 4-percent enrollment rate implies that about one-fourth (4/16) of the school age population is enrolled in school. Values in the 4- to 8-percent range can be taken as signifying a moderate exposure, and values greater than 8 percent indicate substantial exposure. In the figure, to facilitate comparisons among countries, a horizontal broken line is drawn at 4 percent to help identify periods when school enrollment in a country was very low. Differences among countries in peak values, and the trend in these peak values, are of little analytical significance because they chiefly reflect variations in the proportion of the school age population. For this reason, and to reduce confusion in the figure, a country's curve is not plotted after it reaches a fairly high level.

The first impression that emerges from the graph is the very limited extent of formal schooling in most nations throughout much of the period. In 1850, virtually the entire population of the world outside of northwestern Europe and Northern America had little or no exposure to formal schooling. Even by 1940 this was still largely the case in Africa, most of Asia, and a substantial part of Latin America.

Does the graph offer support for the idea that spread of the technology of modern economic growth depended on learning potentials and incentives that were linked to the development of formal schooling? The answer, I believe, is yes. Within Europe the most advanced nations educationally, those in northern and western Europe, were the ones that developed first. Not until the end of the nineteenth century did most of southern and eastern Europe start to approach educational levels comparable to the initial levels in the north and west, and it was around this time that these nations began to develop. Outside of Europe the picture is the same: the leader in schooling is the leader in overseas development, the United States. In Latin America, Argentina, the leader in development there, was in the forefront of educational growth in the last half of the nineteenth century. The leader in economic growth in Asia,

Japan, was also ahead on the education front. Japan's nineteenth-century educational attainment is clearly distinctive in Asia, and this was true even before the Meiji Restoration, though important schooling reforms were introduced in 1872 (Ohkawa and Rosovsky 1965; Passin 1965; Yasuba 1987). In contrast, note the persistently low educational levels in Turkey well into the twentieth century. Throughout the nineteenth century, Turkey was subject in many ways to external economic and political pressures greater than those experienced by Japan but failed to modernize technologically.

There is, of course, the matter of cause and effect: Are we looking here at the effect of education on economic growth, or vice versa? Is the growth of schooling merely induced by the process of economic growth itself? In theory, this could be the case: the higher income accompanying economic growth and increased returns to better educated workers would stimulate the demand for education. But the evidence in Figure 4.1 suggests that the growth of formal schooling often antedated or occurred largely independently of economic growth. Note that in the United States and Germany development of widespread formal schooling clearly preceded the onset of modern economic growth. Note, too, that for several countries the schooling curves show abrupt upswings that are not matched by concurrent surges in economic development; examples are Rumania between 1880 and 1910, the Philippines between 1900 and 1920, and Mexico and Thailand between 1920 and 1940.

There is thus evidence consistent with the notion that formal schooling fosters attributes in a population that are conducive to the acquisition of modern technology. There remains, however, important questions about the type of schooling and attributes.[4] Is it true, for example, that "the spread of technological knowledge, narrowly considered, is not a matter of mass education, but of the training of a small elite?" (Parker 1961). If mass education is important, does it have its effect via training in functional skills such as "the three Rs," through "screening," or via political socialization, either of a broad sort, or more narrowly, in instilling a discipline appropriate to factory work?[5] Or is the function

[4] For valuable discussion of some of the questions in this paragraph, see Anderson and Bowman (1965, 1976); Bowman and Anderson (1977); Cameron (1975); Carnoy (1977); Harbison and Myers (1964); Stone (1976); World Bank (1980).

[5] Bowles and Gintis (1976); Carnoy (1974); Coleman (1965); Dreeben (1968); Foster (1965); Graff (1979); Katz (1971).

of education, as some sociological studies suggest, one chiefly of creating a basic change in human personality – a "modern man" who acquires aspirations and attitudes especially favorable to the adoption of new technology? (Form 1979; Inkeles 1973; Inkeles and Smith 1974; McClelland 1966).

The present state of knowledge does not, I think, provide satisfactory answers to the question of what types of education have what specific effects on economic growth, and clearly the answers to the preceding questions need not be mutually exclusive. It seems likely, however, that a substantial primary education system is essential for sustained economic growth. The reason for this is clear if one contrasts the process of achieving higher income levels with that of raising life expectancy. Thanks to modern public health and medical technology, it has proven possible to improve life expectancy markedly even among large populations through measures such as use of pesticides, water purification, and establishment of sewage systems that require knowledge and action by relatively few specialists (see Chapters 6 and 7). In contrast, raising productivity levels involves active participation in new production methods by large numbers of the population – by workers in agriculture, industry, transportation, and so on. This is not to say that secondary and higher education can be ignored; clearly, one needs technologists as well as mass education. But increases at higher levels of education typically go together with the expansion of primary education. In contrast, education of the elite without mass education is unlikely to foster economic growth.[6]

It also seems that the content of education conducive to economic growth is secular and rationalistic. Although such content has usually characterized an expansion in mass education, this has not always been true. Among the countries in Figure 4.1, Spain stands out as a country whose rate of educational development seemingly exceeded its economic growth. A closer look at Spanish education, however, reveals that, until the twentieth century, it remained closely controlled by the Roman Catholic Church: "[T]he children of the masses received only

[6] In the nineteenth century, educational modernization in the Ottoman Empire, to the extent it occurred, stressed education of the elite; see Kazamias (1966). The 1950s data for India presented by Harbison and Meyers (1964, 47) suggest a disproportion of secondary and higher education relative to primary.

oral instruction in the Creed, the catechism, and a few simple manual skills. ... [S]cience, mathematics, political economy, and secular history were considered too controversial for anyone but trained theologians" (Thut and Adams 1964, 62). One consequence of this is that literacy in Spain fails to show an increase commensurate with what one might expect from the data on primary school enrollment; even by 1900 almost two-thirds of the population remained illiterate.

DETERMINANTS OF FORMAL EDUCATION

In simplest terms, the argument to this point is that the spread of the technology underlying modern economic growth depended in considerable part on the extent to which the populations of different countries had acquired appropriate traits and motivation through formal schooling. But even if the plausibility of this view is tentatively granted, it only leads to a more fundamental question: How can one explain the immense differences among the countries of the world in the timing and growth of formal education?

If, to answer this question, one follows the approach of the new economic history, then the appropriate guidelines are those currently offered by economic theory. This theory centers largely on decision making in one social institution, the family, and sees the expansion of schooling as a voluntary response to growing payoffs to education generated by economic growth. Government, if it comes into the picture at all, is seen largely as implementing or ratifying private household decisions through public action.

Economic incentives may be one of the causes of expansion of mass education. But the sizable payoffs to child labor in many countries should caution against placing primary reliance on this explanation because such payoffs created an incentive to put children to work rather than to send them to school. Hence, there is need to consider possible motives to promote education by social institutions other than the family. Foremost among these other institutions is the government. Education is a powerful instrument for influencing the minds of individuals in their formative years. This elementary fact has hardly escaped the attention of those in society interested in obtaining or maintaining political, social, and economic power (Field 1979). The result has been that the establishment and growth of mass education have often been the product chiefly not of market forces but of political conflicts in which major groups in a society – groups that frequently vary from one country to the next – are ranged against each other. At the risk of oversimplification, let me try to illustrate this point in terms of Figure 4.1.

The most obvious shift in political power with which growth of mass education has been linked is the establishment of independence from a former colonial power. This is suggested by the histories of several countries in southeastern Europe that freed themselves from Turkish rule in the period before World War I (exemplified in Figure 4.1 by Rumania and Yugoslavia), in the Middle East in the 1920s and 1930s (as illustrated by Egypt), and in Asia and Africa after World War II (see India, Indonesia, Burma, and Nigeria).[7] This implies that colonialism was a major deterrent to the growth of mass education and lends support to the "imperialism" explanation for underdevelopment. But the data in Figure 4.1 also suggest reasons against too hasty a generalization of this sort. First, there are cases, though not many, in which colonial governments promoted mass education. The clearest illustration is the American takeover of the Philippines from Spain; another example is Japanese policy in Korea (Etō 1980; Grajdanzev 1944). Second, Latin America's decolonization in the nineteenth century, with country after country becoming independent, was not followed by a great upsurge in mass education; hence, colonialism cannot be the scapegoat there. Third, there is the counterfactual issue: In the absence of colonial rule would mass education have been promoted vigorously by independent governments? It is noteworthy that the historical record for Iran and Turkey in Figure 4.1 does not differ clearly from that for Egypt when it was under colonial domination. The same is true of the record for China compared with colonial India, and of Ethiopia vis-à-vis colonial Nigeria. Even a casual glance at historical experience makes clear the need to consider other factors that may have impeded mass education besides colonialism.

One such impediment is absolute monarchy. The independent countries I have just mentioned – Turkey, Iran, China, and Ethiopia – were all absolute monarchies, and in none of these did a substantial trend toward mass education set in until after autocratic rule ended. To judge

[7] Flora (1973) notes the close association in several countries between the date of independence and the date when compulsory education was established.

from Figure 4.1, one sees that the same is true of Russia and Thailand. Absolute monarchs seem usually to have regarded mass education as potentially subversive of their power. In contrast, communist governments have vigorously promoted mass education as an instrument of political socialization (Azrael 1965; Hans 1964, 1965).

Another deterrent to mass education appears to have been a situation in which the Roman Catholic Church exercised substantial secular power. This has already been touched on in the case of Spain; in Latin America, it was perhaps the dominant factor. The rapid rise of mass education in Argentina after 1880 and in Mexico after 1920 both occurred in conjunction with a substantial shift in power from church to state. Speaking in 1934, Mexican general and ex-president Plutarco Calles said, "it is absolutely necessary to drive the enemy out of that entrenchment where the clergy has been, where the Conservatives have been – I refer to Education."[8] In the Middle East, Islam too frequently appears to have been a negative influence in the development of formal schooling.[9]

For the countries where mass education was already fairly well established by the early nineteenth century (represented in Figure 4.1 by Germany, England, France, and the United States), sufficient data are not available for analyzing their prior historical patterns of educational growth. One can ask, however, about the factors that set these countries apart from the rest of the world so early and contributed to their relatively high levels of schooling. Three influences stand out in the literature: Protestantism, humanism, and central government efforts at national integration. One of the main tenets of early Protestant thought, as shaped by leaders like Calvin and Luther, was that "the eternal welfare of every individual depends upon the application of his own reason to the revelation contained in the Scriptures."[10] In practice, this led to advocacy of formal schooling in the vernacular language

[8] As quoted in Mecham (1934, 406). In Brazil, however, a shift in power from church to state does not seem to have played as critical a role in the growth of mass education; there a shift in political control from conservatives to liberals appears to have been more important. See Burns (1970, 290, 302–03).

[9] On Turkey, see Kazamias (1966, 73–74), and on Iran, see Farmayan (1968, 123). In Egypt, Islam seems to have been less of an obstacle to educational change; see Vatikiotis (1969, 69–70).

[10] Japan seems to have had its own version of the "Protestant ethic"; see Bellah (1957).

so that each individual would have personal access to the Bible. Humanism, which reached fullest expression with the philosophers of the eighteenth-century Enlightenment, preached the ultimate perfectibility of humanity and thus also fostered a view favorable to mass education. Finally, some governments saw mass education as a means of securing allegiance to the central government at the expense of local authorities or the church.

The weight of these influences differed from country to country, and not all operated in each. The role of Protestantism was strongest in Germany and the United States. It was weaker in England, where the established Protestant religion was an Anglican version of Roman Catholicism and the vigorous proponents of education were the nonconformists. The influence of Protestantism was weaker still in France, which was predominantly Roman Catholic, although the separation of church and state was achieved fairly early. The role of humanism was strongest in France[11] and the United States, less so in England, and least influential in Germany. Nationalism and national integration was a potent force in Germany and perhaps France but largely absent in England and the United States (in the latter, formal education systems were established on a state-by-state basis).

England's laissez-faire philosophy is thought by some to explain its lag in educational growth relative to other countries in northwestern Europe such as Germany. The high educational attainment of the United States, which also lacked a national education policy, clearly calls this view into question. The factor that distinguishes the United States and Germany most clearly from England is the different nature of Protestantism – the much larger representation in Germany and the United States of what in England would be called nonconformist religions, religions in the tradition of Calvin and Luther, with their emphasis on each individual's ability to be able to read the Bible on his or her own.[12]

Earlier, in touching on the question of incentives for learning, I suggested that the expansion of formal schooling often signaled a positive

[11] Cf. Thut and Adams (1964, 113): "In the end, Frenchmen committed themselves to the ideas derived from humanism, rather than from Roman Catholic or Protestant theologies, a development which had profound educational consequences."

[12] The leading role of nonconformists in the British industrial revolution is emphasized in Hagen (1962, Chap. 13).

shift in the incentive structure. This survey of the determinants of mass schooling makes clear the reasoning underlying this statement. A major commitment to mass education is frequently symptomatic of a major shift in political power and associated ideology in a direction conducive to greater opportunities and upward mobility for a wider segment of the population. This is not to say that it signals complete democratization of opportunity, but it often represents a sizable break with conditions of the past. From this point of view the absence of mass education systems for so long in so many countries of the world is indicative of a double impediment to the spread of the technology underlying modern economic growth: lack of opportunity as well as limited aptitudes to learn and master new technology.

Major advances in mass education are thus likely to signal sizable changes in both incentive structures and aptitudes favorable to modern economic growth. At the same time they are symptomatic of powerful new political and ideological forces at work in the cultures of the various countries. The educational system is therefore a key link between modern economic growth, on the one hand, and a society's culture, on the other. Study of the evolution of mass education provides an important clue as to when the net balance of the principal cultural forces in a society shifts in a direction favorable to economic growth.

Some economic historians may object that the study of educational systems and the forces that shape them leads away from the traditional concerns of economic history. To this, one may reply that, if this is what the problem demands, then traditional orientations have to go. In a broader sense, however, it can be argued that such study is, in fact, a return to traditional economic history, to economic history in the spirit of scholars like Marx, Sombart, Weber, and Tawney.

CONCLUSION

In sum, the worldwide spread of modern economic growth has depended chiefly on the diffusion of a new body of knowledge concerning methods of production. The acquisition and application of this knowledge by different countries have been governed largely by whether their populations have acquired traits and opportunities associated with the establishment of mass schooling. From the historical experience of the world's twenty-five largest nations, it is evident that the establishment and expansion of formal schooling has depended in large part on political conditions and ideological influences. Thus, the limited spread of modern economic growth before World War II has been due, at bottom, to important political and ideological differences throughout the world that affected the timing of the establishment and expansion of mass schooling. Since World War II, modern education systems have been established almost everywhere, the diffusion of modern technology has noticeably accelerated, and the growing worldwide disparity in living levels has slowed markedly.

5

Kuznets Cycles and Modern Economic Growth

In the last two centuries modern economic growth has brought about an unprecedented shift in the location of economic activity. Before 1800, the vast majority of the population – more than nine out of ten – lived and worked in rural areas on farms and in villages. Today, among the countries leading in economic growth, the situation is virtually reversed, for eight out of ten people are in urban areas.

This immense redistribution of population and economic activity did not take place linearly. Rather, in the historical experience of the leaders, urbanization proceeded at an irregular wavelike pace, erupting intermittently in a financial crisis and collapse. These long swings in economic growth are commonly termed Kuznets cycles in recognition of Simon Kuznets's pioneering work (Kuznets 1930, 1958).[1] Recent work has linked these Kuznets cycles to even longer-term Kondratieff movements of around 50 years' duration (Schön 1998).

In this chapter, I start with the long-term factors making for locational restructuring of the economy during modern economic growth and then describe the mechanisms that caused this process to proceed in wavelike fashion in market economies. The need for similar research on the current experience of today's less developed economies is then noted.

Reprinted with permission in revised form from "Locational Restructuring and Financial Crisis," *Structural Change and Economic Dynamics* 11 (2000): 129–38.

[1] Other early contributors include Burns (1934), Isard (1942a,b), and analyses of the building cycle surveyed in Abramovitz (1964).

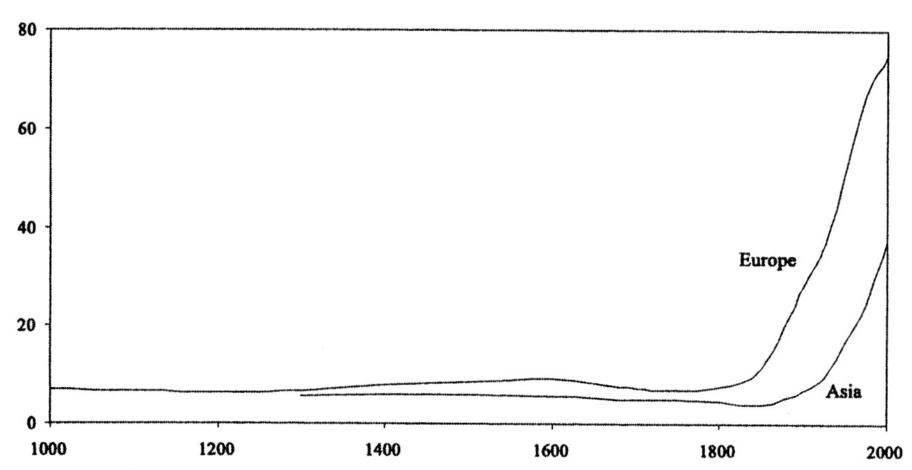

Figure 5.1. Percentage of population in urban places, Europe and Asia, 1000–2000.
Source: 1000–1925: United Nations 1977, p. 13; 1950–2000: United Nations 1988, p. 90.

LONG-TERM CAUSES OF LOCATIONAL RESTRUCTURING

The dramatic impact of modern economic growth on the location of economic activity is illustrated in Figure 5.1, which presents remarkable time series on urbanization in Europe and Asia spanning a millenium. In Europe, in the eight centuries before 1800, the percentage of population in urban places (those with 5,000 or more inhabitants) hovered around 7 percent; thereafter, with the onset of modern economic growth, this figure rose in less than two centuries to an average for Europe as a whole tenfold greater, or to 70 percent. For western and northern Europe, the leading areas in economic growth, the urban proportion at the end of the twentieth century exceeded 80 percent (United Nations 1998, 93). In the twentieth century, as economic growth spread to Asia, a similar shift began there – from less than 10 percent at the start of the century to 30 percent at its end.

The basic cause of this locational restructuring of the economy was the new technology underlying modern economic growth, especially manufacturing and transportation technology. In preindustrial conditions, manufacturing was done for small local markets by artisans working with hand tools in shops, at home, or as itinerant craftsmen. Hence, manufacturing activity was widely distributed among towns and villages.

Aside from commerce, the few cities that existed offered little in the way of special locational advantages for economic activity.

The new manufacturing technology that came into being with the era of modern economic growth has dramatically altered the locational distribution of economic opportunities, producing sharp geographic cost and revenue differentials that especially favor cities and towns with good access to transportation or certain mineral resources. The underlying market forces reflect changes both in supply and demand conditions (Easterlin 1999b; Kelley and Williamson 1987).[2]

On the supply side, the key element has been the widespread implementation of mechanized production based on the new inventions of the First and Second Industrial Revolutions – especially those in power and industrial materials (Table 5.1). The new industrial technology shifts the balance sharply in favor of urban locations partly because it involves sizable economies of scale that have led a growing number of industries to replace shops by factories as mechanization supplanted hand production. Because of their larger scale of operation, factories, unlike shops, require access to a major population, such as that of a town or city, for their labor supply and product markets. Urban locations for manufacturing have also been favored because the new technology requires natural resource inputs, especially minerals, that are much less ubiquitous than the agricultural and forest resources on which preindustrial manufacturing is based. Hence, location is typically favored at or near the sources of the new industrial inputs or at transport points that make these inputs cheaply available and also provide access to high-population–density product and labor markets.

As producers have responded to new opportunities, a corresponding shift to urban areas has occurred in the geographic distribution of the demand for labor. The supply of labor, however, remains disproportionately concentrated in rural areas because rates of natural increase of the population there have been as high or higher than that of urban population. The resulting demand–supply labor imbalance has caused an

[2] It is encouraging to note an upsurge of interest among economists in the causes of city growth (Glaeser 1998; Krugman 1998). Perhaps in the future this work will begin to explore the links between the substantive nature of technological change and city growth, past and future, drawing on related work by demographers and economic historians.

Table 5.1. Major locational determinants of manufacturers and locational outcomes before and after the First Industrial Revolution

	(1) Before First Industrial Revolution	(2) After First Industrial Revolution	(3)
		19th Century	20th Century
I. Determinants			
A. Firm technology			
Energy inputs	Human, animal, wind, water	Steam power	Internal combustion engine, electricity
Material	Wood	Coal, iron, steel	Petroleum, natural gas, nonferrous metals, plastics
Transportation and communication	Water, wagon, and road	Railroad, telegraph	Motor vehicles, telephone, computer, telecommunications
B. Demand	Low income, leading to consumption of a high proportion of food products	Rising income, leading to shift toward manufactured products	Rising income, leading to shift toward services
II. Locational outcome	Villages, farmsteads	Urban growth, monocentric cities, eventual rural depopulation	Greater dispersal of urban centers, polycentric cities, central city depopulation, suburbanization, rural revival

excess of urban over rural wages and induced migration to urban areas. City and town growth has been reinforced by several factors. First, application of the new technology to internal transportation has led to the emergence of a transport grid accentuating the cost advantage of cities located at key junctions in the network. Second, "agglomeration" economies have added to the opportunities in cities and towns. For example, industries serving consumers, such as printing and publishing, have been attracted to cities and towns by the concentration of workers and consumers that have been induced to locate there by the new manufacturing and transport technology.

The new technology also has an impact on location via consumer demand because it gives rise to an unprecedented growth in real productivity and thereby in real per capita income. With income rising, consumer demand grows more rapidly for high-income-elasticity manufactured products than for low-income-elasticity food products. Also, the relatively higher price elasticity of demand for manufactures reinforces the favorable effect on the market for manufactured goods. Because production of manufactured products is becoming more heavily concentrated in urban areas, the effect of the shift in demand toward manufactures is to reinforce the centralizing tendency of the new technology. The result is to expand the job opportunities further in urban areas and hence the attractiveness of these areas to rural job seekers, adding to the flow of migrants to towns and cities.

CAUSES OF WAVELIKE MOVEMENTS IN LOCATIONAL RESTRUCTURING

Over the long term, the combined impact of the new technology and rising incomes associated therewith has been a great impetus to geographic concentration of production, centering on cities and towns. But the process of urbanization does not proceed monotonically. Rather, under free-market conditions, the introduction of the new technology and the associated rise in urbanization occurs in a succession of investment booms and busts. In the history of today's free-market developed countries, these investment fluctuations took the form of Kuznets cycles, typically averaging about 15–25 years in duration. These movements are clearly discernible in the early development of the United States in the period from 1840 to World War I in series for major economic

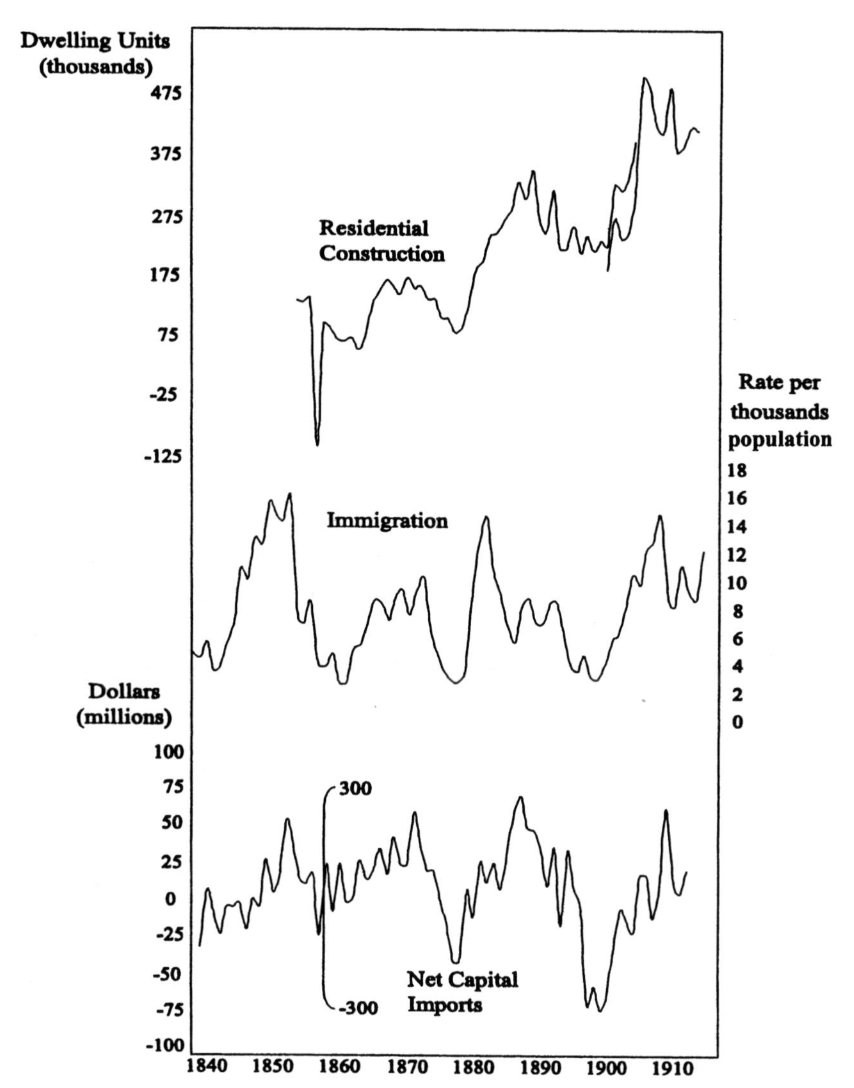

Figure 5.2. Residential construction and labor and capital inflows, United States, 1840–1913.
Source: Easterlin 1968b, p. 218.

magnitudes relating to output, such as residential construction, and inputs, such as immigration and net capital imports (Figure 5.2). The roughly synchronous movements in these magnitudes cannot be a statistical artifact; only raw annual data are plotted in the figure and each series comes from a different statistical source.

The key to understanding the mechanisms underlying a Kuznets cycle is that real investment occurs in a two-stage sequence – investment in a new production technology followed by investment in urban infrastructure, the latter brought on by a surge in new household formation due chiefly to rural-to-urban migration (Easterlin 1968b). The second stage of infrastructure investment reinforces and sustains the growth of aggregate demand set off by the first-stage investment in new technology and dampens the tendency toward shorter-term business cycle recessions in the economy. It is particularly during the second stage of the investment boom that the locational restructuring of the economy takes place.

The sequence of events during a Kuznets cycle takes the following stylized form (for specific evidence, see Easterlin 1968b). At the start, an upsurge in investment in a new technology raises the growth rate of aggregate demand. The demand for labor rises in the urban centers situated favorably for the development of the new technology. Initially, the growing labor demand in urban centers is satisfied predominantly from local sources by drawing on the pool of underemployed or unemployed workers, by greater labor force participation of marginal workers in urban centers, and by lengthening hours of work. Marriages by city dwellers that had been postponed because of previously adverse labor market conditions are now consummated, giving rise to an increase in household formation and births.

There remains, however, a fundamental imbalance in the locational distribution of labor demand and supply: the growth of demand is concentrated largely in urban areas, whereas the growth of population and labor supply is more marked in rural areas. As the local reservoir of labor in urban areas is depleted, this demand and supply imbalance heightens, and the growth rate of real wages in urban areas rises. Younger workers from nearby and, eventually, more distant rural areas are attracted to the better-paying employment opportunities in the newly expanding urban centers. The result is an upsurge in rural–urban internal migration, and, also, in the case of the United States, immigration from abroad. The inflow of migrants raises the growth rate of urban population and provides a major new impetus to urban household and family formation.

In turn, the upsurge in urban household and family formation in urban areas further stimulates the growth of aggregate demand. New residential building booms. Municipal spending on roads, water supply, sewage disposal, and schools rises. Private investment in consumer-oriented businesses is promoted such as retail trade, entertainment, and personal services. There is a bunching of household spending on home furnishings, appliances, and the like, as new homes and families are established.

This induced growth of spending due to new household formation and urban development sustains and reinforces the expansion set off by the first-stage investment in new technology. A real estate boom takes shape. Banks and other lenders are increasingly drawn to the new profit opportunities, and short- and long-term funds from abroad are attracted. As confidence soars with the protracted boom, lenders become more lenient in assessing applications for new credit or credit renewal, and speculative lending for real estate and other purposes mounts. At the same time, however, the best opportunities from the first-stage investment in the new technology are becoming gradually exhausted, and rising labor and capital costs are starting to cut into profit margins. Loan defaults begin to rise. Banks start to call in loans, business bankruptcies turn up, and some banks begin to fail. Foreign capital begins to pull out as the threat of default mounts. A financial crisis erupts, and the boom collapses.

In the resulting recession-depression, economic slack reemerges. Factor input costs become lower, setting the stage for a new burst of private investment. According to some analysts, a new Kuznets cycle is born from the old one (Schön 1998, 2000). In the first Kuznets cycle – a "transformation" phase – a new production technology, such as electricity generation and transmission, is refined to the point at which the prices of the new capital embodying the technology eventually drop sharply. The relatively cheap cost of the new technology, that is, electricity, starts to induce its widespread adoption in many industries – a "rationalization" phase – in this case the electrification of manufacturing production. Associated with the general adoption of the new technology is a new pattern of central locations and rural–urban population redistribution, leading to a new urban boom and a new Kuznets cycle expansion. The two successive Kuznets cycles, the transformation cycle followed by the rationalization cycle, produce in combination a roughly 50-year movement that has come to be called a Kondratieff.

IMPLICATIONS FOR TODAY'S LESS DEVELOPED ECONOMIES

It is over three decades since Moses Abramovitz announced "The Passing of the Kuznets Cycle" in the United States (his 1968 paper is reprinted in Abramovitz 1989, Chap. 9). The onset of modern economic growth in many parts of the less developed world, however, raises the possibility of a rebirth of Kuznets and Kondratieff cycles there as the demands of modern technology induce an urban restructuring of the economy under largely free market conditions.

The 1990s debacle in southeast Asia is widely interpreted as a purely financial crisis (cf. Dow 1998 and references therein). Strangely lacking in the extensive postmortems is reference to the nonfinancial side of the economy. Yet clearly, capital flight was a product of financial system weakness that, in turn, had its roots in the inability of nonfinancial businesses to meet their loan obligations. What was the nature of the problems leading to widespread loan default?

I do not know enough about southeast Asia to answer this question, but it is possible that the real-economy origins of the crisis lay in the locational restructuring of the economy engendered by modern economic growth. What immediately brings to mind the parallel of recent southeast Asian experience to the earlier experience of the United States is the marked upsurge in capital inflows followed by precipitous collapse that occurred in both places (regarding the American experience, note the bottom panel of Figure 5.2).

But there are several other parallels. Rapid urbanization has been taking place in southeast Asia accompanied by substantial rural–urban migration (Chen, Paolo, and Hania 1998; Pernia 1998; United Nations 1998). Also, in southeast Asia, as in the nineteenth-century United States, government regulation of the banking system and of private foreign borrowing was weak or nonexistent. In both places, rapid economic expansion led to surging imports and thereby a worsening balance of payments (Parker 1998; Williamson 1964). Labor shortages induced rising immigration in the nineteenth-century United States as in parts of southeast Asia at the close of the twentieth century (Mochizuki 1998).

A thorough exploration of the relevance of the Kuznets cycle hypothesis to southeast Asia, or less developed economies more generally, requires the compilation and analysis of detailed time series on magnitudes such as private investment, government expenditure, and household spending by type; urban labor force growth by industry, occupation, and component of change; urban household formation; marriages and births; wage rates, unemployment rates, and average weekly hours in urban labor markets; as well as a myriad of financial statistics. But the foregoing may be enough to suggest that there are symptoms in southeast Asia of real-side economic developments similar to those that eventuated in major financial crises in the historical experience of developed economies.

True, the world environment today is different from that of the past. Capital markets are more highly integrated throughout the world. Aggregate demand management via domestic and international macroeconomic policy is a new force, and governments generally play a larger role in the domestic and world economy. Perhaps most important, today's less developed economies have available a varied pool of accumulated production technologies that were introduced sequentially in the historical experience of the developed countries – technologies with somewhat different urbanization patterns (cf. Table 5.1, columns 2 and 3). This technological pool makes it possible, in principle, to forestall the exhaustion of profit opportunities specific to a given technology by transitioning seamlessly to another. Such a passage, however, calls for a high degree of flexibility in the real stock of human and physical capital, the existence of which seems doubtful. It is perhaps time to return to the study of Kuznets cycles. The rapidly growing economies of the less developed world offer a laboratory of vast potential.

6

Industrial Revolution and Mortality Revolution: Two of a Kind?

Ever since the establishment of economic history as an independent discipline, the causes of the Industrial Revolution have been its Holy Grail. The reason for this quest is not hard to find, for the Industrial Revolution marks the onset of an epochal change in the material well-being of humanity, the era of modern economic growth. In northwestern Europe, where the Industrial Revolution first occurred, the improvement in the level of living of the average person over the past two centuries has been tenfold or more, representing a rate of advance unprecedented in human history.

In demographic history, however, a quite different revolution has been the focus of attention, that in human life expectancy. Since 1870, life expectancy at birth in many areas of the world has soared from values around 40 years or less to 70 years or more. The reduction in mortality has been accompanied by an associated improvement in health as the incidence of contagious disease has dramatically lessened. This lengthening of life and associated reduction in morbidity brought about by the "Mortality Revolution" has meant at least as much for human welfare as the improvement in living levels due to modern economic growth. Certainly the Mortality Revolution has substantially affected a much wider segment of the world's population.

Surprisingly, the Mortality Revolution has gone largely unremarked in the discipline of economic history. The indexes and tables of contents

Reprinted with permission in revised form from "Industrial Revolution and Mortality Revolution: Two of a Kind?" *Journal of Evolutionary Economics* 5, 4 (1995): 393–408.

of economic history textbooks and of scholarly overviews of modern economic history reveal a startling absence of entries relating to mortality, life expectancy, health, morbidity, public health, and the like. Economic historians have, of course, made major contributions to demographic history; one need only refer to the classic study of Wrigley and Schofield (1981) and the large literature associated therewith. But almost all of the attention of economic historians working on demographic topics has focused on the period before the Mortality Revolution, when advances in life expectancy, to the extent they occurred at all, were much smaller in magnitude, irregular, and limited in geographic scope.

One might claim that economic historians' emphasis on the Industrial Revolution is justified because the Mortality Revolution is simply an effect of the Industrial Revolution. In this view the improvement in living levels, and particularly in nutrition brought about by modern economic growth, led inevitably to improved health and mortality. This argument is often attributed to the British scholar of medical science Thomas McKeown (1976). Work on physical stature by Robert Fogel and several of his collaborators has also been charged with this view (Perrenoud 1991 and citations therein), although later work by Fogel (1993) appears noncommittal. But even if the Mortality Revolution were simply an effect of the Industrial Revolution, there is no reason for passing so lightly over a development of such unique significance for human welfare. Moreover, the improvement in health associated with the Mortality Revolution may itself have had a significant, independent impact on productivity and thus on economic growth (Easterlin 1996, Chap. 7; Over et al. 1992).

In the first serious attempt to deal quantitatively with the sources of mortality improvement, Samuel Preston (1975) found, contrary to the McKeown thesis, that economic growth played a very small role in the improvement of life expectancy, although his focus was on a somewhat later period, the 1930s to the 1960s. Critical assessments specifically of McKeown's analysis have raised important doubts about major parts of his argument (Kunitz 1987; Szreter 1988). A wide-ranging synthesis of work on European demographic history also reached a largely negative view of the McKeown position (Schofield, Reher, and Bideau 1991).

This chapter, though siding with the conclusions of the latter camp, proposes a somewhat different conception: that the Industrial and Mortality Revolutions should be seen as the result of technological breakthroughs in their respective areas. These breakthroughs should, in turn, be viewed as resulting from a common source, the emergence and growing dominance of a scientific approach to the quest for human knowledge. Also, by noting parallels and contrasts between the Industrial and Mortality Revolutions, this chapter aims to make the point that comparative study of the two should prove fruitful.

The question of whether the Mortality Revolution has been due to modern economic growth is addressed first, and the conclusion presented is that neither facts nor theory support this position. Next considered is how Preston's analysis of the sources of mortality change has a direct counterpart in Robert Solow's earlier pioneering article on the sources of economic growth and how qualitative evidence supports their virtually identical conclusions that technological change in the relevant area was the prime mover. Finally, the Industrial and Mortality Revolutions are linked to the emergence of an empirically bound approach to knowledge followed by a discussion of how the differences in timing of the two revolutions are related to the evolution of different fields of scientific knowledge.

ECONOMIC GROWTH AND MORTALITY

In assessing whether the Mortality Revolution is an effect of modern economic growth, it is helpful to start with some of the principal facts. Around the middle of the nineteenth century, life expectancy at birth for both sexes combined in the major regions of the world fell in a band extending from the low 20s to the low 40s. By 1990, the range for these areas extended from the high 50s to the high 70s except for sub-Saharan Africa. Even there, the last area in which the Mortality Revolution has taken place, life expectancy had broken out of the lower band and by 1990 was almost 50 years.

Although the Mortality Revolution started later than modern economic growth – in the latter part of the nineteenth century rather than the late eighteenth – the geographic pattern of diffusion is similar. Broadly speaking, the Mortality Revolution spread from northwestern Europe and its overseas descendants to eastern and southern Europe and Japan, then to Latin America, followed by the Middle East and Asia, and finally sub-Sahara Africa. But the spread of the Mortality Revolution has been much more rapid than that of modern economic growth. Because of this, the widening in international differences in life expectancy that occurred before World War II has been greatly reduced. In several Third World areas today, life expectancy is not far from the developed areas average of 74 years.

If the Mortality Revolution were simply an effect of modern economic growth, it is hard to explain its later start and much more rapid spread. Moreover, the international convergence in life expectancy that has been occurring stands in marked contrast to the persisting large differences between most leading and following areas in economic growth, as measured by real GDP per capita (cf. Chapter 3, Table 3.3).

Historical demographers identify an earlier phase of improvement in mortality from the late seventeenth to early nineteenth centuries. But this improvement appears to have been confined to a few countries of northwestern Europe, and even in some of these areas, the mid-nineteenth century witnessed stable or even worsening mortality conditions (Schofield et al. 1991; Vallin 1991). Moreover, in the countries where life expectancy improved in the early period, the rate of improvement was only about a third of that in the century after 1870 (United Nations 1973, 111). In Great Britain, the improvement was little more than a return to the level of life expectancy prevailing in the Elizabethan period (Wrigley and Schofield 1981). Thus, the evidence that economic growth caused a concurrent improvement in life expectancy in the areas where the Industrial Revolution first occurred is, at best, mixed. This supposed association is also undermined by the continued occurrence of major advances in life expectancy between World Wars I and II in several developed countries despite stagnant economic growth.

Note also that, before World War II, the Mortality Revolution appears to have occurred in some areas of the Third World under conditions of little or no economic growth. Survival rates of the Korean population improved before 1940 despite declining living levels (Kimura 1993). Similarly, in British Guiana, Cuba, the Philippines, Sri Lanka, and Taiwan, life expectancy improved noticeably before 1940 with little or no evidence of sustained economic progress (Balfour et al. 1950; Barclay 1954; Diaz-Briquets 1981, 1983; Mandle 1973; Newman 1965; Sarkar 1957). This occurrence of the Mortality Revolution in the absence of modern economic growth is true of parts of sub-Saharan Africa in recent decades (see Chapter 7, Figures 7.3 and 7.4).

Thus, the facts of historical experience do not fit well with the view that the Mortality Revolution is largely an effect of modern economic growth. There is the noticeably later onset of the Mortality Revolution than modern economic growth and the mid-nineteenth-century stagnation of mortality in the leading areas of economic growth. There is also the much more rapid spread of the Mortality Revolution than modern economic growth and the occurrence of the Mortality Revolution at quite low and in some cases stagnant levels of economic development.

Nor is it clear analytically that modern economic growth would necessarily lead to improved life expectancy. The argument for this linkage stems from focus on only one feature of modern economic growth, the increase in real per capita income. The resulting improvement in food and nutrition, clothing, and shelter, it is argued, must have increased resistance to disease and thus raised health and life expectancy.

But in the disease environment prevailing at the time of the Industrial Revolution, another systematic feature of modern economic growth, urbanization, tended to affect life expectancy adversely. In every country that has experienced modern economic growth, a predominantly rural population has been transformed into a primarily urban one, and factory production has replaced manufacturing in homes and shops (see Chapter 5). Before the Industrial Revolution and throughout most of the nineteenth century, urban mortality rates were much higher than rural. For example, in the three departments of France containing the cities of Paris, Marseilles, and Lyon, life expectancy at birth was seven to eight years less than that in France as a whole throughout the first six decades of the nineteenth century (Preston and van de Walle 1978; see also Chapter 7, Figure 7.1 herein).

From an epidemiological point of view, the effect of the redistribution of population to urban areas and concentration of manufacturing production in factories in the nineteenth century was to increase the exposure of the population to contagious disease markedly. Schofield, Reher, and Bideau (1991) put it this way:

[T]he rapid process of industrialization and urbanization in nineteenth-century European society created new obstacles to improved health. Towns had always been characterized by higher mortality rates due mainly to greater population densities which facilitated infection and filth; and during the nineteenth century increased proportions of the population were living in these urban centers. The poor living conditions of the age were probably one of the principal reasons why mortality ceased to improve during most of the central decades of the century. (Schofield et al. 1991, 14; see also 170, 179)

A more comprehensive assessment of linkages between modern economic growth and life expectancy (e_0) before the Mortality Revolution would thus look as follows:

(6.1) Economic growth → higher per capita income → higher resistance → higher e_0
(6.2) Economic growth → urbanization → greater exposure to disease → lower e_0

Thus, although modern economic growth may have increased resistance to disease, it also increased exposure, and the net balance of these two factors is not clear.

This argument is consistent with evidence of decreasing mortality in the first part of the nineteenth century in some geographic subdivisions of Great Britain, or, indeed, in the rural and urban sectors generally (Woods and Woodward 1984). At any given time overall mortality is a weighted average of mortality in rural and urban areas with the weights comprising the shares in total population of the rural and urban sectors. Over time, a growth in the share of the higher mortality urban sector raises mortality. At the same time, mortality may be declining within the rural sector, urban sector, or both if economic growth is raising living levels and resistance to disease. The net result of the shift between sectors and the within-sector change is ambiguous. In actual historical experience, the overall outcome appears to have been stagnation or, at best, mild improvement in life expectancy evident throughout most of the nineteenth century in the areas undergoing rapid economic growth.

BIOMEDICAL TECHNOLOGICAL CHANGE AND MORTALITY

If the Mortality Revolution is not due to the Industrial Revolution, what then is its cause? In considering this, it is useful to proceed with parallel attention to the sources of mortality change and of modern economic growth.

In the study of modern economic growth, Solow's (1957) partitioning of the sources of economic growth into technical change and input growth is widely recognized as a classic. In his analysis, Solow

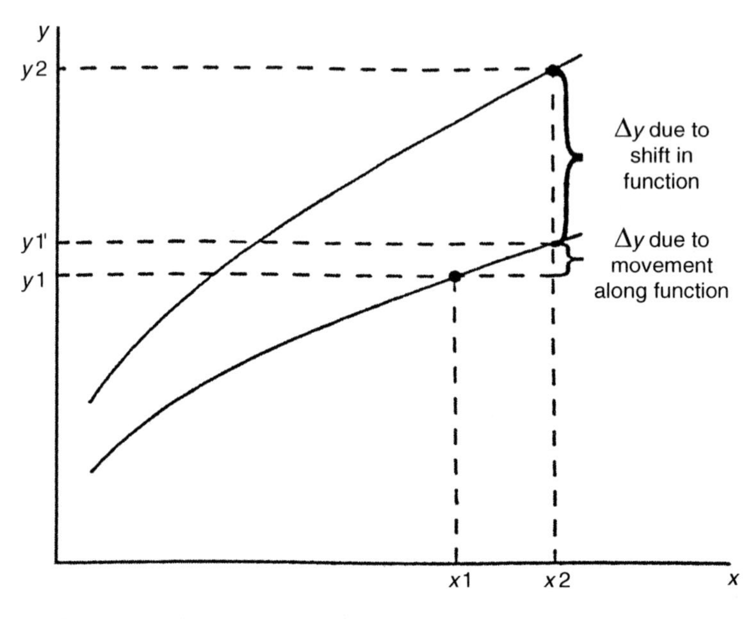

Figure 6.1. Sources of economic growth (Solow 1957) and sources of increased life expectancy (Preston 1975).

differentiated between the growth in output per man-hour due to (a) movements along a production function as inputs per man-hour increased and (b) shifts in the production function associated with "technical change." An analogous undertaking, done independently of Solow's work and no less deserving of classic status, is Preston's (1975) division of the advance in life expectancy into that due to improvements in health technology and that due to modern economic growth as measured by real national income per capita. The parallel in the analytical conception of the two studies is brought out in Figure 6.1. Preston reasoned that, with health technology given, an improvement in real per capita income would tend to raise life expectancy, a movement along the lower curve in Figure 6.1, which might be thought of as a "health production function" relating input (per capita income) to output (life expectancy). However, at given levels of per capita income, advances in health technology would also raise life expectancy (an upward shift of the curve in

Figure 6.1). Using cross-sectional data for several countries in 1930 and 1960, Preston arrived at an empirical result for world life expectancy remarkably similar to Solow's for American economic growth from 1909 to 1949, namely, about 75 to 90 percent of the advance was attributable to technological change.

In discussing how modern economic growth itself might affect life expectancy, Preston, like other scholars, stressed the role of improved living levels. One might claim that there are other links between economic growth and the Mortality Revolution not captured in Preston's estimate and that the causal role of economic growth in raising life expectancy is consequently greater than he estimated. One such argument is that the higher income resulting from modern economic growth is essential to financing increased private and government expenditures associated with improved health technology. But the measures necessary to implement advances in health technology do not seem to have required, on average, anything like the capital expenditures necessary for modern economic growth. If they did, then less developed countries (LDCs) would have been hard put to implement public health programs in the twentieth century without substantial external aid. Although such aid existed, its quantitative significance was trivial. An assessment published in 1980 concluded that "total external health aid received by LDCs is less than 3% of their total health expenditures" (Preston 1980, 315; see also Chapter 7 herein). Clearly, despite their low levels of economic development, LDCs were able almost entirely on their own to fund implementation of advances in health technology.

Against this argument aimed at raising the contribution of economic growth to longer life expectancy, one can set the counterclaim that Preston's analysis overstates the contribution of economic growth because the twentieth-century data he uses do not fully reflect the aforementioned nineteenth-century differential between urban and rural mortality. As discussed later in this section, from the latter part of the nineteenth century onward, improvements in health technology progressively reduced the excess of urban over rural mortality. The eventual effect of this was to eliminate the adverse impacts on life expectancy associated with the increase in urbanization accompanying modern economic growth and to allow the positive effects due to higher living levels to predominate; in other words, relationship (6.1) came to dominate relationship (6.2). Stated in terms of Figure 6.1, the effect of improved health technology in reducing the excess of urban over rural mortality was to increase the slope of the curve relating life expectancy to real national income per capita. In using cross-sectional data for 1930 or later years to estimate the effect of economic development on life expectancy, Preston's analysis fails to allow for this. Consequently, Preston's estimate understates the role of technological change and overstates the contribution of economic growth. Conceivably, the relationship between life expectancy and real national income per capita will be altered once again as degenerative diseases replace infectious diseases as the focus of health technology.

Both Solow's and Preston's analysis assess the quantitative contribution of technical change as a residual, that is, the change in the variable on the y-axis that is not explained by that in the variable on the x-axis. Both authors acknowledge the uncertainty in identifying technological change with the residual. Solow's article, as is well known to economists, set in motion a substantial train of research on "growth accounting." This work seemed destined for a time to replace technological change as the primary source of economic growth with factors such as capital accumulation and improved labor quality. Eventually, Richard Nelson pointed out the high degree of interdependence between technical change and these factor inputs and suggested that an appropriate conception would recognize technical change as the "binding constraint" on the system and as being primarily responsible for the changes observed in the factor inputs (see Nelson 1973 and the citations to the growth accounting literature therein).

All of this work has in common a black box approach to technological change. But if technological change, whether in production methods or health technology, is, in fact, the prime mover in the Industrial and Mortality Revolutions, then the literature specifically on production methods and mortality should itself provide microlevel evidence of important and widespread technological innovations. This, of course, is what one finds, and this finding provides the crucial positive support for Solow's and Preston's conclusions as well as Nelson's. In economic history, the Industrial Revolution is typically defined by the occurrence of three major technological developments – steam power, wrought iron, and textile machinery – and the account of subsequent economic growth is built around a history of continuing and widespread invention and innovation (Landes 1969; for a good chronology of major economic inventions, see Woodruff 1967, 200–63). In like fashion, but less well known to economic historians and economists, the Mortality Revolution is marked by several major technological developments in the control of communicable disease. What follows are some of the highlights; a fuller description appears in Chapter 7.

The spearhead of technological change was "the sanitation movement," which, from the 1850s onward, gained increasing momentum, leading to the gradual establishment in urban areas of effective sewage disposal, pure water supplies, paved streets, and safer food supplies. A critical engineering innovation of the sanitation movement was the construction of ceramic pipes through which sewage could be carried away to distant locations by the use of water (McNeill 1976). This, in turn, required more abundant supplies of water.

In economic history it is not hard to find examples of technological advances that precede understanding of the underlying scientific mechanisms. In demographic history the sanitation movement provides a similar example. Its foremost exponent, Edwin Chadwick, based his proposals for cleaning up the cities on epidemiological evidence of the association between "filth" and disease that he interpreted in terms of the miasmatic theory of disease, which linked disease to bad smells and "vapors." The theory was wrong, but the policy conclusions that he drew were correct.

In the second half of the nineteenth century the work of Pasteur, Koch, and others gradually established the validity of the germ theory of disease and identified the role of carriers (vectors) in the dissemination of disease (Biraben 1991). This work laid the foundations for major breakthroughs in the control of contagious disease in numerous ways. It reinforced and expanded the budding public health movement. It strengthened the sanitation movement and efforts to quarantine and isolate disease victims. It established the fundamental importance of pure water and safer food supplies as well as the need for pest control such as via swamp drainage and rodent control. It led to the growth of public education in personal hygiene and the care and feeding of infants. In medicine, it advanced the work of Lister and others, leading to the development of aseptic surgery, and brought about increased cleanliness in hospitals. It also resulted in a new medical research strategy: identification of the causal agent and carrier, and, based on this, the development of new preventive or therapeutic measures. One of the first payoffs from this work was that, from the 1880s onward, immunization started to become practicable against a growing number of diseases (diphtheria, cholera, pertussis, etc.).

Many of these measures first affected the health and mortality conditions of the urban population. This was because the measures tended to focus especially on urban conditions, as in the case of the sanitation movement, or because the urban population, by virtue of its greater density, could more readily be reached, as in the case of immunization and education measures. The result was a progressive narrowing of the urban–rural mortality differential in the latter part of the nineteenth century (see Chapter 7, Figure 7.1).

It is sometimes possible to link specific advances in health technology to reductions in the prevalence of specific diseases; a notable example is the effect of the purification of water supplies on typhoid fever (Condran, Williams, and Cheney 1984). But many of these advances affected a variety of diseases, and thus a one-to-one association between a given innovation and specific disease mortality is not easily found. In this respect, several of the advances in health technology are similar to general purpose inventions in production technology, such as those in power and materials, that in time affect productivity in numerous industries.

Other similarities and differences between the two revolutions come to mind. One is new types of organization. In many manufacturing industries, implementation of the new production methods entailed the replacement of shop or home production by the factory. With regard to public health, one of the early authorities in the field, C.E.A. Winslow, has "argued that, in assigning responsibility for rapid health progress, the discovery of the possibility of widespread social organization [i.e., the public health system] to combat disease could almost be placed alongside the discovery of the germ theory in importance" (Preston and Haines 1991, 207). The growth of universal schooling, too, played a part in both revolutions, but female education appears to have been much more important than male in the Mortality Revolution (Cleland and van Ginneken 1988; Sandiford et al. 1995). This difference is due to the traditional gender division of labor in which males are primarily responsible for market work and females for management of the household and thus for personal hygiene and health conditions in the home (Ewbank and Preston 1990).

Clearly, both revolutions also required entrepreneurial skill and initiative of the Schumpeterian type to bring about technological innovation. But although the profit motive and private property are often featured as key movers in the Industrial Revolution, their role in the Mortality Revolution is more problematic. In the early phase of the Mortality Revolution, private property and the pursuit of profit were more of an obstacle than a stimulus (see Chapter 7). Successful public health measures often required overriding personal property rights, such as those of slum landlords in the case of sanitary reform (Kearns 1988), or farmers in the case of tuberculosis-infected cows. It is pertinent to note social historian Michael Flinn's report of the views of economist Nassau Senior, one of the foremost mid-nineteenth-century advocates of laissez-faire in the economic realm:

> Accepting the horrifying descriptions [of the great towns in] reports of 1838 as essentially accurate, Senior asked "What other result can be expected, when any man who can purchase or hire a plot of ground is allowed to cover it with such buildings as he may think fit, where there is no power to enforce drainage or sewerage, or to regulate the width of streets, or to prevent houses from being packed back to back, and separated in front by mere alleys and courts, or their being filled with as many inmates as their walls can contain, or the accumulation within and without, of all the impurities which arise in a crowded population?" He concluded that "with all our reverence for the principle of non-interference [laissez-faire], we cannot doubt that in this matter it has been pushed too far. We believe that both ground landlord and the speculating builder ought to be compelled by law, though it should cost then a percentage of their rent and profit, to take measures which shall prevent the towns which they create from being the centres of disease." (Flinn 1965, 39)

The eighteenth-century Industrial Revolution was succeeded in the nineteenth and twentieth centuries by a continuing flow of inventions in production, distribution, and transportation, leading to ever-growing economic productivity. Much the same is true of the Mortality Revolution and its effect on life expectancy. Analogous to the Second Industrial Revolution of the late nineteenth century, demographers identify a Second Mortality Revolution toward the middle of the twentieth century. John Durand (1960, 345) observed that "a second revolution in the technology of disease control began about 1935 and progressed rapidly during the 1940s and 1950s, with major advances . . . in the fields of immunization, chemotherapy, and chemical control of disease vectors." It is common to think of the First Industrial Revolution as being due largely to empirical advances, and the second as influenced more by advances in basic science. Similarly, the scientific basis of the Second Mortality Revolution appears to have been greater than that of the first. More recently, innovations in the prevention and treatment of coronary disease have resulted in sharp increases in life expectancy at older ages – perhaps a Third Mortality Revolution to go along today with a Third, computer-based, Industrial Revolution. All of this serves to underscore the point that substantive evidence on technological change points to its central role in both the Mortality Revolution and modern economic growth.

INDUSTRIAL REVOLUTION AND MORTALITY REVOLUTION: TWO OF A KIND!

In a characteristically eloquent essay on "Why Economists Have Not Explained the Industrial Revolution," McCloskey asserts that "we have learned many nots: that industrialization was not a matter of foreign trade, not a matter of internal reallocation, not of transport innovation, not investment in factories, not education, not science" (McCloskey 1994, 20). In elaborating this argument McCloskey treats the Industrial Revolution as sui generis, as do economic historians and economists generally. But if the Mortality Revolution is a development analogous to, but not caused by, the Industrial Revolution, then it would seem useful to ask with reference to possible causal factors, What do the two revolutions have in common? Is it more than mere accident that two such unprecedented events in the long span of human history have occurred fairly close together? And why was the onset of the Mortality Revolution later than that of the Industrial Revolution?

Viewing the two revolutions together, one is immediately forced away from purely economic explanations. Such things as foreign trade, capital accumulation, private property, and the pursuit of profit are, at best, of questionable importance in causing the Mortality Revolution. But what the two revolutions do have in common is, of course, rapid technological change. Moreover, rapid technological change is not a one-time thing; rather, the two revolutions mark the beginning of sustained advances in the underlying technologies of production and disease control.

If new technology is the common denominator of both revolutions, what, then, is responsible for the new technology? The obvious answer is the development of modern science, conceived, in Mowery and Rosenberg's words, not as "rigorously systematized knowledge within a consistently formulated theoretical framework, but as a set of procedures and attitudes, including the reliance on experimental methods and an abiding respect for observed facts" (1989, 22). This methodological approach was the hallmark of the Scientific Revolution of the seventeenth century (Lindberg 1992). Out of this new empirically based approach grew both new technological advances and scientific discoveries. The "traditional linear model," which sees exogenous scientific discoveries as the cause of technological change, has come increasingly into question (David 1993). Thanks to the work of scholars like David (1993); Kline and Rosenberg (1986); Mokyr (1990); Musson (1972); Parker (1984); and others, it is now understood that scientific discovery and technological advance relating to methods of production are mutually interdependent and have to some extent evolved together. In demographic history, one can point to similar interrelations, such as that between the public health movement and the discoveries in medical science of the latter part of the nineteenth century. What the Mortality and Industrial Revolutions have in common is that they are both manifestations of the explosion in empirically based human knowledge, scientific and technological, that dates from the seventeenth century onward.

From this perspective, the answer to the question of why the Mortality Revolution followed, rather than preceded or accompanied the Industrial Revolution, is that advances in medical knowledge occurred later than those in knowledge of physical relationships. This lag is demonstrated by the historical evidence on the number of scientific discoveries in microbiology compared with those in physics (Figure 6.2). Whereas physics took off in the seventeenth century, little happened in microbiology until the nineteenth.

A similar argument has been advanced to account for the changing pattern of technological change within the realm of economic growth itself. Thus, the later occurrence of the Second Industrial Revolution, featuring chemical and electrical inventions, compared with the first, has been attributed to the sequence of advances in physical science in the course of the seventeenth, eighteenth, and nineteenth centuries from mechanics to chemistry and electricity (Parker 1984, 147).

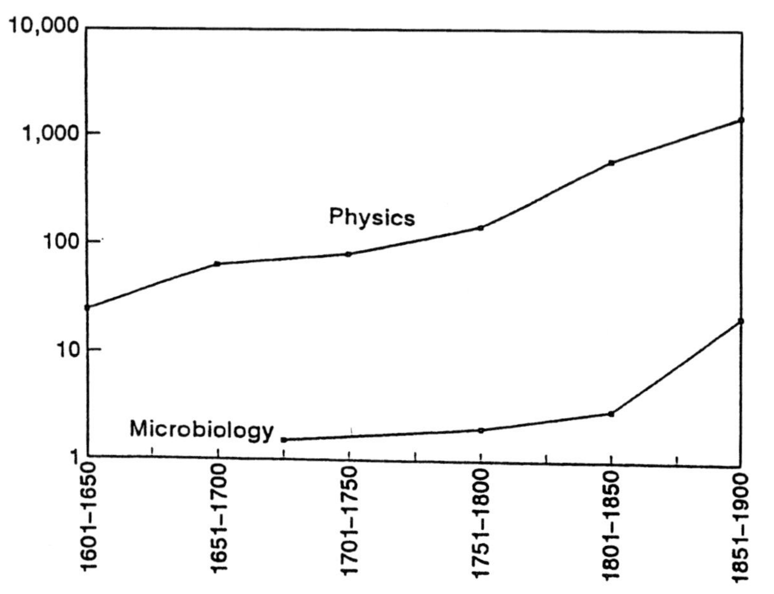

Figure 6.2. Number of discoveries in physics and microbiology, 1601–1900 (rate per half-century).
Source: For physics, Auerbach series as reported in Rainoff (1929). Microbiology: Tolaro and Tolaro (1993).

But how does one explain the different timing in the growth of these fields of knowledge? Why is it that the advance of knowledge progressed from astronomy and mechanics in the sixteenth and seventeenth centuries, to chemistry and electricity in the eighteenth and mid-nineteenth, followed by the medical sciences toward the end of the nineteenth century? Perhaps this pattern is due at bottom to economic factors – to shifts in market forces reflecting the changing nature of human needs, or, to put it differently, that necessity is the mother of advances in knowledge. It is true that one can usually identify after the fact a need that is met in part or whole by a new scientific discovery or invention. But the question is whether, before the fact, the structure of needs dictates the pattern of human inquiry. Is it clear, for example, that the specter of disease was so subordinate to the threat of famine that the advance of the medical sciences should have lagged that in mechanics by more than two centuries? Can market forces explain why chemistry and electricity lagged mechanics and astronomy? It seems doubtful. More plausible is the view that the sequence of advances in human knowledge was linked to differences in the complexity of the problems posed in various scientific disciplines, to the ease with which the human mind might grasp the underlying phenomena, and to the internal logic of scientific inquiry itself. One of the pioneers in the sociology of science, Joseph Ben-David, argues along these lines:

> Certainly political and economic pressures have directed the attention of scientists to important practical problems, but the effect has been much more limited than is usually believed... [A]lthough societies can accelerate or decelerate scientific growth by lending or denying support to science or certain parts of it, they can do relatively little to direct its course. This course is determined by the conceptual state of science and by individual creativity – and these follow their own laws, accepting neither command nor bribe. (Ben-David 1971, 11–12)

If correct, this suggests that the growth of scientific knowledge has been shaped much more by internal factors than external factors such as market forces.

CONCLUSION

In summary, the Industrial and Mortality Revolutions are two of a kind. Both mark the onset of accelerated technological change in their respective fields. Both reflect the cumulation of empirically tested knowledge dating from the seventeenth century onward. They have occurred largely independently of each other, and the later occurrence of the Mortality Revolution is due to the later growth of medical knowledge vis-à-vis knowledge of the physical world. The shifting direction of technological change in each field after the initial revolutionary breakthrough has been shaped in large part by the evolution of the underlying fields of science. The more rapid diffusion of the Mortality Revolution, despite its later start, is due to the much more modest resource commitment that it requires compared with that of modern economic growth.

When the quest for the economic historian's Holy Grail, the causes of the Industrial Revolution, is couched in terms of commonalities in the Industrial and Mortality Revolutions, economic explanations of the Industrial Revolution become less persuasive. In the early stages of the Mortality Revolution, the pursuit of profit and the institution of private property – popular explanations of the Industrial Revolution – were more of an obstacle than a stimulus. In seeking an explanation of both the Industrial and Mortality Revolutions, one must ask what is new on the scene. The answer suggested here is the emergence and growth of modern science – the pursuit of systematic knowledge based on procedures and attitudes that involve an abiding respect for observed facts.

7

How Beneficent Is the Market?

A Look at the Modern History of Mortality

Sweepings from butchers' stalls, dung, guts, and blood,
Drowned puppies, stinking sprats, all drenched in mud,
Dead cats, and turnip tops, come tumbling down the flood.
Jonathan Swift, *A Description of a City Shower*, 1710

Throughout most of the nineteenth century, economic growth had, at best, a minimal impact on life expectancy. The critical causes of the modern rise in life expectancy are the emergence of new knowledge of disease and new technologies of disease control. But were these developments in the control of contagious disease the product of the institutions that are said to be responsible for economic growth, namely, free markets, private property, and freedom of contract? This question was touched on in the previous chapter, but it is considered more fully here. As a basis for forming an answer, I examine in some detail the historical experience of mortality in developed countries (DCs) and developing countries (LDCs) over the past two centuries. Although the experiences of the two sets of countries are almost always treated separately, I see them as a continuum because, in both, all or most of the improvement of life expectancy is due to the great reduction of major infectious diseases. The experience since the 1950s of today's developed countries is not included because of the shift in their disease environment primarily to diseases of older age.

The first section focuses on the particular techniques by which infectious disease has been brought under control and life expectancy has been increased so dramatically. If the institutions of free markets, private property, and freedom of contract are responsible for the modern advance in life expectancy, then these institutions must be linked to the emergence and spread of these specific techniques. The next section therefore considers whether these institutions in fact led either to the adoption or development of the new techniques of disease control. The conclusion that they did not and that public intervention was essential to the control of infectious disease raises the question to which the third section is addressed, namely, whether economic growth has been necessary for improving life expectancy by providing the resources needed to fund public sector spending on the new technology or to fund the research responsible for the advance in medical knowledge. An analysis of the cost requirements of implementing the new technology of disease control and of the basic biomedical research on infectious disease suggests that economic growth has not been essential for either of them.

The bottom line is that improved life expectancy cannot be taken to be simply a byproduct of economic growth or the institutional conditions that foster it. Rather, public policy initiatives have been essential to the improvement of life expectancy, and these can be, and, in fact, have been, undertaken in the absence of economic growth. Life expectancy is an objective to be pursued in its own right by the institutions and policies it requires.

BIOMEDICAL TECHNOLOGICAL CHANGE AND LIFE EXPECTANCY

The starting point for any history of disease control technology must be recognition of the appallingly low state of knowledge of disease in the first part of the nineteenth century. At that time there was no correct knowledge of the causes of disease, very little of the mode of transmission, and almost none of how to treat disease. This is not to say that there were no beliefs on these matters – quite the contrary, there was a firmly established body of doctrine on the nature, causes, and treatment of disease. But these beliefs were as likely to be counterproductive as productive, centering, as they did, on treatment by means of emetics, cathartics, diuretics, and bleeding (Rosenberg 1979, 13). Note the contrast with the state of knowledge regarding methods of production. When modern economic growth began, people already knew how to grow food and manufacture goods; the technology of economic growth increased the ability to do better what people were already doing successfully. However, with regard to controlling disease, the fact is that there was very little useful knowledge before the mid-nineteenth century. Consider the example of a Philadelphia tallow chandler in the fall of 1826 who "complained of chills, pains in the head and back, weakness in the joints and nausea ... [B]efore seeing a regular physician, he

> was bled till symptoms of fainting came on. Took an emetic, which operated well. For several days after, kept his bowels moved with Sulph. Soda, Senna tea etc. He then employed a Physician who prescribed another Emetic, which operated violently and whose action was kept up by drinking bitter tea.[1]

Elsewhere, the author of this passage, in a masterpiece of understatement, observes: "[i]t is difficult to recapture the medical world of 1800 ... a world of thought structured about assumptions alien to a twentieth-century medical understanding" (Rosenberg 1987, 71). A similar gap in medical knowledge existed in the mid-twentieth century between developing and developed countries and persists to some extent even to the present time. For example, a survey of hygienic awareness in Matlab, Bangladesh, in 1986 found that less than 30 percent of mothers believed that contaminated food or water might be responsible for diarrhea, and only 2 percent for dysentery (Bhuyia, Streatfield, and Meyer 1990, 466).[2] Withholding water from infants suffering from diarrhea continues to be a common practice in many parts of the world. None of this is to say that before the nineteenth century there had been no improvement whatsoever in knowledge relevant to the control of disease, but given the long history of humanity, the advances that had occurred were surprisingly recent and had yet to have much practical effect (Ackerknecht 1968; Dixon 1978, Chap. 2; Hall 1967). The most important practical advances had been the use of quarantine and *cordons sanitaires* in the fourteenth century to prevent the spread of plague and the development, in the latter part of the eighteenth century, of inoculation, and then vaccination, against smallpox.

[1] Rosenberg (1979, 13); cf. also Starr (1982, 32–7); Warner (1986).

[2] Study of developing countries' knowledge and beliefs about health has been an important concern of medical anthropology (Caldwell et al. 1990; Landy 1977; Paul 1955; for recent work in other fields on these topics, see Pebley, Hurtado, and Goldman 1996; Weiss 1988). A brief historical overview is given in Roemer (1993, 3 ff).

The major breakthroughs that were eventually to bring infectious disease under control took three principal forms:

1. New methods of preventing the transmission of disease, including education of the public, starting around the middle of the nineteenth century;
2. New vaccines to prevent certain diseases, starting in the 1890s; and
3. New drugs to cure infectious disease (antimicrobials), starting in the late 1930s.

The first major step in preventing the transmission of infectious disease came with what has come to be called the "sanitation revolution." This movement aimed at cleaning up cities through purer water supplies, better sewage disposal, paved streets, education in personal hygiene, and the like. Although this revolution was based on a misguided theory of disease transmission – the miasmatic theory, which linked disease to bad smells and vapors – its emphasis on cleaning up public places and homes led to a gradual reduction in the transmission of waterborne and airborne diseases. The sanitation revolution is usually dated from Edwin Chadwick's landmark 1842(1945). *The Sanitary Condition of the Labouring Population of Great Britain*. This report and similar studies elsewhere (e.g., Citizens' Association of New York 1866; Griscom 1845 (1970); Shattuck et al. 1850) assembled demographic data and the testimony of medical experts to document the association between filth and high mortality. The domestic household counterpart of the sanitation revolution was a new emphasis on cleanliness.[3]

Next came a series of discoveries establishing how certain diseases were specifically transmitted (Table 7.1, Panel A). Two critical mid-nineteenth-century breakthroughs were the discoveries of Snow and Budd that identified impure water as a vehicle for the transmission of two highly feared killers, cholera and typhoid. The specific designation of impure water as a carrier of disease helped strengthen the case for the reforms being urged by the sanitationists. Also, in 1867, Joseph Lister, influenced by Pasteur's contemporary research on the bacteriological

[3] "If sanitary engineering associated with Chadwick represents the public face of the public health movement, the less well-known private aspect is represented in the efforts of the voluntary health visitors and sanitary workers who, entering the homes of the poor, tried to scour the inhabitants as well as their flats" (Wohl 1983, 66; cf. also Tomes 1990).

Table 7.1. Discoveries in the control of major fatal infectious diseases since 1800: Mode of transmission and causal agent

A. Mode of transmission, 1800–1909		
Date	Disease	Investigator
1847	Measles	Panum
	Puerperal fever	Semmelweiss, Holmes
1854	Cholera	Snow
1859	Typhoid fever	Budd
1867	Sepsis (surgical)	Lister
1898	Malaria	Ross, Grassi
	Hookworm	Looss
1900	Yellow fever	Reed
1906	Dengue	Bancroft
	Rocky Mountain spotted fever	Ricketts, King
1909	Typhus	Nicolle

B. Causal agent, 1880–1900		
Date	Disease	Investigator
1880	Typhoid (bacillus found in tissues)	Eberth
	Leprosy	Hansen
	Malaria	Laveran
1882	Tuberculosis	Koch
	Glanders	Loeffler and Schutz
1883	Cholera	Koch
	Streptococcus (erysipelas)	Fehleisen
1884	Diphtheria	Klebs and Loeffler
	Typhoid (bacillus isolated)	Gaffky
	Staphylococcus Streptococcus	Rosenbach
	Tetanus	Nicolaier
1885	Coli	Escherich
1886	Pneumococcus	A. Fraenkel
1887	Malta fever	Bruce
	Soft chancre	Ducrey
1892	Gas gangrene	Welch and Nuttall
1894	Plague	Yersin, Kitasato
	Botulism	van Ermengem
1898	Dysentery bacillus	Shiga

Source: Duffy (1992), Rosen (1958), Winslow (1943).

origins of disease, introduced antiseptic surgery, starting a trend toward sharply diminished mortality in surgical procedures by reducing the transmission of infection during surgery (Biraben 1991; Gariepy 1994).

By the last quarter of the nineteenth century, the discoveries of Pasteur, Koch, and others, and the laboratory techniques and methodology

Table 7.2. Discoveries in the control of major fatal infectious diseases since around 1800: Vaccines and drugs

A. Vaccines			B. Drugs		
Date	Disease	Developer	Date	Drug	Developer
1798	Smallpox	Jenner	1908	Salvarsan	Ehrlich
1881	Anthrax	Pasteur	1935	Sulfanomides	Domagk
1885	Rabies	Pasteur	1941	Penicillin	Fleming, Florey, Chain
1892	Diphtheria	von Behring			
1896	Cholera	Kolle			
1906	Pertussis	Bordet-Gengou	1944	Streptomycin	Waksman
1921	Tuberculosis	Calmette, Guerin	1947–	Broad spectrum antibiotics[a]	
1927	Tetanus	Ramon, Zoeller			
1930	Yellow fever	Theiler			
	Typhoid fever	Weigl			
1948	DTP	(Multiple)			
1950	Polio	Salk			
1954	Measles	Enders, Peebles			

[a] Lappé (1982, pp. 22–4) provides a lengthy tabulation of major antibiotics in use in the United States during 1975–81. See also Brumfitt and Hamilton-Miller (1988).
Source: Baldry (1976), Parish (1965), Plotkin and Mortimer (1988).

that had been developed, had laid the foundation for the new science of bacteriology and essentially validated the germ theory of disease. For the first time the causal agents in several major diseases were identified (Table 7.1, Panel B). Further breakthroughs also occurred in identifying the mode of transmission of certain diseases – most notably, of malaria and yellow fever (Panel A). A basis was laid for the systematic development of immunology, and a new approach opened for the prevention of disease by the development of vaccines (cf. Parish 1965; Plotkin and Mortimer 1988). The conquest of diphtheria by von Behring in 1892 was the first in a series of developments that brought several major infectious diseases under control via immunization (Table 7.2, Panel A). These developments gave increased impetus to educational measures regarding home hygiene, infant and childrearing, care of the sick, and the like (Mokyr and Stein 1997).

The developments summarized so far were techniques that reduced mortality through the prevention of disease, but the ability to cure those who did contract infectious diseases remained elusive. In the early twentieth century, as in the past, physicians could do little to help those who were seriously ill (Thomas 1983, Chaps. 3–5). The successful development of antimicrobials that could attack the newly identified causes of disease without harmful side effects was the next major step in bringing infectious disease under control, but it did not come until almost a half century after the causes of a number of diseases had been found. The most important breakthrough was the development of penicillin in 1941 and the long list of other antibiotics to which it subsequently gave rise (Table 7.2, Panel B; Baldry 1976; Böttcher 1964).[4]

Thus, in little more than a century the ability to control infectious disease was totally transformed – first by sanitation techniques that prevented the spread of certain major infectious diseases, then by vaccines that protected people from contracting some of these diseases, and, finally, by the development of cures. Writing in 1983, a medical historian concludes: "In a single century the understanding of disease increased more than in the previous forty centuries combined. The two crucial developments in this regard were the rise of technology and the application of the basic biological sciences to medicine, using new rules of experimentation and new criteria of proof" (Hudson 1983, 121; cf. also Preston and Haines 1991, and Schofield et al. 1991).

The Epidemiological Transition in Developed Countries

As these new techniques of disease control were introduced, mortality rates plunged, life expectancy took off, and noninfectious gradually replaced infectious disease as the leading cause of death. This development, known as the "epidemiologic transition" or "health transition," is illustrated here by cause-of-death data for England and Wales (Table 7.3; Bobadilla et al. 1993; Caldwell et al. 1990; Omran 1971). Note that most of the mortality decline in England and Wales took place before 1940 (line 1); hence, much of the control of infectious disease was accomplished by preventive measures before the introduction of antimicrobials.

[4] For a striking demonstration of the advance in medical therapy after the 1930s, compare the recommended treatments of major infectious diseases in Winslow (1931) with those in Beeson (1980). The development of antimicrobials is, of course, not necessarily the last step in the control of infectious disease. It is possible, for example, that antibiotics will eventually be replaced by bacteriotherapy – the use of genetically modified strains of nonpathogenic microorganisms to compete against virulent pathogens (Wainwright 1990, 188).

Table 7.3. Death rate and percent distribution of deaths by cause, England and Wales, 1871–1951 (age standardized)

	1871	1940	1951
Death rate (per thousand)	22.4	9.3	6.1
All causes	100	100	100
Infectious diseases	31	10	6
Bronchitis, pneumonia and influenza	14	16	13
Diseases of the circulatory system	9	24	36
Diarrhea and enteritis	6	2	1
Accidents	4	10	6
Neoplasms	2	10	15
Other causes	36	29	24

Source: Caselli, 1991.

One would expect that the new techniques of disease control would improve life expectancy more rapidly in urban than rural areas and that the gap between the two areas would consequently narrow. This is because the sanitation revolution was first and foremost a drive to clean up the cities. Moreover, efforts to educate the public on the importance of personal hygiene were directed especially at, and more easily reached, the highly concentrated urban rather than the widely dispersed rural population. And, in fact, the historical shortfall of urban compared with rural life expectancy was steadily eliminated (Figure 7.1).[5] The initial differential and subsequent trend in rural versus urban life expectancy is the opposite of what one would expect based on per capita income. Although per capita income was initially lower in rural areas (Williamson 1981, 1982), life expectancy was higher. And though rural income grew more rapidly, converging toward urban levels, life expectancy grew more slowly (Preston, Haines, and Pamuk 1981; Preston and van de Walle 1978, 279; Sawyer 1981).

Under the mortality regime prevailing in the first half of the nineteenth century before the onset of sustained advance in the knowledge

[5] Some pioneering historical studies exploring the effect on mortality of urban environmental improvements are Cain and Rotella (1990); Condran and Crimmins-Gardner (1978); Condran et al. (1984); Higgs (1979); Janetta and Preston (1991); Johansson and Mosk (1987); Meeker (1970); Mosk and Johansson (1986); Preston and van de Walle (1978); Wells (1995).

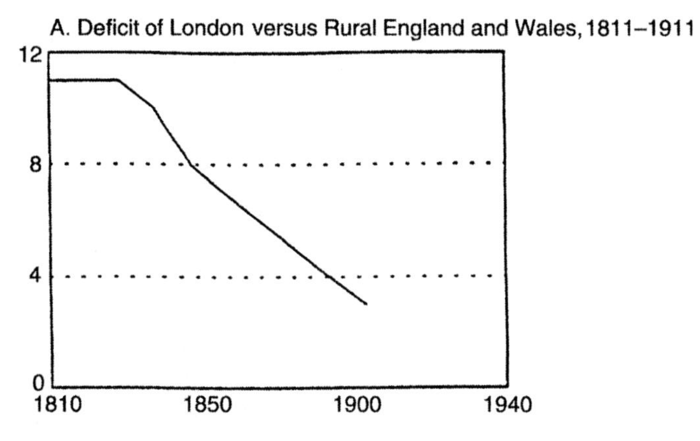

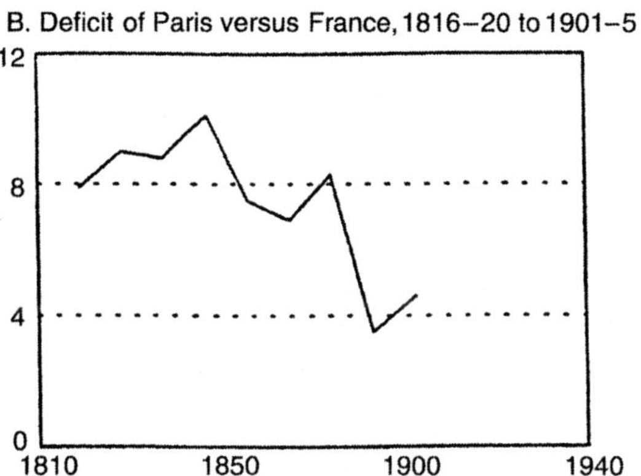

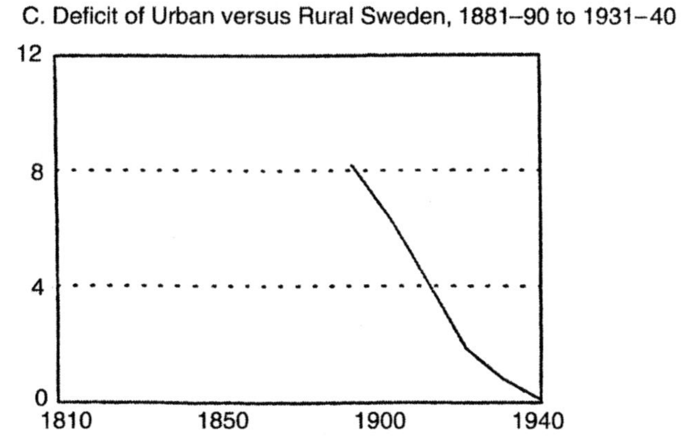

Figure 7.1. Shortfall of urban life expectancy; specified country and period (in years).

Sources: England and Wales, Woods (1985), p. 650; France, Preston and van de Walle (1978), p. 277 (Paris data are those for departement of Seine): Sweden, United Nations (1973), p. 133.

and technology of disease control, the positive relation between life expectancy and income that would be expected on the basis of improved living levels was undercut by the positive association between urbanization and per capita income (see Chapter 6). The subsequent differential trend between rural and urban mortality significantly altered the city–countryside relationship. As unfavorable urban conditions were removed by the new techniques of disease control and excess urban mortality was eliminated, the adverse effect of urbanization on life expectancy evaporated, leaving the positive effect of per capita income via higher living levels. Thus, the new technology of disease control had the effect of increasing the slope of the functional relationship between life expectancy and per capita income as well as shifting that relationship upward (cf. Mosk and Johansson 1986, 420).

Associated with the epidemiological transition there was also a take-off in stature much like that in life expectancy. Work by economic historians on stature has increasingly shifted from the view that stature is determined chiefly by diet to recognition that stature depends also on the incidence of disease because illness seriously affects the capacity of the body to retain nutrients (Engerman 1997; Steckel 1995; Steckel and Floud 1997). A microlevel illustration is the carefully documented growth history of a Gambian infant in Figure 7.2, which reveals that lapses from a normal growth trajectory are primarily associated with periods of infection, particularly diarrheal disease. Because the epidemiological transition especially reduced mortality and illness of the young, among whom the incidence of infectious disease is highest, one would expect this transition to have had beneficial effects on stature, and it did. Stature took off at the same time as life expectancy. In the six European countries for which historical estimates are available, the average improvement in male stature in the century before the third quarter of the nineteenth century was 1.1 centimeters. In the subsequent century – the period of the epidemiological transition – it was 7.7 centimeters (Easterlin 1996, 82). In every one of the six countries, the rate of improvement in stature was considerably higher in the more recent century than in the earlier. The earlier improvement in stature, that before the late nineteenth century, may also partly reflect a reduced incidence of infectious disease as smallpox vaccination became more widespread in the six countries.

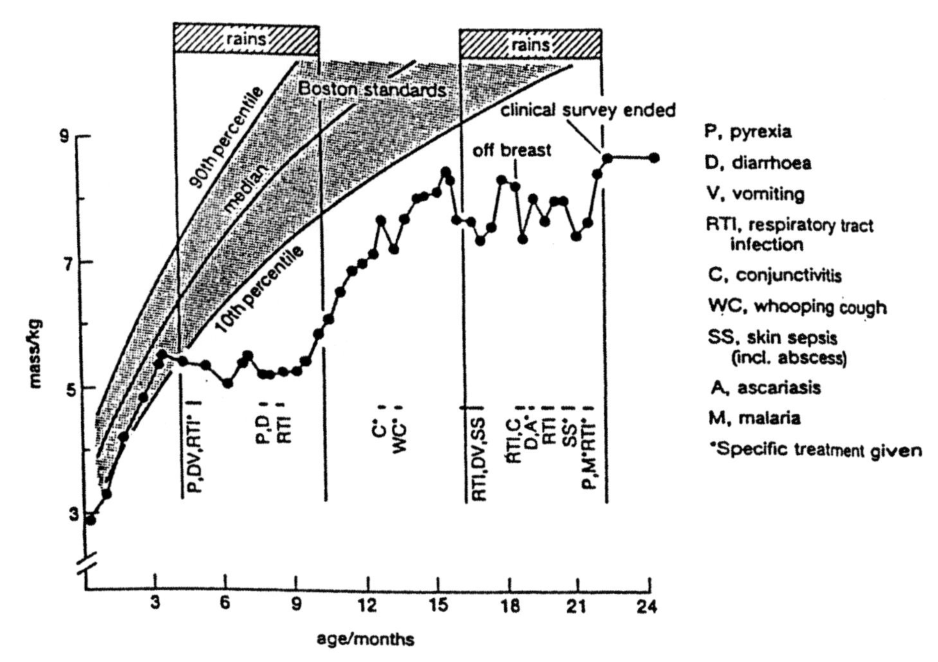

Figure 7.2. Body mass, history of infection, and age of a rural Gambian infant. *Source:* Reproduced from Lunn (1991), p. 133.

Advances in Infectious Disease Control in Today's Developing Countries

Since World War II there has been a sustained improvement in life expectancy in every one of the four major developing regions (Latin America, Asia, sub-Saharan Africa, and the Middle East plus North Africa) at a rate ranging from 3.4 to 6.6 years per decade (Figure 7.3).[6] The contrast with trends in real GDP per capita is noteworthy (Figure 7.4). In three of the four regions GDP per capita turns downward in 1985–95, but life expectancy continues to rise at the same pace as in the prior interval, which is a disparity between trends in life expectancy and

[6] The averages in Figures 7.3, 7.4, and 7.6 are for around 80 developing countries, as determined by the availability of data, with 1990 populations greater than 900,000 – about 14 in Asia, 21 in Latin America and the Caribbean, 13 in the Middle East and North Africa, and 40 in sub-Saharan Africa.

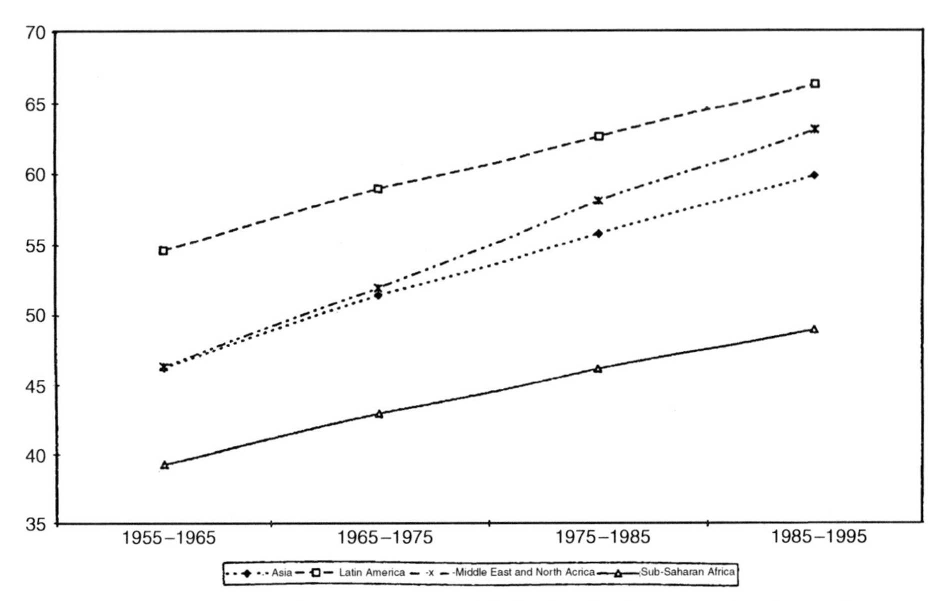

Figure 7.3. Average life expectancy at birth, developing countries, by region, 1955–65 to 1985–95.
Source: United Nations 1995.

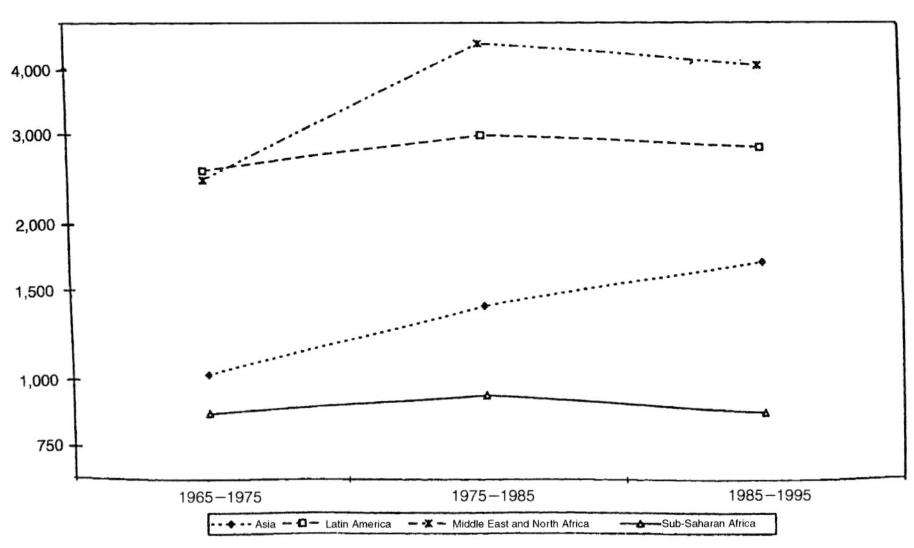

Figure 7.4. Average real GDP per capita, developing countries, by region, 1965–75 to 1985–95 (1985 dollars).
Source: Summers and Heston 1991.

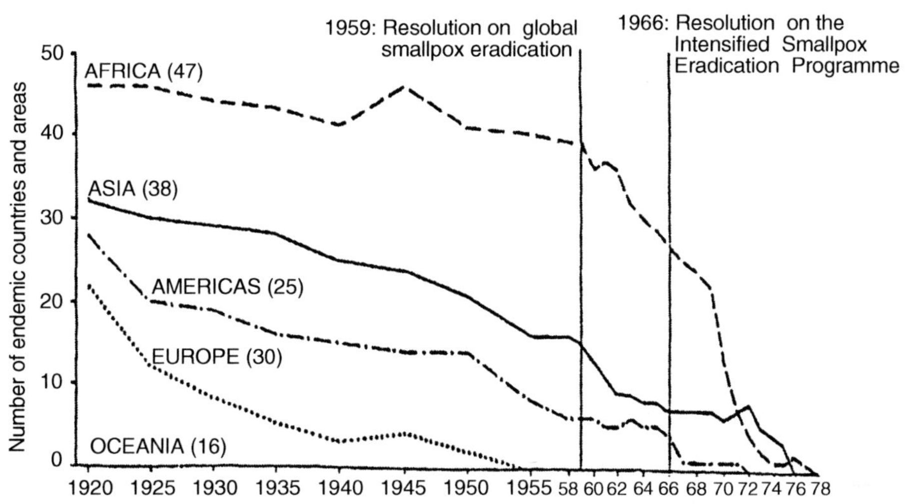

Figure 7.5. Number of countries and territories in which smallpox is endemic, by continent, 1920–78 (figures in parentheses are the total number included in each continent.)
Source: Reproduced from Fenner et al. (1988). p. 171.

economic growth reminiscent of those in the historical experience of the developed countries between World Wars I and II (see Chapter 6).

This improvement in life expectancy in developing countries has been accomplished by the introduction of essentially the same techniques of infectious disease control as were used in the developed countries.[7] For the early post–World War II period, analysts give prominent attention to efforts to bring malaria, smallpox, and other epidemic diseases under control as illustrated here in Figure 7.5 by the diffusion of smallpox immunization (United Nations 1952, 1957, 1961, 1963a, 1973; cf. also Bulatao 1993; Gray 1974; Haines, Avery, and Strong, 1983; Preston 1980, 293–301). Also, since 1965, when data first become more plentiful, access to pure water supply has improved markedly (Figure 7.6, Panel A). So too has female education, which is an indicator of improved control of disease transmission – especially in the home (Panel

[7] Cf. Arriaga and Davis (1969); Chen, Kleinman, and Ware (1994); Gribble and Preston (1993); Mosley and Chen (1984); United Nations (1982, 1985, 1991, 1992). Modifications have, of course, also occurred; cf. Cairncross (1989), Commission on Health Research for Development (1990, 15).

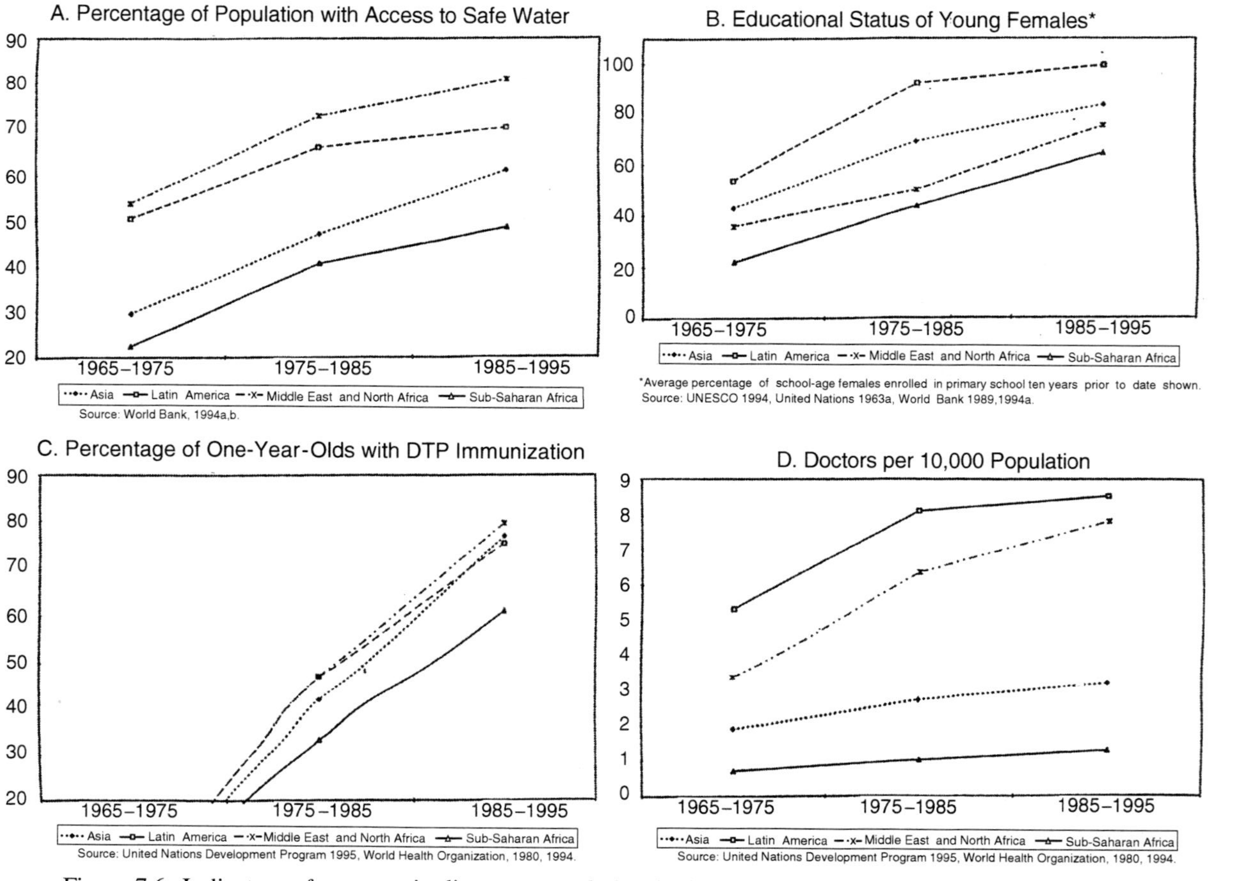

Figure 7.6. Indicators of progress in disease control, developing countries, by region, 1965–75 to 1985–95.

B).[8] Progress in regard to immunization of children is evidenced by the sharp rise in DTP immunization over the last three decades (Panel C). Closely associated with this has been the spread of other immunization measures and oral rehydration therapy (World Health Organization 1992). Although trend data relating directly to the supply of drugs are not available, a proxy, doctors per 10,000 population, improves considerably (Panel D). These indicators of technological change in the control of infectious disease, though by no means comprehensive, signify advance along the same lines in developing countries as those in developed countries – an advance consistent with the rapid rise in life expectancy in developing countries.[9]

Data on public health spending are not available for the full period covered here, but public health spending is likely to be less meaningful than the specific indicators shown, which have been chosen, so far as possible, to relate specifically to technological change in disease control. Public health expenditures are less meaningful because a fair proportion of public health spending in developing countries appears to benefit chiefly the middle- and upper-income classes such as expenditures on urban hospitals and on highly specialized equipment and drugs. Also, some expenditures that have been effective in reducing mortality, such as those on improved water supply and sewage disposal (reflected in Panel A of Figure 7.6), are often not classified as public health expenditures.[10]

The indicators in Figure 7.6 underscore the similarity between the developed and developing countries in the techniques used to control infectious disease. However, in the developed countries, the timing of

[8] In Figure 7.6, Panel B, data on primary school enrollment of school-age females are shifted forward a decade to approximate the trend in years of schooling of young homemakers.

[9] Various studies relate one or more of the indicators in Figure 7.6 to mortality. On water, see Esrey et al. (1991); female education, Caldwell et al. (1990, Chaps. 19–23); Chen et al. (1994, Chaps. 11–13); Cleland and van Ginneken (1988); Hobcraft (1993); Jejeebhoy (1995, Chap. 6); Sandiford et al. (1995); Ware (1984); immunization, Boerma and Stroh (1993); doctors, Doan (1974); Gilliand and Galland (1977).

[10] Piachaud (1979) suggests that there has been a serious misallocation of public health spending in the developing world. Roth (1987, 128) estimates that at most 30 percent of health spending in developing countries is for the preventive measures that have been so important in reducing infectious disease (cf. also De Ferranti 1985, 61; Dréze and Sen 1989, 251; Musgrove 1996, 44).

the various innovations in control of contagious disease was quite different from that in developing countries. This is because the leading countries in life expectancy, as with economic growth, sequentially experienced technological advances that occurred more nearly simultaneously among a large number of followers in the last half of the twentieth century. The increased options available to today's developing countries no doubt helps account for their more rapid rate of improvement in life expectancy than in the developed countries despite their having per capita incomes far below those of today's developed countries at the onset of their rapid life expectancy improvement. Moreover, the adverse effect on life expectancy of the rapid urbanization accompanying economic growth has probably been less. This is because urban areas in LDCs benefited earlier than those in DCs from the new technology of disease control. As a result, the positive effect of economic growth on life expectancy is likely to be greater in today's LDCs than in the historical experience of the DCs.

LIFE EXPECTANCY AND THE MARKET

There is currently a broad consensus among economists that economic growth is fostered by free markets, private property, and enforcement of contracts (North 1990; Rodrik 1996). Were these same institutions at work on the problem of infectious disease? In today's developed countries, incomes were rising in the nineteenth century and disease was an important concern; wasn't it, then, profitable for firms to attack the problem of disease?

It is this issue – the role of the free market in the great improvement of life expectancy – to which this section is addressed. By the "free market" I mean supply and demand conditions operating within the institutions of private property and free contract to allocate resources via the incentive of private profit to the satisfaction of human wants – in this case wants with regard to the elimination of disease and reduction of mortality.

To form a tentative judgment on the role of the market, I focus on the specific techniques identified in the previous section that reduced infectious disease so dramatically (control of the mode of transmission, immunization, and antimicrobials) and consider the extent to which the free market allocated resources to each. The answer, as will be seen, is that the market appears to have functioned poorly. Infectious disease is a subject replete with all the classic sources of market failure – information failures, externalities, public goods, and free rider problems (Stiglitz 1988). Because of this, public sector initiative has been critical in implementing new techniques of disease control. Moreover, the market imperfectly registers the needs of those most vulnerable to disease: infants and children, the poor, and the elderly.

I also take up the question of whether the market might have stimulated the invention of the new methods of disease control. The answer to this again appears to be negative. The sequence of innovation in disease control suggests that it was the changing feasibility of innovation that was responsible for technological progress, and feasibility depended chiefly on the evolution of scientific knowledge in the biomedical area and of research techniques in the biomedical field, not external market forces.

Control of the Mode of Transmission of Disease

For the present purpose, it is helpful to classify the techniques under this heading into those requiring a change in the contaminating behavior of individuals, firms, and other agents and those calling for correction of environmental conditions.

The contaminating behaviors of individuals encompass such things as coughing, sneezing, spitting, and nose blowing; toilet habits; sexual practices; behavior in regard to personal washing and bathing; practices regarding the sources and handling of drinking water and milk; methods of food handling and preparation; customs regarding the care and feeding of infants and children; practices relating to care of the sick; and attitudes toward rodents and insects. In the nineteenth century, everyday behavior in virtually all of these respects generated significant negative externalities with regard to infectious disease. For example, spitting on the floor at home and in public places was often an accepted behavior (Sundin 1995). The fly, rather than being regarded as a carrier of disease, was thought of affectionately as the "friendly fly" (Rogers 1989). Writing of the habits of the poor in Wakefield, England, in 1869, Sir John Simon reports, "people are seen easing their bowels into the beck [stream] which afterwards supplied them with drinking water" (Wohl 1983, 94).

At the firm level, worker and management practices fostering the spread of disease (often unwittingly) were also common. As an example, here is a statement by Stephen Smith, a physician reporting on the results of a sanitation survey in New York City in 1865:

> I hold in my hand a list of cases of smallpox found existing under circumstances which show how widespread is this disease. Bedding of a fatal case of smallpox was sold to a rag-man; case in a room where candy and daily papers were sold; case on a ferry-boat, woman was attending bar and acting as nurse to her husband who had smallpox; girl was making cigars while scabs were falling from her skin; seamstress was making shirts for a Broadway store, one of which was thrown over the cradle of a child sick of smallpox; tailors making soldiers' clothing, have their children, from whom the scabs were falling, wrapped in the garments; a woman selling vegetables had the scabs falling from her face, among the vegetables, etc. etc. (Smith 1911, 108–9)

A description of mid-nineteenth-century London's "town dairies" – "half-underground dens and cellars in which the cows were kept for the greater part of the year, standing knee-deep in filth" – states that "it was difficult to find a sample of London milk which would fail to show the presence of blood or pus when examined under the microscope" (Drummond and Wilbraham 1939, 299–300).

Such behaviors and practices, of central significance for the transmission of disease, are not a simple function of income and prices. They are rooted in the established norms of society and its customs and beliefs. Each generation, as it is raised, internalizes various health beliefs and learns what is socially acceptable behavior. Historically, the market, by crowding people more closely together in towns, cities, and factories, magnified the negative externalities of disease-transmitting behaviors and practices. Writing in 1842 on *The Condition of the Working Classes in England*, Friedrich Engels observed, "Dirty habits . . . do no great harm in the countryside where the population is scattered. On the other hand, the dangerous situation which develops when such habits are practiced among the crowded population of big cities, must arouse feelings of apprehension and disgust" (as quoted in Wohl 1983, 4).

This set of behaviors cannot be corrected by the simple assignment of property rights. In the absence of knowledge of the mechanisms of disease causation and transmission, such assignment is not even conceivable. But even if such knowledge exists, enforcement is not possible because of the overwhelming magnitude of transaction costs. As Phelps (1992, 418) points out: "If you had to sue everybody who sneezed in your vicinity, you would have no time remaining for any other activity.... [S]ocial customs and 'manners' create society's best control mechanism." But appropriate customs and manners do not arise spontaneously. They result chiefly from increasing awareness among the public of the consequences of one's actions for the spread of disease – awareness that depends on appropriate knowledge of disease. In the nineteenth century, a change in contaminating behaviors had to wait, first, for the emergence of new medical knowledge, and, second, for concrete efforts by public agencies and medical practitioners to disseminate this knowledge to households and firms.

The second principal source for preventing the transmission of infectious disease has been correction of environmental conditions that expose the population to disease. Here, too, the contribution of market forces has been dubious. Some environmental techniques for controlling contagious disease, such as insect or rodent control, are quite clearly public goods. The individual may take defensive measures – the use of screens, mosquito netting, rat traps, and so on – but in situations of dense habitation these are likely to be of limited effectiveness in the absence of community action. What is needed are measures that go beyond most individuals' resources such as swamp drainage and the spraying of insecticides on the breeding grounds of insects (Musgrove 1996, 11).

Some environmental conditions important for the control of infectious disease do involve goods that are or have been provided by the market to some extent. This is notably true with regard to those conditions that were the initial target of the sanitation revolution – improved water supply and waste disposal. Didn't rising income generate a growing demand for these goods and their resulting supply work to remove this source of infectious disease?

In answer to this question, it is helpful to start by recalling that, in the mid-nineteenth century, the flush toilet was a rarity. In cities the most common facility was a vault privy, modeled on its country cousin, the outhouse, but in poor neighborhoods, even these were rare.[11] The result

[11] "[I]n mid-century Darlington: 'In 1 yard 66 persons are obligated to use 1 privy; in another 65, and in a third 63, in a fourth 54, in a fifth 45, in a sixth 41, in a seventh 35 and so on'" (Wohl 1983, 87; cf. also Winslow 1943, 244–5).

was burgeoning accumulations of human excrement as city size rocketed. In some areas, these accumulations, because of their potential use as manure, had value as an economic good; there was even a saying that the "chamber pot is a penny savings bank" (Drummond and Wilbraham 1939).[12] But the resulting market only aggravated the problem of infectious disease because of accompanying negative externalities. It is worth repeating a frequently quoted and apt passage from Chadwick describing conditions in British towns around 1840:

> In the parts of some towns adjacent to the rural districts the cesspools are emptied gratuitously for the sake of the manure; but they only do this when there is a considerable accumulation.... For the saving of cartage, as well as the convenience of use, accumulations of refuse are frequently allowed to remain and decompose and dry amidst the habitations of the poorer classes. *Dr. Laurie* in his report on the sanitary condition of Greenock, furnishes an example. He says, –
>
> The first question I generally put when a new case of fever is admitted, is as to their locality. I was struck with the number of admissions from Market-street; most of the cases coming from that locality became quickly typhoid, and made slow recoveries. This is a narrow back street. . . .
>
> In one part of the street there is a dunghill, – yet it is too large to be called a dunghill. I do not mistate its size when I say it contains a hundred cubic yards of impure filth, collected from all parts of the town. It is never removed; it is the stock-in-trade of a person who deals in dung; he retails it by cartfuls. To please his customers, he always keeps a nucleus, as the older the filth is the higher is the price. The proprietor has an extensive privy attached to the concern. This collection is fronting the public street; it is enclosed in front by a wall; the height of the wall is about 12 feet, and the dung overtops it; the malarious moisture oozes through the wall, and runs over the pavement. The effluvia all round about this place in summer is horrible. There is a land of houses adjoining, four stories in height, and in the summer each house swarms with myriads of flies; every article of food and drink must be covered, otherwise, if left exposed for a minute, the flies immediately attack it, and it is rendered unfit for use, from the strong taste of the dunghill left by the flies. (Chadwick [1842] 1965, 119)[13]

[12] "Dogs'-dung... called 'Pure' from its cleansing and purifying properties" was also valued and collected by specialized workers. See the description of "Pure-finders" in Mayhew ([1851] 1958, 306 ff).

[13] Conditions in American cities were much like those described in the Chadwick Report. See, for example, the reports by Griscom [1845] 1970; Shattuck [1850] 1948; Smith (1911).

The market was certainly at work here, but in a way that increased, rather than reduced, exposure to disease.

It may be thought that such conditions are peculiar to the mid-nineteenth century. An excerpt from an article in the *New York Times* of January 9, 1997, reporting on conditions in some parts of the Third World may serve as a corrective:

> On the Bassac River just outside Phnom Penh is one of the most wretched slums in the world, a putrid slope of mud and excrement that is home to tens of thousands of people packed in rickety shacks on the bank of the river.
>
> There are latrines of a sort, for entrepreneurs have set up little platforms over the water. These are open toilets where men and women squat behind half-barrels.... [T]he toilet owners make money by raising fish on the sewage in fenced-off waters below the toilet platform.
>
> The fish may not sound appetizing, but the worst problem is that the slow river is used by the slum not only as its toilet, but also as its source of drinking water.... [T]he only water available for washing hands is the black liquid taken from between the toilets in the river. (Section A, Page 1, Column 1)

For the provision of water in the mid-nineteenth century, the market was at work via piped water supplied by private water companies. Private vendors also sold water from containers and from local street pumps or taps (Hohenberg and Lees 1985). Privately provided piped water was allocated almost wholly to meet the demands of the middle and upper income groups. Lower income groups living in crowded urban slums might have to walk a quarter of a mile to the one water tap in the neighborhood (Briggs 1985, 134–5; Goubert 1989; Wohl 1983, 61–3). In these circumstances, it is not surprising that working-class families in mid-nineteenth-century Burton-on-Trent "purchased an average of nine buckets of water a week for a family of five or more for *all* purposes" (Wohl 1983, 63, emphasis in original). Note that this statistic relates to working-class families; the poor would have fared even worse. Similarly, according to a World Bank study of today's developing countries, "tens of millions of women and children spend as much as three or more hours daily fetching polluted water" (Roth 1987, 231).

But water supply involves much more than a problem of unequal distribution. As cities grew, and the cost of transporting human waste to rural areas became prohibitive, carters turned for disposal to the closest stream, pond, or river. Water courses in and around large cities were transformed into enormous cesspools. William Budd's contemporary description of the "Great Stench" arising from the accumulation of sewage in the Thames River in the summer of 1858 is worth repeating:

> For the first time in the history of man, the sewage of nearly three millions of people had been brought to seethe and ferment under a burning sun, in one vast open cloaca [sewer] lying in their midst.... Stench so foul, we may well believe, had never before ascended to pollute this lower air.... For many weeks, the atmosphere of Parliamentary Committee-rooms was only rendered barely tolerable by the suspension before every window, of blinds saturated with chloride of lime, and by the lavish use of this and other disinfectants. More than once, in spite of similar precautions, the law-courts were suddenly broken up by an insupportable invasion of the noxious vapour. The river steamers lost their accustomed traffic, and travellers, pressed for time, often made a circuit of many miles rather than cross one of the city bridges. (as quoted in Winslow 1943, 288)

Sewage disposal thus led increasingly to contaminated water supply.[14] The problem was aggravated by industrial wastes from factories (Cain 1977, 375–6). Because pathogenic organisms can exist in water that, to the naked eye is pure, not even the wealthy, despite their ability to pay, were assured of protection from this source of infectious disease.

All of this boils down to a simple point: under the conditions of agglomeration arising from nineteenth-century economic growth, the market could not be counted on for the provision of pure water in adequate amounts or for the proper disposal of sewage. Rather, market forces were tending to increase exposure to infectious disease. It has been suggested that economists "need to do a lot more work on the extent to which economic activity produces ill health as well as goods and services for people to buy"(Williams 1987, 1068). The problem of water supply and sewage disposal in rapidly growing cities would seem to be an appropriate subject for study.

[14] Attempts by cities to go further upstream for water did not necessarily solve the problem of contamination. In the United States, after impure water came to be recognized as a source of disease, it took about half a century before the belief that water purified itself after traveling six miles was replaced by the view that "no river is long enough to purify itself" (Marcus 1979, 192). For an excellent analysis of the interdependent problem of urban sanitation and water supply in the United States, see Cain (1977).

Immunization

On the face of it one might suppose that a newly available vaccine would find a ready market. But this assumes a belief in the efficacy of modern medicine that may not exist. In sub-Saharan Africa in the 1960s, for example, babies were sometimes hidden from the national or international teams dispensing smallpox vaccinations.[15] In addition, those who have appropriate knowledge may be priced out of the market. There is also a free-rider problem: the incentive for vaccination diminishes as others become immunized. Moreover, in the case of the immunization of infants and children, the child must rely on the parents' decision to immunize. Parents, however, may be negligent or simply not have the time needed for a round, say, of three inoculations of DTP or polio vaccine in a year.

Immunization also involves a problem similar to that which arises with hygiene education. One person may opt for the new practice or knowledge, but the failure of others to do so may leave that person at risk. Consider the synergistic relation between smallpox and other diseases. The vaccination of one person may protect him or her against smallpox, but if those who fail to get vaccinated suffer from damage to their immune systems caused by smallpox, they may expose the person who was vaccinated to greater risk from other diseases such as typhoid or tuberculosis.

These considerations add up to a questionable case for reliance on the market to foster the spread of immunization. A recent publication of the World Bank puts it more strongly: "Had it been left to private markets during the last few decades, it is inconceivable that today some 80 percent of the world's children would be immunized against the six major-vaccine-preventable childhood diseases"(Musgrove 1996, 14).

Antimicrobials

Here, at last, one might suppose is an area that can be conceded to the market. To be sure, regarding antimicrobials as well as vaccines there are

[15] Fenner, Henderson, and Arita (1988); cf. also Hanlon et al. (1988) and Cutts et al. (1989). Resistance to modern therapies for reasons other than monetary cost has been common; see Caldwell et al. (1990); Dixon (1978); Landy (1977); Paul (1955).

issues of quality control and of monitoring claims for effectiveness by private producers. But can't one rely, generally speaking, on the market as a vehicle for distributing drugs?

The answer appears to be no. Significant externalities are associated with the private distribution of drugs; most important, the market fails to take adequate account of the fact that the excessive use of antibiotics fosters the growth of drug-resistant bacteria. This problem quickly came to the fore in developed countries shortly after antimicrobials were introduced and seriously undercut the high hopes originally held for these drugs (Lappé 1982). But the problem is most serious in the developing countries, where an uncontrolled free market is typically the primary vehicle of drug distribution. A quotation from a World Bank volume is particularly telling because it comes from a study explicitly devoted to a search for free market solutions:

> The proliferation of modern pharmaceuticals in developing countries can have harmful effects.... [I]n many developing countries medical practitioners do not exercise any control over the use of modern prescription drugs such as antibiotics, as do practitioners in the developed countries. Throughout Latin America, for example, prescription medications, usually manufactured by multinational pharmaceutical firms, can often be purchased over the counter in pharmacies or shops or from medicine vendors. The link between healer and healing resource is not always present, and the products are frequently available in the absence of physicians or other trained practitioners....
>
> [I]n some regions of India, indigenous practitioners supply modern medicines on a large scale. In Mysore and the Punjab 80 percent of the medicines are modern, and 50 percent of the patients receive penicillin injections, generally from unqualified practitioners supplied by pharmacists.... [T]he greatest source of hazard [is] the tendency of "pseudo-indigenous practitioners" to use the most powerful drugs possible, such as chloramphenicol, to obtain quick results. Similar systems of "pharmaceutical medicine" have been reported in Ethiopia. (Roth 1987, 137, citations in original deleted)[16]

Some have suggested that pharmaceutical companies have little motivation to waste money on this problem because the development of drug-resistant bacteria promotes the development and sale of newer drugs (Muller 1982, 115). Moreover, consumers who are ill are likely to

[16] Dixon (1978, 205–13) cites other examples of drug promotion in developing countries by multinational pharmaceutical companies, leading to their misuse. Cf. also Chetley (1990); Lappé (1982, Chaps. 10, 15).

demand what they view as the most powerful drugs without regard to their longer-term effects. In 1990, a report by an international nongovernmental Commission on Health Research for Development (1990, 42), after stating that "there are few factors that affect the cost-effectiveness of health services more than fostering the appropriate use and controlling and reducing the misuse of drugs" went on to say that "[b]ehavioral research is urgently needed to improve the way pharmaceuticals are prescribed, dispensed, and used."

Institutional Innovations in the Control of Contagious Disease

The foregoing suggests that free market institutions have functioned poorly to control major infectious disease. In what is widely regarded as one of the early classics in health economics, Arrow (1963, 947) observed: "[W]hen the market fails to achieve an optimal state, society will, to some extent at least, recognize the gap, and nonmarket social institutions will arise attempting to bridge it." The history of infectious disease bears testimony to the accuracy of this generalization.

I take "institutions" here in North's (1990) sense of both formal and informal arrangements. And, indeed, both types have been required: informal arrangements in the form of a change in social norms relating to responsibility for disease and, also, formal establishment of an apparatus for state intervention. These are taken up in succession below.

One of the effects of the nineteenth-century sanitation movement was a gradual transformation in attitudes toward responsibility for disease (Duffy 1992, 128; Flinn 1965, 59; Griscom [1845] 1970; Hanlon, Rogers, and Rosen 1960, 446; Institute of Medicine 1988, Chap. 3; Rosenkranz 1972; United Nations 1952, 24). Previously, disease had been attributed to "acts of God" or individual failings such as sinfulness, lack of moral character, and the like. However, the growth of knowledge regarding modes of transmission of disease made it increasingly clear that the individual might be the victim of forces beyond his or her control and that these forces were within the purview of social action. As awareness of this possibility grew, so too did support for state intervention in the interest of "public" health (Briggs 1985, II, 150).

What was lacking, however, was an effective mechanism for intervention. It was in the solution of this problem that the sanitation movement made its greatest contribution. The key institutional innovation was the establishment of a network of local boards of health under the supervision of a central authority (usually a national health agency, although in the United States this function was performed by state health boards) armed with the weapon of inspection.[17] In England and the United States, the last half of the nineteenth century saw the gradual emergence of this new public health apparatus (Briggs 1985; Duffy 1992; Kearns 1988; Marcus 1979; Rosen 1958; Wohl 1983).

Initially the focus was on sanitation – especially establishing pure water supplies and sewage disposal and paving streets. But the functions of the public health organization changed over time as knowledge and technology advanced. As the germ theory became more widely accepted, a bacteriological view of public health tended to reinforce "sanitary science" and expand the functions of health departments. Bacteriological laboratories became part of the new municipal health departments, and research and diagnosis of pathogens became significant functions. Regulation of food and milk supply developed as the role of food handling in the transmission of disease became recognized. Recognition grew of the need for housing standards, building regulations, and appropriate enforcement authorities. The production and distribution of vaccines became important. And gradually some of the original activities of health departments were spun off to other municipal agencies such as responsibility for water supply, waste removal, and "nuisances," although oversight and regulation functions continued.[18]

[17] The novelty of the institutional innovation of the public health system is recognized by both contemporaries and historians. In 1890, looking back on the evolution of the public health apparatus, Sir John Simon, "the greatest of the Victorian medical officers" (Wohl 1983, 8), was to observe that "on the new foundations of Science, a new political superstructure has taken form" (Simon 1890, 463). Writing in the mid-twentieth century, George Rosen, author of the classic history of public health, cites Edwin Chadwick's chief contribution as his recognition that "what was needed was an administrative organ to undertake a preventive program by applying engineering knowledge and techniques in a consistent manner" (Rosen 1968, 167).

[18] The association between the growth of knowledge regarding disease and the expansion of government regulatory and educational activities from the latter part of the nineteenth century onward is apparent in several articles written from the comparatively recent perspective of the early 1930s in the first edition of the *Encyclopaedia of the Social Sciences*. See, for example, the articles on food and drug regulations, building regulations, inspection, health education, sanitation, water supply, milk supply, housing, and slums.

For households, the domestic hygiene counterpart of the new sanitary science centered initially on ventilation, disinfection, plumbing, water purification, isolation of the sick, and general cleanliness. Because the new knowledge was not proprietary, the market could not be relied on to disseminate it. Nor were there competitive profit-making pressures on households analogous to those fostering the adoption of new production techniques by profit-making firms. At first, the new knowledge was promoted especially by women reformers through voluntary organizations. But public health agencies gradually assumed an increasing role, and voluntary domestic hygiene was supplemented by compulsory quarantine and disinfection. As knowledge grew, education expanded to encompass food handling and infant and child care, and health programs were introduced into the schools. Because women were principally responsible for household care and childrearing, these educational efforts were especially directed toward women (Mokyr 2000). Thus, in contrast to economic growth, female, rather than male, education has played a central role in the improvement of life expectancy (Cleland and van Ginneken 1988).

Changing patterns of consumer demand are one indication of the success of these educational efforts in shifting the household's "health production function." Mokyr and Stein (1997) point out that, in England, soap consumption rose sharply in the late nineteenth century despite a rising price (cf. also Wohl 1983, 71). In regard to the late-nineteenth-century United States, Tomes (1990, 531) reasons that "the rush to develop and to patent sewer traps, toilet designs, window ventilators and water filtration systems . . . suggests that entrepreneurs found a lucrative market among householders anxious to safeguard their families against infection."

Barr (1992) points out the critical importance of the little-discussed topic of "information failures" as a justification for state intervention. One could hardly find a better case than infectious disease. Throughout much of the history of the world both producers and households have been ignorant of the causes of disease and of the consequences of their actions for the spread of disease. Under these circumstances, education of the public, based on the growth of knowledge regarding disease, has been fundamental in its control, and this educational function has devolved primarily on the public health system and the schools. Regulatory actions enforced by the police power of the state have reinforced education.

The institutional impact of advancing biomedical knowledge went, of course, beyond the official public health system. Voluntary associations arose usually dedicated to a specific purpose such as education in regard to infant care or the diffusion of knowledge about tuberculosis. These voluntary organizations served a useful purpose in supplementing the governmental system and sometimes pointed to new possibilities or needs for action. But, as with hygiene education, the voluntary agencies were for the most part relatively short lived, and it was the governmental system that formed the backbone of the new institutional structure dedicated to the promotion of public health.

As the germ theory became accepted, it revolutionized the training of doctors and nurses and gave birth to today's modern hospital (Abel-Smith 1960, 1964; Haines 1933; Rosen 1958, 374–82; Rosenberg 1987; Vogel 1980). As awareness grew of "community" medicine, professional associations (the American Public Health Association was founded in 1872), schools of public health (the first American school, Johns Hopkins, was established in 1918), and a specialized professional literature arose (Duffy 1992, 253; Rosen 1958, 516–25). The history of public health is filled with "public entrepreneurs" who led in the formation of new institutions or the revamping of old ones to implement the new goals and knowledge (Rosen 1958, 507–15 provides a list of some of these entrepreneurs, whose accomplishments deserve the recognition in economic history currently reserved for industrial tycoons).

From its inception in the sanitation revolution, the public health movement encountered serious opposition because of the necessary expansion of the government's role in the economy. The sanitation revolution was mirrored, in effect, in a clash of ideologies between advocates of laissez-faire and proponents of state intervention, though some public sector proponents such as Chadwick sought to assimilate proposals for intervention to the prevailing laissez-faire philosophy and Benthamite utilitarianism (Briggs 1985, II, Chap. 7; Flinn 1965; Kearns 1988; Szreter 1988). Specific proposals were fiercely debated in the local and national political arenas. The backbone of the opposition was made up of those whose vested interests were threatened: landlords, builders, water companies, proprietors of refuse heaps and dung hills, burial concerns, slaughterhouses, and the like (for Great Britain, see

Briggs 1985, II, Chap. 7; for the United States, Wells 1995; for Germany, Evans 1987, Chap. 2). The opposition appealed to the preservation of civil liberties and sought to debunk the new knowledge cited by the public health advocates, which is a strategy reminiscent of the response a century later by the tobacco industry to evidence of the adverse health effects of smoking.[19]

Sources of Technological Change in Disease Control

Economic explanations of invention have typically focused on demand conditions as the source of technological change. With regard to advances in the control of infectious disease, demand may similarly be assumed to be the main causal factor. As has been seen, in mid-nineteenth-century England, the prior, slow, century-long advance in life expectancy had come largely to a halt as a result of rapid urbanization and industrialization. Health conditions among the poor in urban centers were increasingly recognized as appalling, and epidemic outbreaks of cholera and typhoid aroused concerns generally (Brown 1988; Flinn 1965; Mercer 1990). These problems contributed to a growing search for solutions.

Although demand increased in the nineteenth century, it was not new – sickness and death have been the eternal bane of humanity. As Nathan Rosenberg points out:

> Many important categories of human wants have long gone either unsatisfied or very badly catered for in spite of a well-established demand. It is certainly true that the progress made in techniques of navigation in the sixteenth and seventeenth centuries owed much to the great demand for such techniques in those centuries, as many authors have pointed out. But it is also true that a great potential demand existed in the same period for improvements in the healing arts generally, but that no such improvements were forthcoming. (Rosenberg 1976, 267–8)

That study of the "healing arts" was far from neglected in the sixteenth and seventeenth centuries is suggested by Europe's leading universities at that time having had more salaried chairs in medicine than in science (Ben-David 1971, 52).

[19] Despite the documented success of smallpox vaccination, a strong antivaccinationist movement existed in Great Britain well into the late nineteenth century (Fenner et al., 1988, 270).

The actual sequence of the solutions to controlling disease that were found suggests that it was supply-side developments, rather than demand, that governed advances in the control of infectious disease – specifically, changes in the feasibility of invention arising from advances in knowledge. Obviously, the most intense demand comes from those who are sick and want a cure for disease. As has been seen, however, in the actual sequence of technological developments in the control of infectious disease, the development of cures came last, not first. The first major breakthrough came with regard to the transmission of disease and reflects the lesser difficulty with which knowledge of transmission can be obtained vis-à-vis developing a cure. Typically, the mode of transmission of a disease is more amenable to observation than its causes, and the development of a cure must wait upon identification of the pathogen and physiological mechanisms responsible for a particular disease. This is evidenced today in experience with the newest major infectious disease, HIV, for which the modes of transmission were quickly identified and led to measures directed toward control well before effective therapies started to appear. Before the nineteenth century the only major advances in control of fatal infectious diseases were methods of preventing the transmission of leprosy and plague.

Two early developments underlying the growth of epidemiological knowledge were the emergence of vital statistics dating from the work of Petty and Graunt in the seventeenth century and of new statistical techniques pioneered by analysts such as William Farr and Adolphe Quetelet in the first half of the nineteenth century (Briggs 1985, I, Chap. 3; Porter 1986, Chap. 1; Wohl 1983, 144). These, together with the slow growth of medical knowledge, laid the basis for epidemiological studies of the type done by Chadwick, Snow, Budd, Villermé, Shattuck, and other health analysts in the early industrializing countries.[20]

Knowledge of the causes and mechanisms of disease and their application to the development of systematic immunization and chemotherapy had to wait upon the founding of microbiology. This, in turn, depended on advances in instrumentation (especially the microscope), development of laboratory research techniques, and the growth of

[20] Rosen (1958, 210) states that "Chadwick saw clearly that accurate statistical information could be exceedingly important in disease prevention."

related disciplines such as chemistry, anatomy, and physiology. The sequence in the advance of knowledge – from epidemiological studies to identification of causes and mechanisms – is apparent in recent experience with regard to both HIV and the health effects of smoking. It is this sequence in the development of basic knowledge that principally explains the chronology of advances in the control of major infectious disease, not demand conditions.

ECONOMIC GROWTH AND LIFE EXPECTANCY REVISITED

This section returns to the causal role of economic growth in the historical improvement in life expectancy. New knowledge of disease and a new technology of disease control were the basic causes of the great advance in life expectancy since the nineteenth century. But if public initiative was essential to disseminating knowledge and implementing the new technology, was economic growth perhaps necessary to finance the new public spending that was required? Beyond this, there is the question of whether economic growth was needed to finance the research responsible for the advance in knowledge underlying the new techniques of disease control. These questions are taken up in turn next.

Cost Requirements of Life Expectancy Improvement

New government activities of the type required for public health are not costless. Implementing the new technology of disease control may necessitate an increase in the share of government spending in GDP in much the same way as the technology of economic growth requires a rise in the proportion of GDP devoted to new capital investment. If more government health spending is needed, economic growth might be necessary to generate the additional tax revenue required for this spending. Even though economic growth may not be a sufficient condition for rapid advance in life expectancy, isn't it a necessary condition?

In considering this proposition, let me immediately concede the obvious. Economic growth makes the expansion of public health programs easier by relaxing the public budget constraint; economic stagnation or decline may lead to the curtailment of already established public health programs, as happened in some Third World countries in the 1980s, though with smaller adverse effects than one might have expected.[21]

But this concession does not make economic growth a necessary condition for life expectancy improvement. The counterargument – that it is not – is based on two considerations.

First, since at least the mid-1950s, the cost requirements of major improvement in life expectancy have probably been no more than 2 percent of GDP, even in the poorest countries. This contrasts with the roughly 15 to 20 percent of GDP needed for the capital requirements of economic growth. The cost figure for life expectancy here is derived from estimates by public health specialists of the cost of a broad set of health programs considerably more ambitious than those needed to raise life expectancy per se.[22] The low cost of life expectancy improvement is illustrated dramatically by the experience of China, which raised life expectancy from around 40 years in the early 1950s to 60 years by the late 1960s. At the end of this period, China's income level was about three-fourths of the 1820 level in Western Europe, where life expectancy averaged under 40 years. According to Drèze and Sen (1989, 251), China was allocating an estimated 2 percent of GDP to health spending during this period of rapid improvement in life expectancy.

Second, many cases of significant improvement in life expectancy have occurred in the absence of marked economic growth. In sub-Saharan Africa, despite an epidemic outbreak of AIDS, life expectancy increased from 46 to 53 years between 1970–5 and 1990–5, whereas per capita income declined on the order of 10 percent (Figures 7.3 and 7.4; cf. also Sen 1994). Earlier, in the first half of the twentieth century, several colonial powers introduced public health programs in some of

[21] A National Research Council (1993) study found that economic reversals in the 1980s had an impact on child mortality in only two of seven sub-Saharan countries studied.

[22] In the early 1990s the cost to a poor country of "a minimum package of public health and clinical interventions, which are highly cost-effective and deal with major sources of disease burden," amounts to about 1.5 percent of the GDP of sub-Saharan Africa in 1992 (Bobadilla et al. 1994, 171; Maddison 1995, 116, 192, 221). A 1951 estimate suggests that about the same order of magnitude of expenditure requirements for public health have prevailed since the middle of the twentieth century (Winslow 1951, 68). Leading demographic scholars in the late 1950s were impressed with how much could be done in poor countries to reduce mortality at quite low cost (Taeuber 1962, 4; Thompson 1959, 28).

their colonies that significantly improved life expectancy generally even though there was little income growth among the bulk of the population.[23]

These considerations suggest that economic growth is not a necessary condition for improved life expectancy and that public programs can achieve substantial improvements in life expectancy at very low income levels and in the absence of economic growth. A World Bank publication entitled *Public and Private Roles in Health* says as much:

> There is a small but extremely important collection of health-related activities *which must be financed by the state* if they are to be provided at all, or provided at the socially optimum level of consumption. These interventions appear to account for much of the impact of health spending on health improvements. (Musgrove 1996, p. 2, italics added; cf. also World Health Organization 1991)

After comparing recent experience in developing countries with regard to mortality reduction and economic growth, Sen (1994, 315) concludes that "economic growth can certainly help reduce mortality . . . , but that help is not invariably utilized, and it is not the only possible route." Put succinctly, income growth without appropriate public policies does not substantially reduce mortality, whereas appropriate public policies without income growth, can.

Economic Growth and the Advance of Biomedical Knowledge

Scientific research requires resources. Was economic growth needed to finance the discoveries that lay behind the technological breakthroughs in the control of infectious disease? Certainly the location and timing of these discoveries – in northwestern Europe starting in the mid-nineteenth century – are generally consistent with the idea that economic growth was necessary.

[23] Cf. Barclay (1954) on Taiwan; Diaz-Briquets (1981, 1983) on Cuba; Kimura (1993) on Korea; Mandle (1973) on Guyana; and Meegama (1981) on Sri Lanka. Other frequently cited cases of sizable life expectancy improvement with little or no economic growth are Costa Rica from 1920 to 1950, Chile between 1960–5 and 1980–5, and the post–World War II experience of the Indian state of Kerala (Behm and Soto 1991; Castañeda 1985, 1992, Chap. 3; Mata and Rosero 1988). The experience of many of these places is reviewed in the proceedings of a 1985 conference on "good health at low cost" sponsored by the Rockefeller Foundation (Halstead, Walsh, and Warren 1985; see also Caldwell 1986).

Yet, if one thinks of the first great discoveries of modern science (those of Copernicus and Kepler in astronomy and the Newtonian Revolution in mechanics), these clearly antedated the period of modern economic growth and did not require the enormous resources generated by such growth. The roots of these discoveries go back to earlier intellectual undertakings that were supported by the societies of the Middle Ages (Lindberg 1992). That medical inquiry was not neglected is evidenced by the statistic cited earlier: in the sixteenth and seventeenth centuries the number of university chairs in medicine exceeded those in science.

The evidence indicates that, before the last half of the twentieth century, the resources required to fund scientific research were quite small. In 1929, research and development spending in the United States, the country that was undoubtedly the leader in such spending at that time, was 0.2 percent of GDP (OECD 1968). This includes spending by profit and nonprofit organizations for both basic and applied research and development in all fields of science. Clearly, spending on biomedical research would be a much smaller fraction. When one considers the rudimentary laboratories of scientists like Pasteur, Koch, and Fleming, it is hard to believe they involved requirements that much exceeded those of their predecessors two centuries earlier. What was different was the knowledge that they could bring to bear – that of optics embodied in the microscope; of chemistry, reflected in the methods and materials with which they worked; of prior epidemiological research based on new statistical data and techniques; and of new knowledge in subjects such as physiology and anatomy. The history of science suggests that it was primarily the internal evolution of knowledge, not the resources provided by economic growth, that was responsible for the great discoveries leading to the control of infectious disease.[24]

CONCLUSION

Let me summarize some of the impressions from this look at the modern history of mortality. The improvement of life expectancy, like economic

[24] Dependence of biomedical research on the resources generated by economic growth may have increased since the mid-twentieth century in the developed countries with the shift in the disease environment to noninfectious diseases.

growth, has been based on a new technology involving new institutional, capital, and labor requirements. But for life expectancy, the nature of the new technology and associated requirements is quite different from those for economic growth. The technology comprises new methods of controlling major infectious disease. The institutional requirements center on the establishment of a public health system. The capital requirements involve new public expenditures, and the labor requirements are for the bearers of the new technology: specialized personnel in the fields of public health and medicine and homemakers educated in personal hygiene and household sanitation.

The point of departure for understanding the vast worldwide improvement in life expectancy in the last century and a half must be the abysmal state of knowledge that prevailed throughout the world at the start of this period and still exists today in many places. The causes of the major infectious diseases were not known, and almost nothing was known about the way in which these diseases are transmitted. In the absence of valid knowledge of what economists call the "health production function," resources allocated to the prevention or cure of disease were probably totally ineffective. These differences in knowledge persist to the present day, both among and within developing countries, and obviously call into question cross-sectional analyses that assume a uniform state of knowledge everywhere (Behrman and Deolalikar 1988; Bhargava 1997; Strauss and Thomas 1995).

The phenomenon of modern economic growth burst on the world scene at the end of the eighteenth century. Because of its favorable impact on living levels, one might have expected resistance to disease to have grown and life expectancy to have been raised in the areas undergoing economic growth even though health knowledge remained negligible and health practices were of questionable value. But this reasoning regarding the effect of economic growth on life expectancy is incomplete, for it fails to take account of the agglomeration requirements of the new methods of production on which economic growth was based (see Chapter 5). The rapidly rising concentration of population in urban centers sharply increased exposure to disease and largely vitiated any effect of increased resistance.

Only with the growth, first, of epidemiological and then bacterial knowledge did effective techniques emerge for bringing infectious disease under control. These techniques focused primarily on the prevention of the spread of disease – first via controlling the mode of transmission and subsequently via immunization. It is these methods of prevention that have been chiefly responsible for the great improvement in life expectancy throughout the world and in eliminating the excess of urban over rural mortality. In the last half-century the advance of knowledge has also added methods of curing disease to the arsenal available to fight infectious disease, particularly with the development of antibiotics, but the great bulk of the reduction in infectious disease has been accomplished largely by preventive methods. Economic growth in today's developing countries usually occurred after this new technology of disease control had started to be introduced and the historical excess of urban over rural mortality had consequently been largely eliminated. As a result, the positive effect of economic growth through increasing resistance to disease is likely to have been greater in today's developing countries than in the past.

As is recognized in the health literature, the control of infectious disease involves serious issues of market failure such as information failures, externalities, public goods, free-rider problems, and so forth. The market cannot be counted on for such things as the provision of pure water and milk, the proper disposal of sewage, control of pests such as mosquitoes and rats, the supply of uncontaminated food and other manufactured products, immunization of children and adults against major infectious diseases, and the dissemination of new knowledge regarding personal hygiene, infant and child care, food handling and preparation, care of the sick, and the like. Moreover, those most vulnerable to infectious disease – the poor, children, and the elderly – have typically had a disproportionately small voice in market decisions. There is also a serious market failure problem with regard to the distribution of antimicrobials because of negative externalities associated with the development of disease-resistant bacteria.

The title of this chapter poses the question, How beneficient is the market? The ubiquity of market failure in the control of major infectious disease supplies the answer. If improvement of life expectancy is one's concern, the market cannot do the job. Because of market failure, public intervention has been essential to achieve a major reduction of mortality of the type experienced in the last century.

Implementation of the new techniques of disease control has required the development of new institutions centering on the public health system. The functions of this system have included, in varying degrees, health education, regulation, compulsion, and the financing or direct provision of services. The establishment of a public health system has required acceptance of social responsibility for the control of major infectious disease. This shift in norms came about as the advance of biomedical knowledge increasingly pointed to factors beyond individual control as the primary source of disease in much the same way that progress in economics in the twentieth century has led to increased acceptance of social responsibility for unemployment and inflation. In time, intervention in the interest of public health came to be seen as positive and necessary, not simply as a residual function, doing "what the market can't or won't do" (Institute of Medicine, 1988, 46).

The cost requirements of the new technology of disease control are much less than those of economic growth and amounted in the last half century to probably less than 2 percent of GDP in poor countries. Absent a public health system to implement the new technology of disease control, income growth associated with economic development probably has at best a small positive impact on life expectancy. Given a public health system, life expectancy can be raised substantially without economic growth. Economic growth can make the improvement of life expectancy more feasible by facilitating the financing of public interventions, but to assert that "Wealthier Is Healthier" (Pritchett and Summers 1996) and imply that economic growth will raise life expectancy without reference to the central role of public sector intervention is seriously misleading. There is an essential set of governmental decisions that are not mechanically triggered by rising per capita income. Caldwell (1986, 210) makes the point quite simply: "[L]ow mortality for all will not come as an unplanned spinoff from economic growth."

Nor does it seem that economic growth has been indirectly responsible for life expectancy improvement by providing financing for public spending via international aid to developing countries. Such aid has been a small proportion of public health spending in developing countries (see Chapter 6), and, in fact, a sizable share of such spending in these countries has gone to relatively low-productivity expenditures on urban hospitals using developed countries' technology. It is doubtful, too, that economic growth was needed to fund the advances in biomedical knowledge underlying the breakthroughs in controlling infectious disease. The resource requirements for the research underlying the discoveries leading to the control of fatal infectious disease were small – perhaps not much different from those invested in inquiries into the "healing arts" in the sixteenth and seventeenth centuries.

None of this is to say that the situation with regard to public sector intervention for the control of infectious disease has been, or is, optimal. Mention has just been made of the low-productivity nature of much public health spending in developing countries (which is why correlations of total public health spending with mortality are frequently poor). The substantial increase in life expectancy almost everywhere confirms that a relatively few low-cost interventions have been highly productive. But the solution to inefficiency in the public sector is not necessarily to turn things over to the market. What is needed is careful assessment of the cost effectiveness of different policy interventions and attention to their political feasibility and compatibility with existing health knowledge and beliefs.[25] In such work the market may be found to have a contributing role. But the assumption that the market, in solving the problem of economic growth, will also solve that of health and life expectancy is belied by the lessons of experience. Rather than a story of the success of free market institutions, the history of mortality is testimony to the critical need for collective action.

[25] Cost-effectiveness concerns are prominent in the research of public health specialists on developing countries. Cf. Chen et al. (1994); Feachem and Jamison (1991); Feachem, Graham, and Timaeus (1989); Jamison et al. (1993). On political aspects, see Nathanson (1996); Reuschemeyer and Skocpol (1996); Szreter (1997); on cultural beliefs, see Note 2 above.

PART THREE

DEMOGRAPHY

8

An Economic Framework for Fertility Analysis

How relevant to human fertility behavior is economic theory? The answer is, I believe, not as much as it could be. In this chapter I try to extend the mainstream, demand-oriented economic theory of fertility to improve its applicability to a wider range of childbearing behavior in time and space.

In the first two decades after World War II, most theoretical work on the economics of fertility derived from seminal studies by Harvey Leibenstein (1957) and Gary S. Becker (1960) in which the economic theory of consumer behavior was applied, in one form or another, to childbearing decisions (see also Easterlin 1969; Robinson and Horlacher 1971). The conventional theory of consumer behavior views the individual as trying to maximize satisfaction given a range of goods, their prices, and his or her own tastes and income. In the application of the theory to fertility analysis, children are viewed as a special kind of consumer durable good, and fertility is seen as a response to the consumer's demand for children relative to other goods. In the mid-1960s, a special variant of this approach emerged, deriving chiefly from an article by Becker (1965) and distinguished by use of the concept of a "household production function" (T. W. Schultz 1973, 1974). In this chapter, the term economic theory of fertility refers to both the older and newer variants.[1]

Reprinted with permission in revised form from "An Economic Framework for Fertility Analysis," *Studies in Family Planning* 6, 3 (March 1975): 54–63.

[1] The newer variant generated some critical discussion by economists, usually in a sympathetic vein; see, for example, Nerlove (1974), T. P. Schultz (1973), and T. W. Schultz

Although the economic theory of fertility based on consumer choice has noticeable limitations, I believe that a more comprehensive economic framework incorporating this theory remains the best point of departure for systematic fertility analysis. Such a framework, however, must be able to include the principal concepts of demographers, sociologists, and other scholars of human fertility. And it must be relevant to fertility behavior in a wide range of circumstances, past and present – to the trends, fluctuations, and differentials in fertility observed throughout human history. Thus, the empirical concern here is not only with present or recent fertility in the United States, on which most economic research has focused, but also with the demographic transition and premodern fertility differences and movements. Is it fair to apply such a sweeping standard of empirical relevance? I think so. Aside from the social urgency of understanding developments like the demographic transition, I am dealing here with the scope of the subject of fertility as viewed by noneconomists. Economists' claims of a superior theory of fertility behavior are customarily assessed by noneconomists in terms of this wide-ranging set of problems.

Before proceeding, let me make clear that I think the application of the economic theory of household choice to fertility problems has resulted in several valuable contributions. First, economics has clarified the appropriate concept of income for analyzing fertility decisions, namely, "full" or "potential" income, and has shown, for example, that for many purposes, total family income is a less pertinent measure than husband's income or variant measures of the household's earning potential. Second, economic analysis has reduced the conceptual confusion between cost of children and expenditures per child. As with many economic goods, rising income may promote the acquisition of both greater quantity (more children) and higher quality (greater expenditures due to the purchase of more goods per child). This rise in child outlays due to higher income is not an increase in the price of children. It is only when the prices of the goods for childbearing and childrearing rise relative to the prices of other goods that one can appropriately speak of an increased price or cost of children. Third, economics has clarified causal

(1973). Leibenstein's (1974b) review adopts a more skeptical stance. Ben-Porath's (1974) discussion recognizes the argument in this chapter but does not consider its empirical implications.

interrelations. For example, few economists would speak of lower fertility as "causing" higher female labor force participation, or vice versa, but would view both magnitudes as simultaneously determined by other factors. Finally – a contribution that is attributable especially to research stemming from Becker's 1965 article – economic theory has led to more explicit recognition both of the competition between children and economic goods for the time of father and mother and of the value of that time to each parent.

Because the stress here is positive, on the value of a more comprehensive economic framework (which incorporates fuller attention to the concepts of noneconomists) rather than on the limits of the current economic theory of fertility, I start with a brief sketch of the more comprehensive framework, indicating how the more limited version fits in. Then I take up various empirical problems to illustrate the value of the broader economic framework as well as shortcomings of the usual approach.

THEORY

The standard formulation of the microeconomic theory of fertility emphasizes the demand for children as the key to understanding fertility behavior. It also treats, but less fully and systematically, the costs of controlling fertility. The principal innovation in the present approach, which builds substantially on prior work by Tabbarah (1971), is a more explicit and formal treatment of the production of children, including the possibility of shifts in output independent of demand conditions. Attention to the production side leads to greater recognition of such sociological concepts as natural fertility and of real-world conditions to which the usual demand analysis may be inapplicable.

For brevity, I use the total number of surviving children of a "representative" married couple as the principal dependent variable, for surviving descendants, rather than births, are what parents want. Both spouses are assumed to live throughout the reproductive span of the wife. Questions relating to the formation of reproductive unions and to child spacing are left aside. Although the present framework falls short of encompassing all of the subjects of fertility analysis, it is considerably broader in empirical scope and more consonant with the views of noneconomists than the usual economic theory of fertility. The exposition here is highly condensed; for other studies in which the theoretical analysis is discussed in fuller detail, see Easterlin (1978) and Easterlin et al. (1980).

The determinants of fertility are seen as working through one or more of the following:

1. Desired family size (the demand for children), C_d, the number of surviving children parents would want if fertility regulation were costless;
2. Potential family size, C_n, the number of surviving children parents would have if they did not deliberately limit fertility; and
3. Costs of fertility regulation, *RC*, including both subjective (psychic) costs and objective costs, namely, the time and money required to learn about and use specific techniques.

Desired Family Size, C_d

In keeping with the economic theory of household choice, the immediate determinants of the demand for children are income, prices, and tastes. Desired family size is seen as depending on the household's balancing of its subjective tastes for goods and children against externally determined constraints of price and income in a way that maximizes its satisfaction. Variations in the basic taste, price, and income determinants will cause differences in desired family size among households at a given time or for a given household over time. Other factors being constant, the number of children desired would be expected to vary directly with household income (on the assumption children are a "normal" good), directly with the price of goods relative to children, and inversely with the strength of tastes for goods relative to children.

It is through tastes or subjective preferences that attitudinal considerations stressed by sociologists operate such as norms regarding family size and the "quality" of children (standards of child care and rearing). Nothing in the usual presentations of economic theory precludes the analysis of tastes. The overriding emphasis of economists, however, in both theoretical and empirical work, has traditionally been on price and income variables rather than on preferences, and in this way economists have subordinated consideration of tastes. The household production function variant of fertility theory, moreover, further predisposes its users against the analysis of tastes, for it lends itself to reformulating the influence of preferences partly in terms of household technology.[2] In another article, I developed the argument that the formation of tastes should have high priority in fertility research and that such work would help bridge the economics and sociology of fertility (Easterlin 1969). Leibenstein's (1974b) critique of the household production function approach stresses the importance of studying taste formation, as do a few other economists such as Ben-Porath (1975) and Lindert (1978). I still believe in the need for research on taste formation; however, the emphasis in this chapter is on an additional link between the economics and sociology of fertility arising from the production side.

As noted, the principal dependent variable here is surviving children because parents are ultimately interested in grown offspring, not number of births. Birth behavior may be linked to desired family size through the rate of infant and child survival. For households to achieve a given number of surviving children, the necessary number of births would be higher the lower the level of infant and child survival. Even though tastes, prices, and income remained unchanged, birth behavior might vary because of changes in the survival prospects of children. Other things being equal, the higher the survival prospects, the lower the birth rate.

It might be argued that the child survival rate is determined by household decisions. Historically, and for many households in developing countries today, this is patently false because people have not known what caused disease or how to treat it (see Chapters 6 and 7). In the past century, new knowledge of disease has been gradually diffusing, especially in the more developed countries, but even today most

[2] The household production function takes the traditional outputs of economic theory, namely, market goods (including children) as inputs. These are combined in the home with time supplied by household members to produce more basic "commodities" that directly enter the utility functions of the household members (Becker 1965). In this theory, college education, for example, may be viewed as tending to increase the consumption of operas, not by changing tastes, but by improving consumption technology through an increase in the efficiency with which the inputs, consisting for a given household of an opera and the time spent attending it, are consumed. A general critique of the household production function approach has been given by Pollak and Wachter (1975), who argue, among other things, that where there is no operational concept of "commodity," Becker's formulation introduces at best an unnecessary and at worst a misleading additional concept into the traditional chain linking utility directly to market goods and time.

households have limited control, at best, over infant and child mortality. Hence, the child survival rate is taken here as basically determined by factors beyond the typical household's control.

So far it has been assumed implicitly that the family size decision refers to children of a standard "quality," that is, children embodying a given set of inputs of time and goods. Allowance can be made for variations in child quality by viewing it as an additional good along with number of children. An increase in income would then be expected to raise both the number of children desired and the standard of child quality, whereas a rise in the relative prices of inputs required for children would lead to substitution against both child numbers and child quality. Also, subjective preferences relating to child quality might change, leading, for example, to greater emphasis by parents on the quality of children at the expense of number of children.

Potential Family Size, C_n

On the production side of fertility determination, the key analytical concept is potential family size, that is, the number of surviving children a household would have if fertility were not deliberately limited. This depends, in turn, on natural fertility and the probability of a baby's surviving to adulthood. If, for example, a typical couple that is not deliberately controlling its fertility would have eight births over the childbearing span, and three out of four infants, on average, survived to adulthood, then potential family size would be six children. Given natural fertility, an increase in infant survival prospects due, say, to public health measures, would increase potential family size. Similarly, given survival prospects, potential family size would vary directly with natural fertility, as governed, say, by breastfeeding norms.

The immediate determinants of natural fertility are different from the factors governing desired family size. They are (a) frequency of intercourse, as affected by sexual desire and involuntary abstinence due to such factors as impotence or illness; (b) fecundity or infecundity as affected by involuntary causes; and (c) fetal mortality from involuntary causes. (Sociologists will recognize that the terminology here is that of the well-known Davis and Blake article, 1956.) Natural fertility is independent of deliberate controls on coital frequency, fecundity, or fetal mortality because it relates to the number of births a household would produce in the absence of intentional limitation of fertility.

Natural fertility depends partly on physiological or biological factors and partly on cultural practices. Biological factors would include those that influence natural fertility through such mechanisms as genetic effects on fecundity or the effect of disease and malnutrition on coital frequency and the ability to carry a fetus to term. Cultural factors would include various social customs or events that inadvertently affect coital frequency, fecundity, or fetal mortality such as the belief that sexual intercourse should be avoided while a mother is nursing (an "intercourse taboo"), customary practices regarding length of breastfeeding, and physical separation of partners due to such events as civil strife or seasonal migration for employment purposes. Two societies identical in biological and physiological characteristics might differ in natural fertility because, for example, an intercourse taboo led to a higher prevalence of involuntary abstinence in one society than in the other or the customary length of child breastfeeding differed. Natural fertility in a given society and potential family size are likely to be below the reproductive potential of the population because of both biological constraints and cultural conditions that inadvertently reduce family size.[3]

A household deliberately wishing to reduce family size must necessarily adopt some techniques of fertility limitation; hence, a corollary of any demand-based explanation of fertility is that one should be able to observe the use of fertility-limiting practices. The concept of natural fertility described in the previous paragraph, however, makes clear that the existence in a given society of a practice that reduces fertility below the physiological maximum is not in itself evidence that households are *deliberately* restricting fertility. The critical issue is the meaning attached to the practice by its users. If, for example, abstinence is due to observance of a taboo on intercourse while a mother is nursing in the belief that this is important for the health of mother or child, then there is no deliberate

[3] Some work on the economics of fertility has introduced natural fertility considerations (Rosenzweig and Schultz 1985; Schultz 1981) but confined them to biological constraints in the curious belief that behaviors such as how long a mother nurses her child are practiced knowingly and chiefly with a view to limiting the mother's childbearing, despite evidence to the contrary (Easterlin and Crimmins 1985, 46).

control, and the practice is simply one of various cultural conditions that keep natural fertility below the physiological maximum.[4]

The emphasis here on the intent behind a fertility-limiting practice is not an analytical quibble, for it bears directly on the prospective efficacy of a governmental family planning program. In the abstinence example just given, abstinence arises from observance of a social taboo that is believed to be important for the health of mother or child. Alternatively, abstinence might be used with the deliberate aim of reducing family size. If the basic motive is the health of mother or child, then there is no implicit demand for a better method of fertility control; if the motive is reducing family size, then there is such a demand. Obviously, the response to a family planning program would be negligible in the first case and positive in the second. Nor does it matter whether a particular fertility-limiting practice might have originated historically from some explicit or implicit societal concern about controlling population growth. Whatever the origins of a practice, the current response of its users to a family planning initiative will depend on their present view of the reasons for its use.

Motivation for Fertility Regulation, $C_n - C_d$

Potential family size and desired family size jointly determine the motivation for fertility regulation. If potential family size falls short of that desired, $C_n < C_d$, there is no desire to limit fertility. The typical couple, for example, might want six surviving children but only produce four over the course of the reproductive years. An "excess demand" situation of this type would result in a demand for ways to enhance fertility and for the adoption of children (although these possibilities are usually quantitatively unimportant). Households might know how to limit fertility, but there would be no incentive to practice family size limitation. In this situation, parents would be expected to have as many children as possible; that is, the number of children parents actually have would

[4] In sociology the question of the intent behind a given behavior is formalized by distinguishing between the "manifest" and "latent" functions of the practice, corresponding roughly to the intended and unforeseen consequences. Allied notions in anthropology are the concepts of "emic" and "etic," which refer to the meaning attached to a phenomenon, by, respectively, the actors themselves and independent observers (Harris 1968, 571–5).

correspond to their potential family size. Variation in the number of children parents have would depend on the determinants of potential family size, namely, natural fertility and the probability of an infant's surviving to adulthood.

In contrast, if the potential family size exceeds desired family size ($C_n > C_d$), an "excess supply" situation, parents would be faced with the prospect of having unwanted children and would be motivated to regulate their fertility. A typical couple might want only four surviving children but produce five in the absence of deliberate family size limitation. The prospect of an unwanted child would create an incentive for the couple to restrict fertility intentionally. In an excess supply situation, there is thus a demand for ways of limiting fertility. Whether fertility control will actually be used depends on how the costs of fertility regulation compare with the strength of the motive to limit fertility.

Costs of Fertility Regulation, *RC*

Although motivation is a necessary condition for fertility regulation, it is not a sufficient condition. Fertility regulation imposes costs on the household of two types. There are psychic costs – the displeasure associated with the idea or practice of fertility control – and market costs – the time and money necessary to learn about and use specific techniques. These costs, in turn, depend on (a) the attitudes in society toward the general notion of fertility control and toward specific techniques, and (b) the degree of access by parents to fertility control in terms of both the availability of information and the range of specific techniques and their prices. Typically, a family planning program lowers market costs by increasing information and providing services free or below cost. It also lowers subjective costs by lending legitimacy to the notion of practicing birth control.

Whether fertility control will actually be used in a given excess supply situation depends on how the costs of fertility regulation compare with the strength of the motivation to limit fertility. Given the strength of the motivation, the lower the costs of fertility regulation – that is, the more nearly conditions approach those of the "perfect contraceptive society," where psychic and market costs would be zero (Bumpass and Westoff 1970) – the greater would be the adoption of fertility regulation and the more nearly would the number of children parents have correspond to the number they desire. Conversely, the higher the costs of fertility control, the more nearly would actual conditions approach potential family size, the lower would be the deliberate control of fertility, and the greater would be the number of unwanted children.

Summary

In the present analysis, the determinants of fertility are seen as working through one or more of the following: the demand for children (desired family size) if fertility regulation were costless, potential family size if no conscious effort were made to control fertility, and the costs of fertility regulation. The immediate determinants of desired family size are income, the price of children relative to goods, and subjective preferences for children compared with goods. Potential family size depends on natural fertility and the survival prospects of a baby to adulthood. The costs of fertility regulation include subjective costs ("attitudes") as well as the time and money necessary to learn about and use-specific techniques ("access").

The role of these factors in determining actual fertility differs depending on the comparative state of potential and desired family size. If the situation is one of excess demand (or even of excess supply but the motivation for fertility control falls short of the costs of fertility control), then the number of children parents have corresponds to their potential family size, and the determinants of potential family size (natural fertility and child survival) govern variations in actual family size. If, however, the situation is an excess supply one in which the motivation to regulate fertility exceeds the costs, then deliberate limitation of fertility occurs and the number of children parents have falls below potential family size. As long as fertility regulation is not entirely costless, some parents still have unwanted children. The situation is thus one in which the actual number of children parents have falls short of potential family size, the difference reflecting the extent of conscious fertility control, but the actual number exceeds the desired number, the excess consisting of the number of unwanted children.

The usual economic theory of fertility is confined to two of the three basic determinants identified here, namely, the demand for children and costs of fertility control, although the treatment of the latter varies considerably from one writer to another. Moreover, the emphasis with regard to both of these is typically on objective market circumstances – income and prices (including prices of fertility control) – rather than on subjective attitudes. The present approach stresses the desirability of adding a third set of fertility determinants disregarded in the usual economic theory, namely, those shaping the potential output of children, and also advocates direct study of subjective (taste) considerations.

APPLICATIONS

Nonmarital Fertility

Although the framework, as sketched, relates to marital fertility, it can be used to analyze nonmarital fertility. In comparing the framework with the more usual demand-based economic analysis, it is simplest to start with two empirical problems in this area. The examples make the point, on the one hand, that a framework is needed that explicitly includes consideration of potential family size, and, on the other, that demand factors may sometimes be relevant even for nonmarital fertility.

Let me start with the noticeable rise in teenage nonmarital fertility rates in the United States after 1940. An explanation offered by Cutright (1972) stresses physiological factors. Because of improvements in health and nutrition among young women after 1940, age at menarche fell substantially and the likelihood of conception noticeably increased at ages 15–17. These improvements also increased the probability of a young woman's carrying a fetus to full term. Together, these factors resulted in a substantially increased likelihood that a given rate of sexual activity among teenage women would result in a live birth. Cutright (1972) suggests that these developments played an important part in the rise of teenage rates of fertility outside marriage.

Cutright's hypothesis cannot be expressed within the framework of the usual demand-based economics of fertility because it has nothing to do with the demand for children or with the costs of fertility control. However, it can readily be handled by the present approach. In terms of the present framework, Cutright's hypothesis is that the rise in teenage nonmarital fertility reflects in large measure an increase in the potential output of children (C_n) caused by physiological changes that increased natural fertility.

The validity of Cutright's interpretation is not at issue here.[5] A popular alternative, which also stresses potential family size and is thus outside the demand framework, is that higher teenage nonmarital fertility is due to a breakdown of taboos on premarital intercourse. (In this case the increase in nonmarital fertility occurs via a shift in natural fertility caused by greater frequency of extramarital intercourse due to changed social mores.) My point in mentioning these interpretations is that an economic theory of fertility that disregards potential output precludes reasonable hypotheses like these advanced in disciplines other than economics. On the other hand, the more general economic framework sketched here lends itself readily to the recognition and analysis of these hypotheses.

If an economic framework needs to include potential output considerations to be relevant to nonmarital fertility, does one need the demand analysis that comes with the framework as well? After all, the desired number of children in extramarital unions is typically zero. My answer is that the full framework, including demand, is needed, and not only because of the possibility of cases in which nonmarital pregnancy is sought as a means of fostering a marriage proposal. Let me take, as an example, an argument that quite explicitly discounts the relevance of demand considerations to nonmarital fertility. Shorter, Knodel, and van de Walle (1971), in a valuable study of the long-term decline in nonmarital fertility in Europe since the nineteenth century, note the close parallel between the trends in marital and nonmarital fertility. They argue that the type of economic pressures cited by Banks (1954) to account for the decline in marital fertility cannot be used to explain the trend in nonmarital fertility. Here are their words:

> J.A. Banks' explanation of the decline in marital fertility as a consequence of rising middle-class standards of living and of simultaneous greater educational aspirations of parents for their children is much less plausible when applied to the decline in nonmarital fertility. It is unlikely that higher incomes moved unwed mothers to curb their illegitimate fertility so as to plan better the educational future of their bastards on hand. Possibly improvements in the standard of living during the last quarter of the nineteenth century restricted illegitimate fertility through some other mechanism. But an ad hoc rummaging about for

[5] Tietze, for one, has expressed reservations. (See Tietze 1972, 6 and Cutright's reply in the same publication.)

alternate linkages to an "economic prosperity" model is unlikely to result in any generalizable kind of explanation. (Shorter et al. 1971, 393)

Suppose, however, that a decline in desired family size among married couples, owing to the reasons given by Banks, generated a greater demand for fertility limitation. Suppose, further, that in response to this, a substantial expansion occurred in the supply of abortion services, lowering their market costs and increasing their social acceptability. In addition, improved efficiency in the practice of withdrawal might develop. This reduction in the costs of fertility control would make it easier for unmarried as well as married couples to terminate or avoid pregnancy and would thereby reduce nonmarital fertility. Thus, a decline in nonmarital fertility might arise from the same basic circumstances that caused a decline in marital fertility, that is a decreased demand for children by married couples that resulted in lower costs of fertility control generally. Although this argument does not contradict the emphasis that the article's authors place on the costs of fertility regulation in explaining the nonmarital fertility decline, it does show that changes in fertility control costs might ultimately stem from the effect of a decreased demand for children within marital unions. Again, let me emphasize that I am not arguing for or against any particular hypothesis. Rather, I am trying to show that the present framework lends itself to consideration of all factors potentially relevant to nonmarital fertility, whether they operate via desired family size, potential family size, or fertility control costs.

Premodern Fertility Differentials and Fluctuations

Let me turn to a different set of empirical problems. Time series fluctuations in fertility that are positively associated with the state of the economy in a premodern situation have frequently been noted (Lee 1978). Also, a positive association between fertility and socioeconomic class at a point in time has sometimes been observed in premodern conditions (Stys 1957; United Nations 1961, Chap. 10). The natural inclination of economists is to interpret these findings of a positive income–fertility relationship as being due to demand influences, that is, that variations in household income cause corresponding variations in the number of children that households desire.

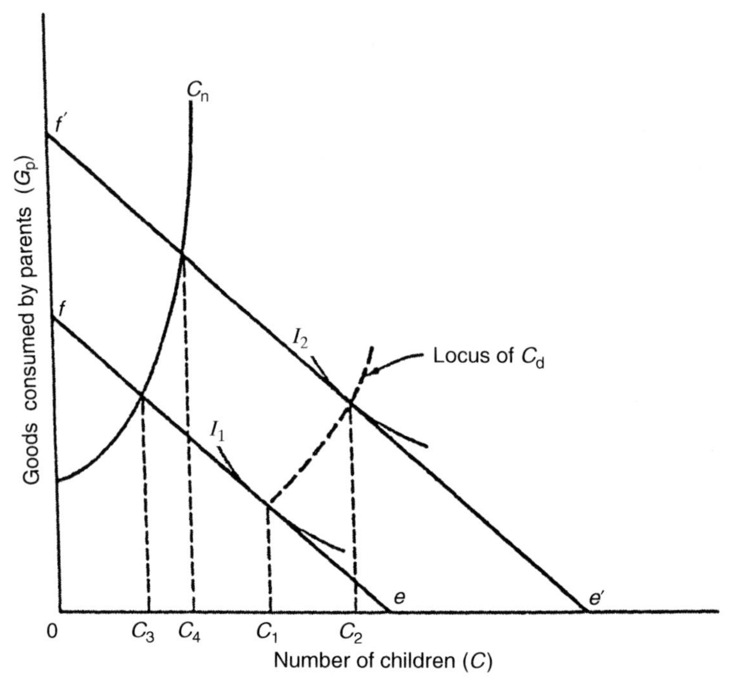

Figure 8.1. "Output" compared with "demand" interpretation of a positive income–fertility relationship.

An alternative interpretation based on potential family size is possible, however. Figure 8.1 contrasts the two interpretations. Consider, first, the demand explanation. (For simplicity, variations in fertility control costs are disregarded.) If one ignores, for the moment, the curve labeled C_n, the figure incorporates the usual graphical version of the economic theory of fertility, though in highly simplified form to bring out the desired contrast. Number of children C is measured along the horizontal axis and goods consumed by parents G_p on the vertical axis. Household desires for children are expressed in terms of an indifference map that represents the degree of satisfaction the household attaches to every possible combination of commodities and children. Only two curves on this map, I_1 and I_2, are shown here, although an entire set filling the quadrant exists at any given time. Any point on a curve expresses the degree of satisfaction attaching to that particular combination of children and commodities, and a curve is drawn so that all combinations on the curve yield the same amount of satisfaction. In other words, an indifference curve is a "constant-satisfaction" curve. Curves farther from the origin (e.g., I_2 compared with I_1) are situations involving both more children and more goods and represent higher levels of satisfaction than curves nearer the origin.

A household's ability to "purchase" combinations of children and goods is represented by a budget constraint, which delimits those combinations within financial reach of the household, based on the household's perceived income prospects and prices of children and goods. Two budget constraints, *ef* and $e'f'$, are pictured, but at any given time only one is applicable, let us say, initially, *ef*. The triangle *Oef* represents all combinations of children and goods within financial reach of the household.

In a purely demand-based economic theory of fertility, the household is seen as choosing, from among the set of combinations within financial reach, that which will maximize its satisfaction according to its subjectively determined preferences. In this case, this is the combination shown by the point of tangency of *ef* and I_1, the latter being the highest attainable indifference curve. Thus, given tastes (as represented in the indifference map) and prices and income (as represented by the budget constraint *ef*), the number of children desired or "demanded" by the household would be C_1.

What would be the effect on the equilibrium number of children of an increase in income with tastes and prices remaining unchanged? This is shown by a parallel outward shift in the budget constraint from *ef* to $e'f'$. With its financial reach now extended, the household moves to a higher indifference curve, the tangency of $e'f'$ and I_2, and enjoys a larger number of children, C_2, as well as more commodities.

The dashed line labeled "locus of C_d" (desired number of children) is the set of equilibrium values that would be traced as income varied with prices and tastes held constant. It shows the relationship between income and purchases of a good that economists take to be normal, namely, a positive one: number of children varies directly with income. Confronted with data showing that fertility varies positively over time or among groups with variations in income, economists would tend to conceptualize the underlying mechanism as that generating movements along the locus of C_d. Let me repeat that I am giving here a very simplified presentation for purposes of contrast.

The alternative interpretation of a positive income–fertility relation under premodern conditions is suggested by the C_n (potential family size) function, which has been added to the usual economic diagram.

This function shows how the number of children a couple has might vary positively with the couples' material living level even if no conscious effort were made to control fertility. (It is assumed that such factors as public health conditions or social customs, which might affect potential family size independently of income, are held constant; changes in such factors would shift the entire C_n function.) Below some minimum living level, natural fertility would be zero. Near-starvation conditions, for example, would drastically lower frequency of intercourse and heighten the likelihood of spontaneous abortion if conception did occur. As the parents' living conditions improved from very low levels, natural fertility would progressively increase, although the increments would become gradually less until eventually a point would be reached at which further living level changes would leave natural fertility unaffected because of biological and cultural limits on a woman's reproductive years. This is the relationship portrayed by the C_n curve in the figure. Starting with a positive intercept on the *y*-axis at which potential family size is zero, the curve shows an initial positive relation between C_n and G_p; eventually, however, it reaches a vertical phase in which C_n is unaffected by further increases in G_p. Other than the general shape of the curve drawn here, no claim is made for its realism; my aim is merely to bring out clearly the contrast with the previous demand interpretation.

A movement in the budget constraint from ef to $e'f'$ along the C_n function of Figure 8.1 would produce a positive income–fertility relationship with the equilibrium number of children varying from C_3 to C_4. The mechanism underlying this relationship, however, differs from that discussed earlier in the demand interpretation. In this case the underlying mechanism involves such things as the effect of better nutrition on reproductive capacity, as suggested, for example, by Frisch's work (1974, 2002), or the relaxation of the social custom of young wives' returning to their parents' homes when times are hard. Another possibility is that, at a point in time, higher-income wives may be more likely to resort to wet nursing. As a result, the typical higher-income wife would have a shorter period of temporary sterility after childbirth and consequently higher natural fertility, giving rise to the observed positive association.

In the figure as drawn, the potential output rather than demand interpretation of the positive income–fertility relation is the correct one. At both of the income levels shown (ef and $e'f'$), parents could not produce the desired number of children, which is indicated by the tangency of the appropriate budget constraint and indifference curve. Because desires exceed potential family size, parents would have as many children as possible, that is, the amount given by the intersection of the relevant budget constraint with the C_n function. (We have here the counterpart in fertility analysis of a rationing situation in the theory of household choice in which a household is unable to attain the consumption pattern that would be optimal under free market conditions because of the restricted availability of one or more goods.) Variations in income (that is, shifts in the budget constraint) would generate variations in number of children as shown by the C_n (potential family size) function, not by the C_d locus.

The C_n function could, however, lie to the right of the C_d locus, if, say, public health conditions or social customs were more favorable to high natural fertility and child survival. In this case the demand interpretation would be the appropriate one because, disregarding fertility control costs, households would be unwilling to produce more children than desired. Variations in income would generate variations in the number of children as given by the C_d locus, not by the C_n function.

Again, I am not concerned here with which interpretation may be more appropriate to a premodern situation. My point is simply to show the alternative interpretations that are possible in order to demonstrate the need for a theoretical framework sufficiently flexible to encompass both.

The Transition from High to Low Fertility

The transition from high to low fertility provides another opportunity for illustrating the influence of both demand and potential output factors on fertility behavior. The leading interpretation of the shift from high to low fertility in modernizing societies is the theory of the demographic transition. In this scheme, a shift to low fertility follows, with a lag, a decline to low mortality levels and is taken to be associated, in a general way, with the process of urbanization and industrialization.

The present framework suggests a more comprehensive view in which the demographic transition model is one of many possible real world patterns. The emphasis here is on identifying different ways in which the process of social and economic development may engender a new type of concern within households with regard to reproduction, that of having unwanted children, and lead to a growing motivation to regulate fertility.

Figure 8.2 shows some hypothetical trends during modernization in the equilibrium values of C_n and C_d. In all of the diagrams, the progress of economic and social modernization is assumed to be correlated with time and corresponds to a movement to the right along the *x*-axis. The diagrams represent only the general nature of the possible relationships during modernization; no implication is intended regarding specific magnitudes.

As we have seen, the motivation for fertility regulation varies with the prospective number of unwanted children, the excess of C_n over C_d. In the upper panels of Figure 8.2, this is shown by the solid line at the bottom of each diagram; in the lower panels this line has been omitted to simplify the presentation; the applicable $C_n - C_d$ line in the lower panels is that in Figure 8.2c. In all of the diagrams in Figure 8.2, the initial situation, that on the *y*-axis, is one in which there is no motivation for fertility regulation because parents are unable to produce as many children as they would like to have. More generally, all positions to the left of point *m* are excess demand situations. In these circumstances there would be a demand, not for ways of reducing fertility, but of raising it, and also for children to adopt. This representation is, of course, vastly oversimplified. A more realistic diagram might show C_n fluctuating widely in premodern conditions and the early stages of modernization and then trending upward as the fluctuations dampen.

Figures 8.2a–c illustrate alternative ways in which the motivation to regulate fertility might emerge and grow in the course of modernization, causing the $C_n - C_d$ curve to cross the *x*-axis and move upward to the right. Figure 8.2a shows a situation in which the moving force is potential family size, C_n, while desired family size remains constant. The rise in potential family size might be due to better child survival or to a rise in natural fertility (due to improved health of mothers or shorter breastfeeding, for example). Figure 8.2b illustrates the contrasting demand situation in which C_n is constant but desired family size shifts from above to below C_n (as a result, say, of an increase in the relative cost of children), leading to the appearance of unwanted children. Figure 8.2c shows a shift from excess demand to excess supply conditions owing to changes in both C_n and C_d.

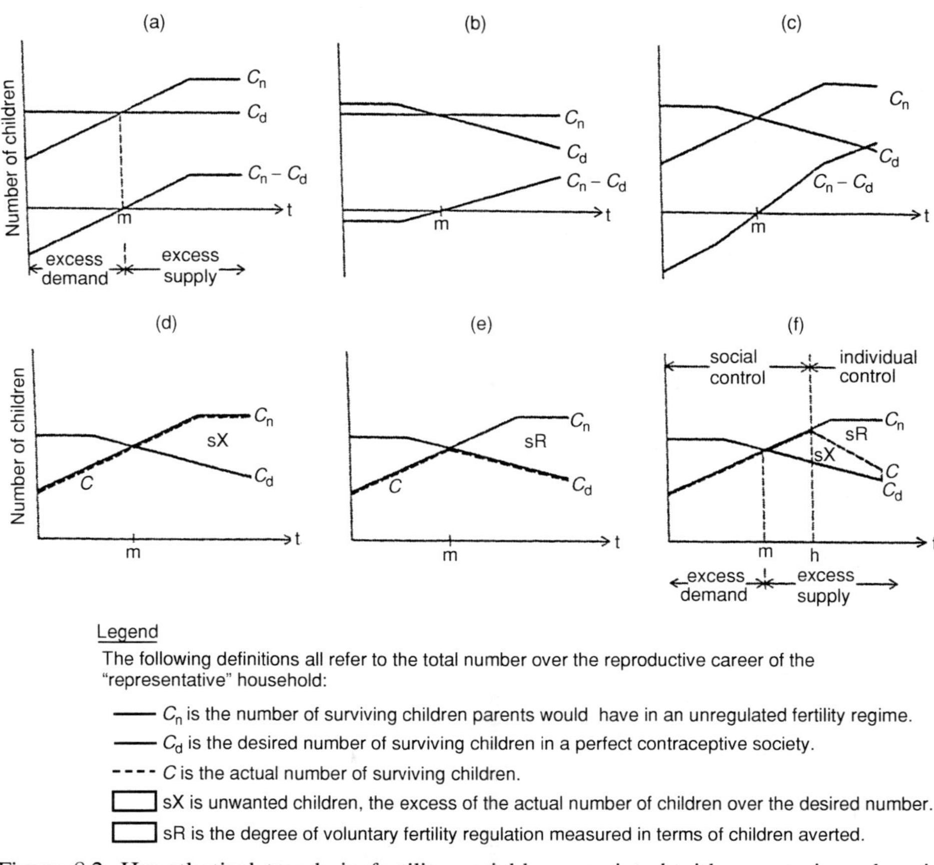

Figure 8.2. Hypothetical trends in fertility variables associated with economic and social modernization.

As noted previously, although motivation to limit family size is a necessary condition for fertility regulation, it is not a sufficient condition. Whether in a given excess supply situation fertility control will actually be used depends on the strength of the motivation compared with the subjective and market costs of fertility regulation. Figures 8.2d and 8.2e illustrate the two extremes with regard to costs of fertility control. In both diagrams, to the left of point *m* parents are not able to have as many children as they would like to have. As a result, to the left of *m* the actual number of children they have, shown by the broken *C* line, is equal to the maximum amount they can produce, as indicated by the C_n curve, and rises as potential family size increases. As one moves to the right of point *m* in both diagrams, a problem of unwanted children emerges, creating the motivation to regulate fertility. In Figure 8.2d, it is assumed that the costs of fertility regulation are prohibitive. Consequently, the actual number of children continues to follow the potential family size curve C_n, and unwanted children increase. The number of unwanted children is shown by the vertical distance between *C* and C_d marked *sX*. Figure 8.2e, in contrast, represents the perfect contraceptive society, for subjective and market costs of fertility regulation are zero. As soon as the motivation to regulate fertility occurs, parents immediately start limiting family size. The actual number of children falls short of the maximum possible and follows the C_d curve, turning downward in the case shown. The extent of fertility regulation, measured in children averted, is shown by the vertical *sR* distance between C_n and *C*.

In any real world situation, fertility control costs would be neither zero nor prohibitive. The likely course of the actual number of children for a given level of fertility costs is shown in Figure 8.2f. Initially, as the potential family size curve C_n edges above the desired number of children C_d to the right of point *m*, the motivation to regulate fertility is not great enough to offset the costs. The actual number of children continues to be governed by the C_n curve with unwanted children increasing as shown by *sX*. As the movement to the right continues, however, a point is reached at which the loss in welfare due to unwanted children begins to exceed that associated with the costs of fertility regulation. In effect, a threshold of fertility regulation, labeled *h* in the diagram, is reached (Kirk 1971). Deliberate fertility control is begun, and the *C* curve turns downward in the direction of the C_d curve with fertility regulation practiced to the extent shown by the vertical distance *sR*. As long as costs of fertility control are positive, however, there will continue to be some unwanted children, indicated by *sX*. Given the C_n and C_d curves, the effect of a reduction in the costs of fertility regulation would be to shift point *h* to the left, and, for any given excess of C_n over C_d, to reduce unwanted children *sX* and increase the amount of fertility regulation *sR*.

This sketch attempts to bring together systematically the factors that may operate to induce a motivation for fertility limitation during modernization. The advantage of the present approach is that it directs equal attention to the possible roles of desired family size, potential family size, and fertility control factors. By making different assumptions regarding changes in the basic fertility determinants, it is possible to bring out within the present framework alternative sources of change from high to low fertility. The typical demographic transition pattern, a shift from high to low mortality preceding a corresponding movement in fertility, may be most simply generated, if, with other fertility determinants given, one assumes mortality is sharply reduced in a situation of initially high mortality and fertility. The accompanying increase in child survival prospects, and perhaps also in natural fertility of mothers due to better health, would raise potential family size and would shift the typical household into an excess supply situation of the type shown to the right of point *m* in Figure 8.2a. As the prospect of unwanted children continued to grow, the typical household would, in time, reach and cross the fertility control threshold *h*, and fertility rates would start to move downward, thus following with a lag the decline in mortality.

By contrast, there are situations of the type noted by Coale (1969) in which historically the fertility decline apparently accompanied or preceded the mortality decline. Such a pattern might arise from changes in the economic and social structures that give rise to unwanted children by shifting desired family size below potential family size in the manner shown to the right of point *m* in Figure 8.2b.

On the basis of the data on the fertility decline in Taiwan presented by Freedman and Takeshita (1969), a variant of the Figure 8.2a pattern may be applicable there. The decline through 1970 appears to be due to factors increasing potential family size and reducing the costs of fertility regulation rather than to changes in desired family size. Perhaps this pattern is representative of the early phases of the fertility decline in today's developing nations because of the earlier onset of social modernization (public health and education measures) relative to economic development (see Chapter 9). However, in the United States, where mortality conditions appear to have been relatively favorable from an early date, it may be that a decline in desired family size of the type represented in Figure 8.2b was predominant in motivating fertility decline. Arguments emphasizing the role of changing land scarcity in inducing rural fertility decline by lowering the demand for children would apply in the American situation (see Chapter 10). The present framework brings out such different possibilities by making clear how a given society may be pushed across the threshold of fertility regulation in different ways – by changes in desired family size, potential family size, the costs of fertility regulation, or combinations thereof.

The framework also brings out the possibility of an upsurge in fertility in the early phases of modernization of the type experienced by many developing countries (Dyson and Murphy 1985; Olusanya 1969; Roberts 1969; see also Chapter 9 herein). This is shown between points *m* and *h* in Figure 8.2f, where C moves upward with the rise in C_n. As illustrated, the upsurge is due to changes on the potential output side. A demand explanation is also possible, however, based on the reasoning stated in developing the dashed line locus of C_d in Figure 8.1. Thus, the present framework brings out the possibility of alternative "demand" and "output" interpretations with regard to a premodern fertility upswing.

The Changing Nature of Fertility Determination

Several scholars have argued that modernization results in a fundamental change in the mechanisms determining fertility. According to Bourgeois-Pichat,

> [f]ertility in preindustrialized societies seems to be strongly determined if not controlled in the sense we give to this word today. It is determined by a network of sociological and biological factors and when the network is known, the result can be predicted. Freedom of choice by couples is almost absent. The couples have the number of children that biology and society decide to give them.
>
> One of the main features of the so-called demographic revolution has been precisely to change not only the level of fertility but also change its nature. Having a child has been becoming more and more the result of free decision of the couple. And this change in the nature of fertility may be more important

than the change in its magnitude. Fertility has left the biological and social field to become part of behavioral science. . . .

For fertility we had for a long while a lot of customs carefully molded in the course of time which almost completely determined the size of families. These customs are still there but they are for the most part useless, as fertility is now under the will of people. (1967, p. 163)

A similar distinction is that made by Wrigley (1969, 192) between "social sanctions" that operate to restrict fertility in a preindustrial situation and "family sanctions" that operate in a modernized society.

The present framework helps clarify these distinctions. The threshold point *h* in Figure 8.2f may be thought of as the dividing line between premodern and modern fertility determination. To the left of point *m*, fertility is "regulated" by a variety of social and biological mechanisms working through natural fertility. Fertility is not yet viewed by the household as involving a potential problem of unwanted children and is, in effect, outside the standard household decision-making calculus. This is not to say that behavior is irrational in the premodern situation. On the contrary, it is rational in the sense that the means are appropriate to the end. Given a conception of the problem as one of having enough surviving children, maximization of output within the existing set of biological constraints and established social practices makes sense. The process of modernization alters not the rationality of the individual but the nature of the problem from one of having too few children to one of having too many. Between points *m* and *h*, a problem emerges of unwanted children, but the loss in welfare due to unwanted children is less than the costs of regulating fertility, and fertility continues to be regulated by mechanisms working through natural fertility. This is a rational outcome based on a weighing of the costs involved.

The modernization process, which eventually shifts the typical household to a position to the right of point *h*, creates a fundamental change in the circumstances of family reproduction, moving the household from a situation in which childbearing is a matter "taken for granted" to one posing difficult problems of individual choice regarding the limitation of family size. To the left of point *h*, although there is a demand for children, the usual demand mechanisms emphasized in the economic theory of fertility are typically not operative, although fertility may be affected by economic variables operating through potential family size. The explanation of fertility in such a situation calls for inquiry along the lines followed by sociologists and other students of natural fertility. To the right of point h, the household decision-making approach comes more into its own. Even here, of course, sociology still has an important part to play, particularly in the investigation of taste formation. To dramatize this contrast, the section to the left of point h in Figure 8.2f has been labeled "social control" and that to the right "individual control," following Bourgeois-Pichat's terminology.

Such sweeping distinctions are never fully satisfactory. Social sanctions operate in both premodern and modern circumstances, and the idea that there is no individual choice whatsoever in a premodern society is too strong (there is some evidence, for example, of deliberate control among some "elite" segments of the population in some premodern societies). Moreover, no society shifts en masse at a single point of time from social to individual control situations; the real-world process is characterized by timing differences between various groups in the population. One of the needed extensions of the present analysis is to take explicit account of this diffusion process. Nevertheless, the present framework is helpful in formalizing the distinction between social and individual control and clarifying its substantive meaning. Moreover, the difference between social and individual control of fertility is a fundamental one, not merely terminological, for it bears, as we have seen, on such questions as the prospective efficacy of a family planning program, which is likely to find little acceptance when social controls prevail.

CONCLUSION

I have chosen several problems in the explanation of human fertility – nonmarital fertility, premodern fluctuations and differentials, and the transition from high to low fertility – to illustrate the need for a framework that directs attention equally to considerations stressed by economists and sociologists, that is, to potential family size along with demand considerations and fertility control costs.

It seems clear that there are many situations in which the usual demand-oriented economic theory of fertility behavior based on the theory of consumer choice may be of dubious relevance. Indeed, considering the history of human fertility as a whole, one might argue that a demand-oriented model has very limited relevance. The basis for this is several studies of premodern and early modern societies, including contemporary family planning surveys, indicating that there is little or no deliberate fertility control in such societies, although households may engage in practices that have the unintentional effect of reducing fertility. Intentional control of fertility is, as we have seen, a necessary element in a demand explanation of fertility. It should be recognized, however, that the same reasoning implies that, in modern societies, where deliberate fertility control is extensive, a demand-based model (including fertility control costs) may be sufficient for analyzing many fertility problems.

A broader economic framework, like that advocated here, is capable of handling real-world conditions to which the usual demand analysis may be inapplicable. This framework, through more explicit and formal treatment of the production of children, including the possibility of shifts in potential family size independent of demand conditions, lends itself to greater recognition of such demographic concepts as natural fertility and to the formulation of alternative hypotheses of the type frequently voiced by sociologists, anthropologists, and other noneconomists.

In the long run, the relevance of this framework can be established only by more empirical study. Whether one can get adequate data to test alternative hypotheses of the demand versus potential output types discussed here remains to be seen. But the effort needs to be made. Unless we can get the necessary data, we will often be unable to choose between competing views of the causes of human fertility.

9

New Perspectives on the Demographic Transition

Since 1900, a revolution has occurred in human childbearing. Today, throughout much of the world, parents deliberately limit their fertility, and the average number of births per woman over the reproductive career is approaching two or less. Before then, and throughout most of human history, parents typically did nothing intentionally to restrict fertility, and women averaged six births or more. What has brought about this remarkable change in human reproduction?

To answer this, I use the theory developed in Chapter 8 to analyze here two high-quality and fairly comparable surveys of fertility and family planning that bridge the early stage of the shift to deliberate control of fertility in a less-developed area. These surveys were conducted in the Indian State of Karnataka in 1951 and 1975 (Reddy and Raju 1977; Srinivasan, Reddy, and Raju 1978; United Nations 1961). Rarely have the economic and demographic circumstances of a pretransition population been professionally surveyed so thoroughly as that of Karnataka in 1951, which was then known as Mysore State. Karnataka's population then was about 9 million, which was larger than that of Australia. In rural areas, which accounted for three-fourths of the state's population, over two-thirds of males were illiterate and nine-tenths of females. The rural population was spread over some 8,000 villages, most of which had less than 500 persons, and was engaged very largely in cultivating rice,

Reprinted with permission in revised form from Richard A. Easterlin, Eileen M. Crimmins, Shireen J. Jejeebhoy, and K. Srinivasan, "New Perspectives on the Demographic Transition: A Theoretical and Empirical Analysis of an Indian State, 1951–1975," *Economic Development and Cultural Change* 32, 2 (January 1984): 227–53.

which accounted for more than three-quarters of the cropland in use. More than eight villages in ten were at least three miles from the nearest town. The one significant departure from pretransition conditions was that in some rural areas antimalarial operations (DDT spraying) had been under way for about four years before the survey. Because of this, infant and child survival rates had already improved somewhat.

The analysis of Karnataka is complemented by a similar one for Taiwan, a country that at the time was further along in the transition to low fertility (Jejeebhoy 1979). The inclusion of Taiwan extends the span of coverage of the fertility transition, though the early experience there is less fully documented.

Two questions are in the forefront of the analysis: (1) Why in the past has there been so little effort to limit fertility deliberately? (2) What developments initiated the shift to intentional fertility control and eventual fertility decline?

CONCEPTUAL APPROACH

In the theoretical approach of Chapter 8, the factors that determine the adoption of deliberate control are seen as falling into three categories:

1. Desired family size (C_d): the number of surviving children a couple would want in a "perfect contraceptive society," one in which costs of family size limitation were negligible. It reflects the taste, income, and price considerations of the usual economic theory of fertility, including both the economic and noneconomic returns from children as well as their costs.
2. Potential family size (C_n): the number of surviving children a household would have if it did nothing deliberately to regulate its fertility. Potential family size is the product of a couple's natural fertility (N) and child survival rate (s). Both natural fertility and potential family size may be well below the biological maximum because of cultural conditions that inadvertently reduce fertility and family size such as prolonged breastfeeding.
3. Costs of fertility regulation (RC): this lumps together a couple's attitudes toward, and access to, fertility control services and supplies. It includes both subjective disadvantages of family size limitation and the economic costs of control.

To simplify the analysis, the theory focuses on the fertility control decision of married couples and assumes fertility control is undertaken to limit family size and not for spacing births. The typical couple's decision whether or not to limit family size is viewed not as a highly formal decision but as a gradual response to the balance between several types of pressures they feel. The excess of potential family size over desired family size ($C_n - C_d$) is the number of unwanted children a couple would have in the absence of deliberate fertility control. The larger this excess, the greater is the potential burden of unwanted children, and consequently the greater is the household's motivation to limit its fertility. It is worth stressing the two-sided view here of how motivation is determined. Demographers sometimes identify the motivation to limit fertility with a desire to reduce family size (i.e., a lower C_d), and it is assumed that only if parents want fewer children will motivation grow. However, an increase in potential family size (C_n) can increase motivation even if desired family size remains constant because greater potential family size increases the potential number of unwanted children. An increase in potential family size may arise from an increase in a couple's natural fertility, improved chances of child survival, or both.

The value of $C_n - C_d$ may be negative, indicating that a household is in a "deficit fertility" situation, that is, that it is unable to produce as many children as it would like to have. In this case, there is no motivation to limit fertility and a couple would have as many children as possible; natural fertility would be a logical outcome of the couple's underlying reproductive conditions.

Even if the value of $C_n - C_d$ is positive, however, it does not necessarily follow that a couple will deliberately control its fertility. Against the pressure to do so must be weighed the costs of fertility control (*RC*), that is, the nonpecuniary and pecuniary costs attaching to the actual use of control. If *RC* is high and the motivation ($C_n - C_d$) low, then a couple may feel that the disadvantages of unwanted children are less than those associated with deliberately restricting fertility and may forego fertility control. In general, the probability of adopting control is higher the greater the degree of motivation (the excess of potential over desired family size) and the lower the costs of regulation.

As applied to the demographic transition, the theory envisages a situation of the following sort (illustrated in Chap. 8, Figure 8.2f). Under early modern or premodern conditions (high infant and child mortality, low literacy, and with labor-intensive agricultural activity predominating) parents may be unable to have as many children as they would like, or, if they can produce more than they want, the drawbacks connected with having unwanted children may be viewed as small compared with those of deliberately regulating fertility. Hence, natural fertility is a rational response to the couple's basic reproductive circumstances.

Modernization causes changes in the basic reproductive conditions, raising the motivation for fertility control and reducing the costs of regulation. The motivation for control may increase because potential family size increases or because desired family size decreases. Potential family size may rise because of higher child survival rates (due, e.g., to public health programs) or higher natural fertility (due, e.g., to reduced breastfeeding as education and urbanization increase or to better health as infectious disease is controlled). Desired family size may decline because expanding education tends to raise the costs of children and shift preferences away from children toward nonfamily-oriented goods. Costs of fertility control may decline as education expands and couples acquire greater knowledge of techniques of fertility control and come to view such techniques as socially acceptable.

The growth in motivation and decline in costs of regulation tend to induce a shift from natural fertility to deliberate family size limitation. However, the negative effect on fertility of contraception may not initially reduce observed rates of childbearing; indeed, use of contraception may at first be accompanied by a rise in observed fertility. This is because the positive impact on observed fertility of rising natural fertility may equal or outweigh the negative impact of deliberate control, especially when control techniques are new and likely to be practiced imperfectly and only toward the end of a couple's reproductive career. Eventually, though, as the motivation for control continues to mount and costs of regulation decline, deliberate family size limitation spreads throughout the population and is practiced more efficiently and earlier in the reproductive career. As this occurs, observed fertility and actual family size start to decline.

The sequence of mortality and fertility change described here is consistent with the usual view of the demographic transition, namely, that reduced mortality precedes fertility decline, but the reasoning also opens the possibility of an early phase of fertility increase, as has sometimes actually been observed (Dyson and Murphy 1985; Olusanya 1969). There is, however, nothing inevitable in the sequence of mortality decline followed by fertility decline. If, for example, socioeconomic development in a country emphasized economic change and education to the exclusion of public health programs, then the relative timing of the mortality and fertility changes might differ.[1]

The theory thus leads to mobilizing data on potential family size, desired family size, and costs of regulation with a view to examining such questions as the following: In an early modern or premodern situation, is the typical household able to have as many children as it wants if it does nothing deliberately to restrict fertility? In other words, does potential family size fall below or exceed desired family size? As modernization progresses, does the motivation for control rise? And, if so, is this due to the trend in potential family size, desired family size, or both? Do costs of fertility control decline? What are the relative weights of motivation and costs of regulation in inducing a shift to deliberate fertility control? To what extent does increasing fertility control translate into actual fertility decline? These and similar questions are the concern of the subsequent empirical analysis.

DATA AND MEASURES

The basic data are from two surveys that covered roughly the same parts of Karnataka state in India: the Mysore Population Study (MPS), conducted jointly by the government of India and the United Nations in 1951–2 and the Bangalore Population Study (BPS) undertaken in 1975 by the Population Center, Bangalore. The study population is continuously married females aged 35–44. The urban data in both surveys are from the city of Bangalore, the largest city in Karnataka.

The principal variables in the analysis are as follows:

1. Fertility (B) is measured in terms of the mean number of births per continuously married woman. Family size (C) is the product of fertility (B) and the child survival ratio (s) measured as the ratio of surviving children to children ever born.
2. Fertility control (U) is any deliberate use of contraception (including abstinence) or contraceptive sterilization. (Induced abortion is not included because data are not available.)

[1] The various links between socioeconomic development and the transition from high to low fertility are discussed more fully in Easterlin (1983).

3. Costs of regulation (*RC*) is estimated as the mean number of fertility control methods known per couple with costs of control assumed to vary *inversely* with methods known.
4. Desired family size (C_d) is measured somewhat differently in the two surveys. In the MPS, each woman was asked the ideal number of children a couple should have without any reference to the number of children the respondent had at the time of the survey. In the BPS, each woman was asked the number of additional children she would like to have, and this figure was added to the number she had at the time of the survey to obtain the desired family size.
5. Potential family size (C_n) is the product of natural fertility (N) and the child survival ratio (s) defined above in paragraph 1. Natural fertility (N) is the mean number of births per continuously married woman that would have occurred in the absence of deliberate family size limitation.[2]

The analysis throughout is based on averages for the population, which is a choice necessitated by the data. Individual households would, of course, vary about the mean – a point that is emphasized at several places in the subsequent analysis.

EMPIRICAL RESULTS

Although the data are imperfect, they form a coherent picture when pieced together in terms of the theoretical framework. The following presentation takes up first the experience of Karnataka and then turns to a comparison with Taiwan.

Karnataka

Potential family size – If a husband and wife were continuously married and did nothing to limit their fertility, then in 1951 they would have had, on average, about 4.3 surviving children by the end of the wife's reproductive career (Table 9.1, Col. 3). Their fertility would have been

[2] Natural fertility is estimated by adjusting the Coale–Trussell standard value of natural fertility downward by their scale factor, *M*, as estimated here for each geographic area from age-specific marital fertility rates. See Coale and Trussell (1974a). This method of estimating natural fertility was first used in Srinivasan and Jejeebhoy (1981).

Table 9.1. Natural fertility, child survival ratio, and potential family size of women 35–44 in rural Karnataka and Bangalore, 1951 and 1975

	(1) Natural fertility (N)	(2) Survival ratio (s)	(3) Potential family size (C_n)
A. Rural Karnataka			
1951	6.27	0.686	4.30
1975	6.58	0.798	5.25
Percentage change, 1951–75	4.9	16.3	22.1
B. Bangalore			
1951	5.94	0.739	4.39
1975	6.85	0.865	5.93
Percentage change, 1951–75	15.3	17.1	35.1

considerably higher (on the order of six births per wife), but high infant and child mortality would have reduced the survivors to about 70 percent of this figure (Cols. 1 and 2).

By 1975, family size in the absence of deliberate control would have been at least one-fourth greater (Col. 3). This growth in potential family size was partly due to an improvement in child survival rates, which occurred at about the same pace in rural as in urban areas (Col. 2). It was also due to increased natural fertility. In urban areas the contribution of natural fertility to raising potential family size was just about the same as that of improved child survival; in rural areas, the contribution, though positive, was considerably less than that of improved child survival (see the percentage changes at the bottom of each panel).

Desired family size and motivation for control – In 1951, parents in urban areas wanted to have about four surviving children; in rural areas, desired family size was somewhat larger, about 4.6 children (Table 9.2, Col. 2). By 1975 the number of children desired had declined in both areas, but by less than half a child. Because of the change in concept noted in the data section, the decline in desired family size is possibly understated.

How did desired family size compare with the number of children that would have resulted from unregulated fertility (i.e., potential family size)? The results for the rural area in 1951 are instructive; on average,

Table 9.2. Potential family size, desired family size, and motivation for fertility control of women 35–44 in rural Karnataka and Bangalore, 1951–75

	(1) Potential family size (C_n)	(2) Desired family size (C_d)	(3) Motivation for fertility control ($C_n - C_d$)
A. Rural Karnataka:			
1951	4.30	4.65	−0.35
1975	5.25	4.20	1.05
Change, 1951–75	0.95	−0.45	1.40
B. Bangalore:			
1951	4.39	4.00	0.39
1975	5.93	3.70	2.23
Change, 1951–75	1.54	−0.30	1.84

potential family size fell short of desired size by about 0.4 children (Table 9.2, Col. 3). This means that the typical married couple was unable to have as many children as were wanted, even if the spouses enjoyed an unbroken marriage throughout the wife's reproductive career and did nothing to limit their fertility. To be sure, this is an average situation. Some couples had as many children as, or more than, they desired, whereas others had a much greater shortfall. And in urban areas the situation was the opposite; on the average, potential family size exceeded that desired by about 0.4 children. However, the rural sector is more representative of India at the time (and of pretransition experience generally) because the rural population accounts for perhaps four-fifths of the population. The implication is that the representative situation in India in 1951 – and, more generally, in pretransition conditions – is one in which many couples have difficulty in achieving their desired family size even in an unbroken marriage.

By 1975, the situation had changed dramatically. In both rural and urban areas potential family size increased, whereas desired family size decreased. In rural areas the initial shortfall below desired family size was replaced by an excess amounting to about one child; in urban areas, the modest initial excess of 0.4 children rose to 2.2 (Table 9.2, Col. 3). Unregulated fertility was therefore likely to result, on average, in one to two more children than were desired, creating a corresponding pressure to reduce fertility.

Table 9.3. Motivation for fertility control and costs of regulation for women 35–44 and percentage of women ages 20–39 and 35–39 controlling fertility in rural Karnataka and Bangalore, 1951 and 1975

	(1) Motivation for fertility control ($C_n - C_d$)	(2) Costs of regulation (RC) (inverted)	(3) Percentage controlling 20–39 (U)	(4) Percentage controlling 35–39 (U)
A. Rural Karnataka				
1951	−0.35	<0.8	3.4	n.a.
1975	1.05	>2.3	21.0	25.6
B. Bangalore				
1951	0.39	0.8	15.3	22.2
1975	2.23	2.3	36.0	48.6

What were the most important sources of the increased motivation to control fertility? Both potential and desired family size contributed, but of the two, potential family size made a much more important contribution (Table 9.2, bottom line of each panel). As has been seen, the rising trend in potential family size was, in turn, due to increases in both child survival and natural fertility rates probably driven by public health programs and perhaps changing breastfeeding practices. Thus, these factors, more than a change in desired family size, were chiefly responsible in this period for pushing families into a potential surplus fertility situation.

Adoption of control – At the start of the period rural couples, on average, could not have as many children as they wanted even if fertility were unregulated; hence, one would expect fertility control to be quite limited in rural areas. This in fact was the case, the percentage reporting any use being only 3 percent (Table 9.3, Col. 3). There was some fertility control even though the average situation was one of deficit fertility because some couples were doubtless above the average in a surplus fertility situation. If rural Karnataka in 1951 is representative of premodern or early modern situations more generally, then the absence of deliberate control in such situations, as is typically reported, is due to lack of motivation – the inability of most couples to have as many surviving children as they want.

One would expect that the appearance and growth of a potential surplus of children would induce motivation for control and thereby increase use, and again, this is the case. In both rural and urban areas, increasing motivation was accompanied by increased fertility regulation (Cols. 3 and 4). Moreover, at both dates urban adoption exceeds rural, as does the motivation for control.

Motivation is, of course, only one factor determining control; the other is the costs of fertility regulation. It is possible that greater fertility control could also result from lower costs of regulation once potential family size exceeds desired size.

The available measure of costs of regulation – number of methods of control known – is far from the ideal, especially because it fails to reflect subjective attitudes. The measure does show, however, a growth in knowledge over the period (that is, *reduced* costs of regulation) and thus a trend that would contribute to greater use of control (Table 9.3, Col. 2). Moreover, the measure shows a very low level of knowledge at the start of the period, which again is consistent with the low use of control at that time. In general, then, costs of regulation as well as motivation appear to have contributed to both low initial use and the growth in use over time.

Given the imperfections in the present measures of motivation and costs of regulation, and the small number of observations, an assessment of the relative importance of motivation versus costs of regulation in inducing fertility control is difficult. However, the data do offer one suggestion that motivation is more important than costs of fertility control. In seeking to account for the consistent excess of urban over rural areas in the use of control, one finds that the motivation measure indicates that more motivation existed in urban areas at both dates. As regards the measure of costs of regulation, however, this favored higher use in urban areas only at the start of the period. The 1951 deficit of rural areas in fertility control knowledge was reversed by 1975, implying that regulation costs there became less than in urban areas. On the basis of costs of regulation alone, one would have expected rural areas to use fertility control more than urban areas in 1975, but rural use of fertility control was actually less in 1975. Hence, at both dates, the rural–urban difference in use of control is consistent with the difference in motivation, but only at one date is it consistent with the difference in regulation costs.

The inference that rural regulation costs dropped below urban costs by 1975 is based on the following data on the percentage of currently married women reporting any knowledge of family limitation methods (Srinivasan et al. 1978):

	1951	1975
Bangalore	38	76
Rural	13	92

Note the striking reversal between 1951 and 1975 in the rural situation compared with urban. The source report comments: "This is possibly because of the fact that mass sterilization camps have been conducted in rural areas in large numbers since 1965 and the sterilization programmes were more well known to the population in the rural areas than in the urban areas" (Srinivasan et al. 1978). An implication of the present analysis – again subject to the caution about possible imperfections of the measures – is that the emphasis of the Indian family planning program on rural over urban areas was misplaced because the program was more handicapped by lack of motivation in rural areas than in urban.

Fertility control and fertility – Despite the rise from 1951 to 1975 in the proportion of the population using fertility control, the number of births per woman either rose, as in rural areas, or remained constant, as in urban (Table 9.4, Col. 3). This does not mean that fertility control was ineffective. As has been seen, natural fertility was rising during this period. The growth in fertility control, although not enough to reduce the absolute number of births per woman, did serve to moderate the increase, especially in the urban sector. In the absence of deliberate control, childbearing in urban areas would have increased by about one birth per woman (Table 9.1, Col. 1). The actual increase in births per woman was zero (Table 9.4, Col. 3).

Note that the absence of a decline in observed fertility should not be taken to mean that the demographic transition was not under way or that fertility control was ineffective. As has been seen, in Karnataka, during this period, inducements to greater regulation of fertility developed and the population responded with a sizable increase in use of control. This increase in control moderated or prevented an upsurge in births that rising natural fertility was tending to bring about.

Table 9.4. Percentage of women ages 20–39 and 35–39 controlling fertility and children ever born, for women 35–44 in rural Karnataka and Bangalore, 1951 and 1975

	(1) Percentage controlling	(2)	(3) Children ever born
	20–39 (*U*)	35–39 (*U*)	(*B*)
A. Rural Karnataka			
1951	3.4	n.a.	5.90
1975	21.0	25.6	6.20
B. Bangalore			
1951	15.3	22.2	5.40
1975	36.0	48.6	5.40

Comparison of Karnataka with Taiwan

Further light can be thrown on these generalizations from Indian experience by comparing the results with those from similar surveys of Taiwan, an area with about the same population as Karnataka (Jejeebhoy 1979). The similarities between Taiwan and Karnataka are noteworthy. From 1957 to 1973, potential family size rises owing to increases in both natural fertility and child survival rates (Table 9.5, Cols. 1–3). Desired family size trends downward after an initial period of stability (Col. 4). At the start of the period, the motivation for control is positive but small – on average, parents would have had 0.3 more children than desired (Col. 5). In the next sixteen years, motivation rises steadily and markedly to the point where, in the absence of deliberate control, parents would have averaged 2.5 unwanted children. The number of methods known rises slightly through 1965 and thereafter quite sharply in conjunction with a marked expansion in the family planning program. This implies a mild downtrend in fertility control costs before 1965 and thereafter a sharp drop. The use of fertility control rises noticeably both before and after 1965. Before 1965 the increase in use is chiefly due to growing motivation and thereafter to both increased motivation and reduced fertility control costs (Cols. 5–7). As in Karnataka, the number of births per woman rises at first, despite the increase in fertility control (Col. 8). After 1965, however, fertility turns noticeably downward as use of fertility control becomes widespread in the population.

Table 9.5. Selected fertility and fertility control measures for women ages 35–9 in Taiwan, 1957–73

	(1) Natural fertility (N)	(2) Survival rate (s)	(3) Potential family size (C_n)	(4) Desired family size (C_d)	(5) Motivation for control ($C_n - C_d$)	(6) Costs of regulation (RC) (inverted)	(7) Percent controlling (U)	(8) Children ever born (B)
1957	5.55	0.843	4.68	4.40	0.28	<3.0	12.0	5.46
1960	5.76	0.874	5.03	4.39	0.64	3.0	22.7	5.61
1965	6.27	0.901	5.65	4.28	1.37	3.7	44.2	5.56
1973	6.31	0.977	6.16	3.66	2.50	6.2	83.9	4.38

Note that the development in which Taiwanese experience departs from that of Karnataka, the eventual sharp decline in births per woman, occurs, roughly speaking, after more than half of the population is limiting family size, that is, at a later stage in the transition to deliberate control than that reached in Karnataka by 1975. The pattern common to both countries is one of rising fertility in the early stages of the transition to fertility control owing to an upsurge in natural fertility that is only moderated by the start of deliberate control. Eventually, however, as Taiwan's experience indicates, a decline in actual fertility sets in.

Differentials by Age and Socioeconomic Status

The analysis to this point has centered chiefly on trends over time with some attention to rural–urban differentials. This section points out briefly some implications of the theoretical framework for trends in fertility differentials by age and socioeconomic status and notes some supporting evidence.

Age – Figure 9.1, Panel A is a hypothetical sketch of how desired family size (C_d) and potential family size (C_n) might vary as the typical woman in a premodern society goes through her reproductive career. As shown, even by the end of her reproductive career, the typical woman has fewer surviving children than are desired, which is a situation like that of rural Karnataka in 1951. If for simplicity of exposition one disregards variations around the mean, then no motivation for, or adoption of, fertility control exists at any reproductive age. This means that the observed

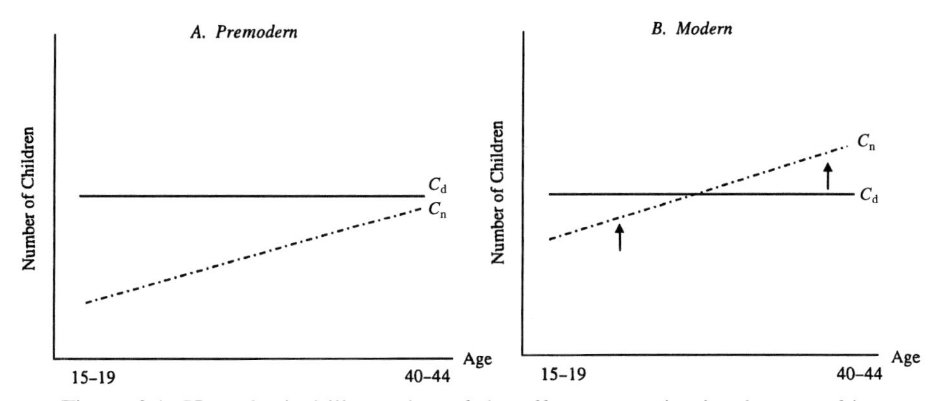

Figure 9.1. Hypothetical illustration of the effect on motivation by age of increase in potential family size during modernization.

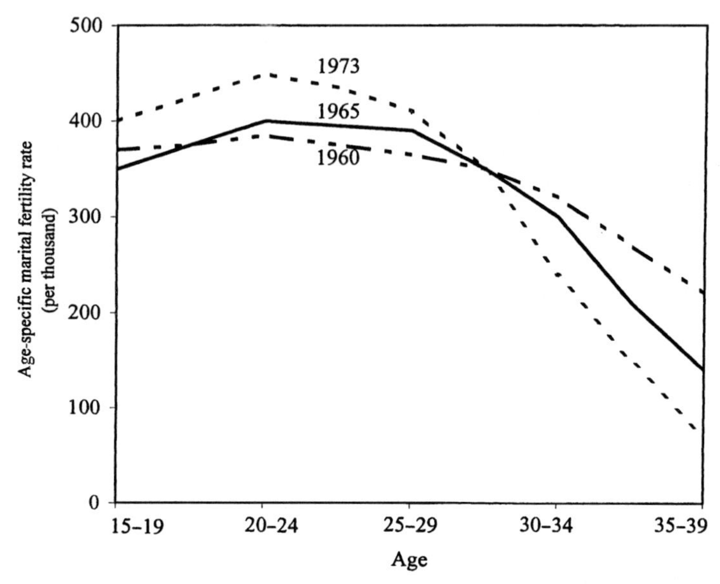

Figure 9.2. Age-specific marital fertility in Taiwan for the cohort aged 35–39 in 1960, 1965, and 1973.

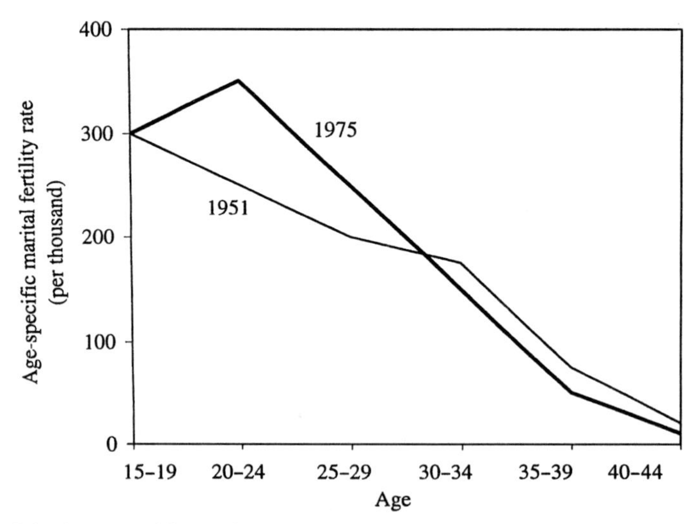

Figure 9.3. Age-specific marital fertility rates for Bangalore City, 1951 and 1975.

Table 9.6. Index of general marital fertility rate by agricultural occupation, rural Karnataka, 1951 and 1975

	(1) 1951	(2) 1975
Low socioeconomic status (laborers or temporary tenants)	90	119
High socioeconomic status (other agricultural occupations)	100	96

age-specific marital fertility schedule would correspond to a natural fertility schedule.

Panel B of Figure 9.1 presents a hypothetical sketch of the same two curves early in the process of modernization. On the basis of the trends in Karnataka and Taiwan, it is hypothesized that the C_n curve shifts upward relative to the C_d curve as natural fertility and child survival improve with modernization. As a result, a motivation to control fertility emerges at the later reproductive ages. With regard to the schedule of age-specific marital fertility, this implies that the *trend* in age-specific fertility rates will, at the younger reproductive ages, reflect developments in natural fertility alone, but the trend at the older ages will be influenced, in addition, by a shift from uncontrolled to controlled fertility.

The actual age-specific marital fertility schedules for both Karnataka and Taiwan show a pattern consistent with the hypothesized developments in Figure 9.1. Over time, there is a tilt upward at the younger ages owing to increased natural fertility, and downward at the older, due to the adoption of deliberate control (Figs. 9.2 and 9.3).

Socioeconomic status – Finally, consider the hypothetical patterns of C_n and C_d by socioeconomic status (SES) shown in Figure 9.4. In Panel A, the premodern case, neither those at low nor high SES are able to have as many children as they would like; hence, those at both levels have as many as they can. Potential family size (C_n) increases with socioeconomic status, reflecting an assumption that both natural fertility and child survival are higher for the higher status group. In this situation, one would expect that observed fertility would vary positively with SES. This positive association appears to have existed in rural Karnataka in 1951, where natural fertility conditions prevailed (Table 9.6, Col. 1).[3]

[3] Compare also the pattern for Indonesia shown in Hull and Hull (1977).

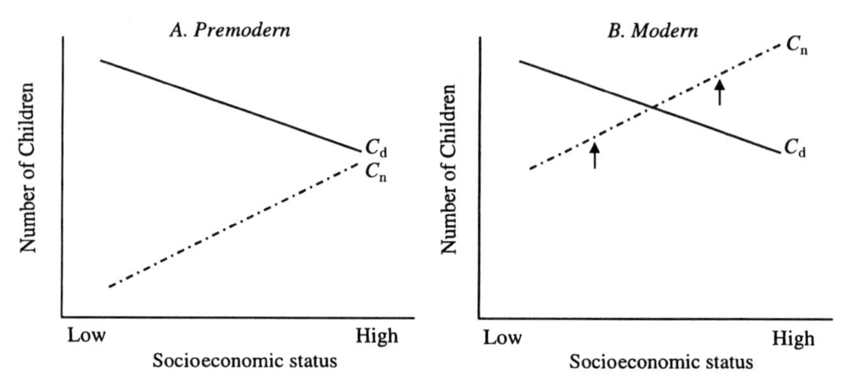

Figure 9.4. Hypothetical illustration of the effect on motivation by socioeconomic status of an increase in potential family size during modernization.

In panel B of Figure 9.4, the early modern case, the C_n schedule is shifted upward relative to the C_d schedule, as was assumed in the previous analysis of differentials by age. The hypothesized result, as was also true in the age analysis, is that natural fertility prevails at the lower end of the distribution and deliberate control at the higher end. The implication is that fertility differentials by SES shift from a positive to a negative association. In actuality, such a shift did occur in rural Karnataka (Table 9.6, Col. 2).

SUMMARY AND CONCLUSIONS

The present results tell a consistent story for both Karnataka and Taiwan in conformity with the theoretical view of the demographic transition in Chapter 8. In general, in a premodern or early modern situation, the typical couple is unable to have as many surviving children as it would like, even if fertility were unregulated, in large part because infant and child mortality is so high. There is no motivation to limit fertility, and natural fertility is a rational response to the couple's basic reproductive circumstances. Also, to judge from the very limited knowledge of methods of fertility control, the costs of control are high; hence, even those couples who are motivated to regulate fertility – whose potential family size exceeds that desired – may prefer to bear the burden of unwanted children rather than incur the difficulties of deliberate fertility regulation. For such couples also, natural fertility is a rational response to their basic reproductive circumstances.

With the expansion of public health programs, mass schooling, and economic development, the typical couple shifts from a situation of deficit to excess fertility, that is, family size in the absence of deliberate control would exceed that desired. This comes about partly through a reduction in desired family size, but more through an increase in potential family size, owing to both increased natural fertility and improved child survival. As a result, the motivation to restrict fertility deliberately emerges and grows. The costs of fertility control decline as knowledge of methods of control expands owing, in today's developing countries, in substantial part to new family planning programs as well as to increased education. The concurrence of rising motivation for control and reduced costs of control leads to the gradual spread of deliberate fertility control throughout the population.

The growth in deliberate family size limitation does not necessarily lead to an immediate reduction in fertility rates because the fertility-enhancing effects of rising natural fertility may offset the fertility-reducing effects of deliberate regulation, which is typically concentrated near the end of a couple's reproductive career. Eventually, however, the effect of growing control prevails and total fertility declines. Fertility differentials by age may initially increase, reflecting the impact at younger ages of increased natural fertility and, at older, of the adoption of deliberate control. Fertility differentials by SES may reverse during the demographic transition, shifting from positive to negative as the natural fertility conditions that initially prevailed throughout the SES distribution are gradually replaced by deliberate fertility control, which occurs first among those of higher status.

10

Does Human Fertility Adjust to the Environment? Population Change and Farm Settlement in the Northern United States

> In the year 1770, I purchased some lands in the county of..., which I intended for one of my sons; and was obliged to go there in order to see them properly surveyed and marked out: the soil is good, but the country has a very wild aspect. However, I observed with pleasure, the land sells very fast; and I am in hopes when the lad gets a wife, it will be a well-settled decent country. Agreeable to our customs, which indeed are those of nature, it is our duty to provide for our eldest children while we live, in order that our homesteads may be left to the youngest, who are the most helpless. Some people are apt to regard the portions given to daughters as so much lost to the family; but this is selfish, and is not agreeable to my way of thinking; they cannot work as men do; they marry young: I have given an honest European a farm to till for himself, rent free, provided he clears an acre of swamp every year, and that he quits it whenever my daughter shall marry. It will procure her a substantial husband, a good farmer – and that is all my ambition.
>
> J. Hector St. John de Crèvecoeur, Letters from an American Farmer

Firmly rooted in the Malthusian origins of economists' views on population is the idea that population expands to fill up empty land until the exhaustion of cultivable soil brings population increase to a halt. On the face of it, American history provides telling documentation of this notion. The vast territorial accessions of the nineteenth century were rapidly absorbed by the process of farm settlement, and then, with the closing of the frontier at the end of the nineteenth century, farm population leveled off and remained about constant from 1910 to 1935. Subsequently, particularly with the advent of the new biochemical technology, farm population trended downward, but that is a subject for a different story.

A little scratching beneath the surface of the American record, however, reveals critical aspects of this process that do not fit the Malthusian model very well. That model, in its simplest form, takes the level of fertility as given, and mortality change governs the rate of population growth. In fact, American experience, so far as it has been established, appears to be just about the opposite. The stabilization of farm population growth was brought about in large measure by fertility decline, not by mortality increase, although migration too played a part. Moreover, the decline in the fertility of the farm population was apparent very early in our history. It was certainly under way in the Northeast by the beginning of the nineteenth century, despite the abundance of cheap farm land to the west (Grabill, Kiser, and Whelpton 1958; Lockridge 1968; Okun 1958; Smith 1972; Taeuber and Taeuber 1958; Wells 1971a,b; Yasuba 1962). The fertility decline in older areas took place at the same time as rural out-migration occured to newer farm lands and urban centers. Over the long run, the stabilization of American farm population growth stemmed primarily from a long-term downtrend in farm family fertility to replacement levels. This fertility decline antedated by at least three-quarters of a century the onset of fertility decline in Europe associated with the demographic transition.

It is the mechanisms underlying this long-term decline in the fertility of the farm population that is the central concern of this chapter. An analysis of this decline is best conducted in the context of the pattern of farm settlement itself. Hence, farm settlement is addressed first and then fertility. The focus is on northern farm areas of the United States because of the more plentiful supply of data for this region and the fairly homogeneous structure of agricultural organization.

THE PATTERN OF FARM SETTLEMENT

The march of population across the northern United States has been characterized by replication of essentially the same pattern of farm settlement in all states. The degree of settlement of a state at any date can be measured by the ratio of the rural population at that date to the maximum rural population eventually attained. On the basis of this

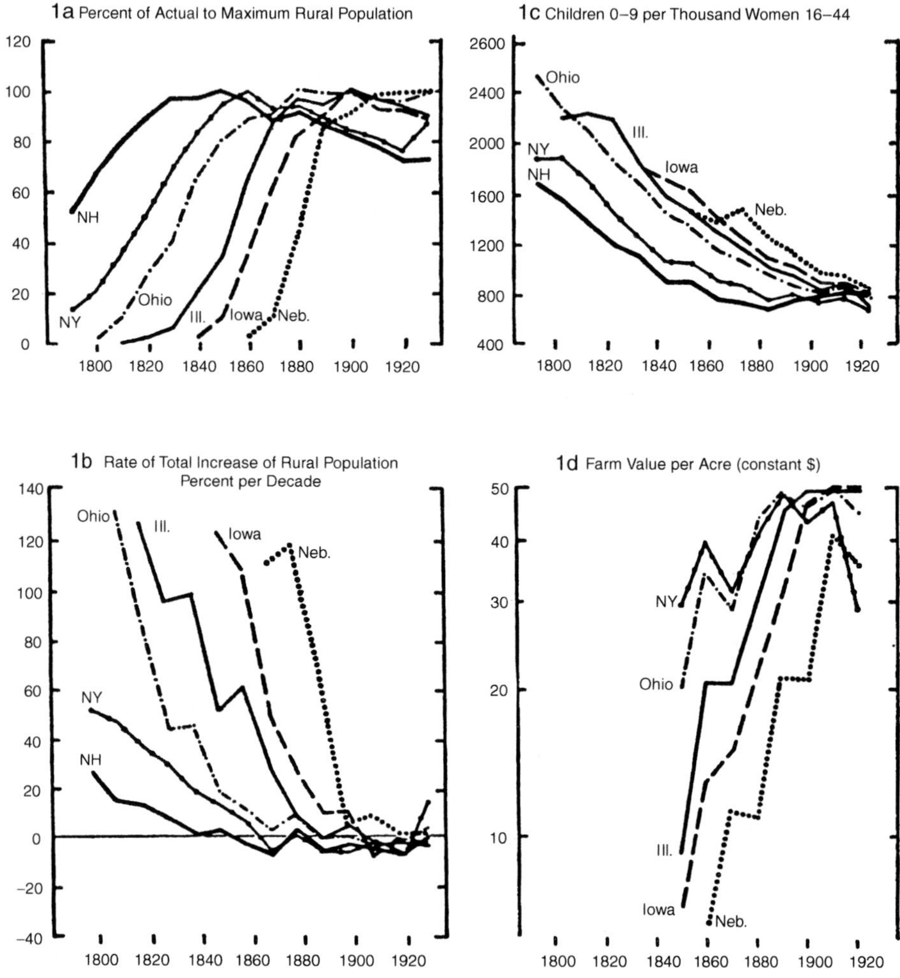

Figure 10.1. Measures of economic and demographic change, six states, 1790–1930.

measure, the successive settlement of six states is depicted in Figure 10.1a. A similar progression in rural rates of total population increase – in this case from initially high levels to convergence toward zero growth rates – is shown in Figure 10.1b. The states also exhibit a corresponding sequence of fertility declines, converging toward a common level (Figure 10.1c). Figure 10.1d gives the settlement picture for an economic magnitude, the constant dollar value of farm property per acre of land in farms, available only for a somewhat shorter period, from 1850 onward. In this case there is a repeated pattern of rising farm values followed again by convergence toward a rather similar level.[1]

Figure 10.1 suggests some tentative generalizations about settlement patterns: the length of the process, the point at which out-migration usually starts, when the fertility decline starts and ends, and when farm values first reach specified levels. Panel A of Table 10.1 presents dates relating to these events for each state. In Panel B, on which the discussion will center, the date for each event is differenced from that when the state was at 90 percent of settlement, thus facilitating comparisons among states.

Column 1 of Panel B presents a measure of the duration of the settlement process, that is, how long it took for the state to move from being 10-percent settled to 90 percent. There is a clear indication that settlement occurred more rapidly in states being settled later, which is also apparent from the progressively steeper slopes of the curves in Figure 10.1b. The faster rate of settlement occurred even though western states had more farm land available for settlement. An obvious reason why the speed of settlement increases over time is that the later a state enters the settlement process, the larger is the population base in older states available for migration to the new state.

Column 2 of Panel B indicates that fertility decline sets in early in the settlement process while in-migration is still occurring, sometimes even before the state is 10-percent settled. The initial fertility level is usually lower in the states being settled later. There is little evidence of a lower initial rate of rural population growth in those states, implying that a higher in-migration rate offsets a lower fertility rate.

As a rough measure of the initiation of out-migration, I have used here the date at which the rural rate of total population increase falls below 20 percent per decade. The underlying assumption is that, throughout most of the nineteenth century, a minimum figure for the rate of natural increase (the excess of the birth rate over the death rate) is

[1] New Hampshire is omitted from Figure 10.1d. The New Hampshire series for farm value per acre is level (though fluctuating) from 1850 onward, but at a much lower level than is reached in the other states perhaps because of the comparative inferiority of farm land in that state or the much later settlement stage observed.

Table 10.1. Date of specified event in settlement process and years intervening between event and date when state was 90-percent settled, six selected states

	(1) 10% Settled	(2) Start of decline in child–woman ratio	(3) Value/acre about $20	(4) Start of out-migration	(5) 90% Settled	(6) Value/acre about $40	(7) Child–woman ratio about 900
			A. Date of Specified Event				
New Hampshire	n	n	n	1800	1820	n	1845
New York	1786	1805	n	1834	1846	1860	1865
Ohio	1810	1795	1850	1845	1860	1878	1885
Illinois	1833	1815	1860	1870	1873	1886	1900
Iowa	1848	1835	1877	1879	1888	1896	1905
Nebraska	1868	1875	1889	1894	1897	1909	1920
			B. Years before (−) or after (+) State Was 90-Percent Settled				
New Hampshire	n	n	n	−20	0	n	+25
New York	−60	−41	n	−12	0	+14	+19
Ohio	−50	−65	−10	−15	0	+18	+25
Illinois	−40	−58	−13	−3	0	+13	+27
Iowa	−40	−53	−11	−9	0	+8	+17
Nebraska	−29	−22	−8	−3	0	+12	+23

n = not available.

20 percent per decade; hence, if the rate of total increase, is lower than the assumed 20-percent rate of natural increase, one can fairly confidently infer the existence of out-migration. By this measure, out-migration sets in before a state is 90-percent settled and usually occurs between the 2/3 to 4/5 points of the settlement process (Col. 4).

Column 3 indicates that farm values usually rise above $20/acre a few years before out-migration occurs. Farm values reach a level of $40/acre about a decade and a half after the 90-percent settlement stage (Col. 6) and fertility hits its minimum about a decade following that (Col. 7). Unlike the events that occur before the settlement process is 90-percent completed, there is little or no evidence for the last two events of a shortening of the timing in the states being settled later.

The evidence for the different states thus tells essentially the same story of settlement, although the duration of the settlement phase becomes shorter in the course of time. Of special interest here is the marked decline in the rate of population growth, signaling the stabilization of farm population in an area. If one asks what it is that brings the rural rate of total increase to such low levels, the answer is that during the settlement phase proper, it is primarily the shift from high in-migration to out-migration. Over the longer run, however, the secular decline in fertility must be given principal credit. If the fertility decline had not occurred, much higher out-migration rates would have been necessary to stabilize population. Although there have been few attempts to make refined estimates of farm family fertility, it is clear that the decline in childbearing as farming areas "aged" eventually brought fertility close to the replacement level (Bash 1955, 1963; Spengler 1930; Sydenstricker 1932).

Over the longer run, therefore, adjustment of population to the farming opportunities in a given area was substantially accomplished by the reduction of fertility. This decrease in fertility was entirely a matter of private voluntary behavior. No central authority was publicizing the need for population control. On the contrary, the prevalence of legislation against birth control signifies that the official stance was one of hostility to fertility reduction. Thus, the answer to the question of the factors responsible for the cessation of population growth in an established agricultural area basically requires an explanation of the sources of the voluntary reduction in farm family fertility.

THE FERTILITY PATTERN IN CROSS-SECTIONAL DATA

At any given time, states along an east–west geographic axis are at different stages of the settlement process (Figure 10.1). Consequently, by pooling state data at a point in time, one should be able to reproduce in fair degree the time series pattern of settlement. For example, if one were to read off the 1860 values for each state from Figures 10.1a and 10.1c, six paired observations on stage of settlement and the child–woman ratio would be obtained. The bottom curve in Figure 10.2 presents such a set of paired observations, using a settlement measure based on improved acreage, chosen so as to improve comparability with series used subsequently in the figure. The plot shows an inverse relation between fertility and degree of settlement, conforming in general to the relationship revealed in time series data. The negative relation does not appear at the earliest stage of settlement, which is a phenomenon that is sometimes true in time series data (compare Figure 10.1c).

That cross-sectional state data roughly reproduce the settlement process over time means one can go beyond the published census data and explore interrelationships during the process of settlement more fully by drawing on the massive cross-sectional sample of farm and village households taken from the 1860 manuscript census by Fred Bateman and James D. Foust (1974). The sample covers all households living on farms or in rural villages in each of 102 townships scattered across sixteen northern states from New Hampshire to Kansas. The data for each household in the sample include almost all information from the free-population census schedule, and, for each farm household, from the agricultural schedule as well. The availability for individual farm households of matched demographic and economic data and the unusually large sample size offer exceptional analytical opportunities for historical analysis.

To simplify the current presentation, I have grouped the households in the Bateman–Foust sample according to the stage of settlement of the townships in which the households lived as measured by the ratio of improved agricultural land in 1860 to the maximum ever-improved and then classified households into each of five stage-of-settlement groups.[2]

[2] Because data at the township level were not available, the ratio is computed for the county in which each township is located.

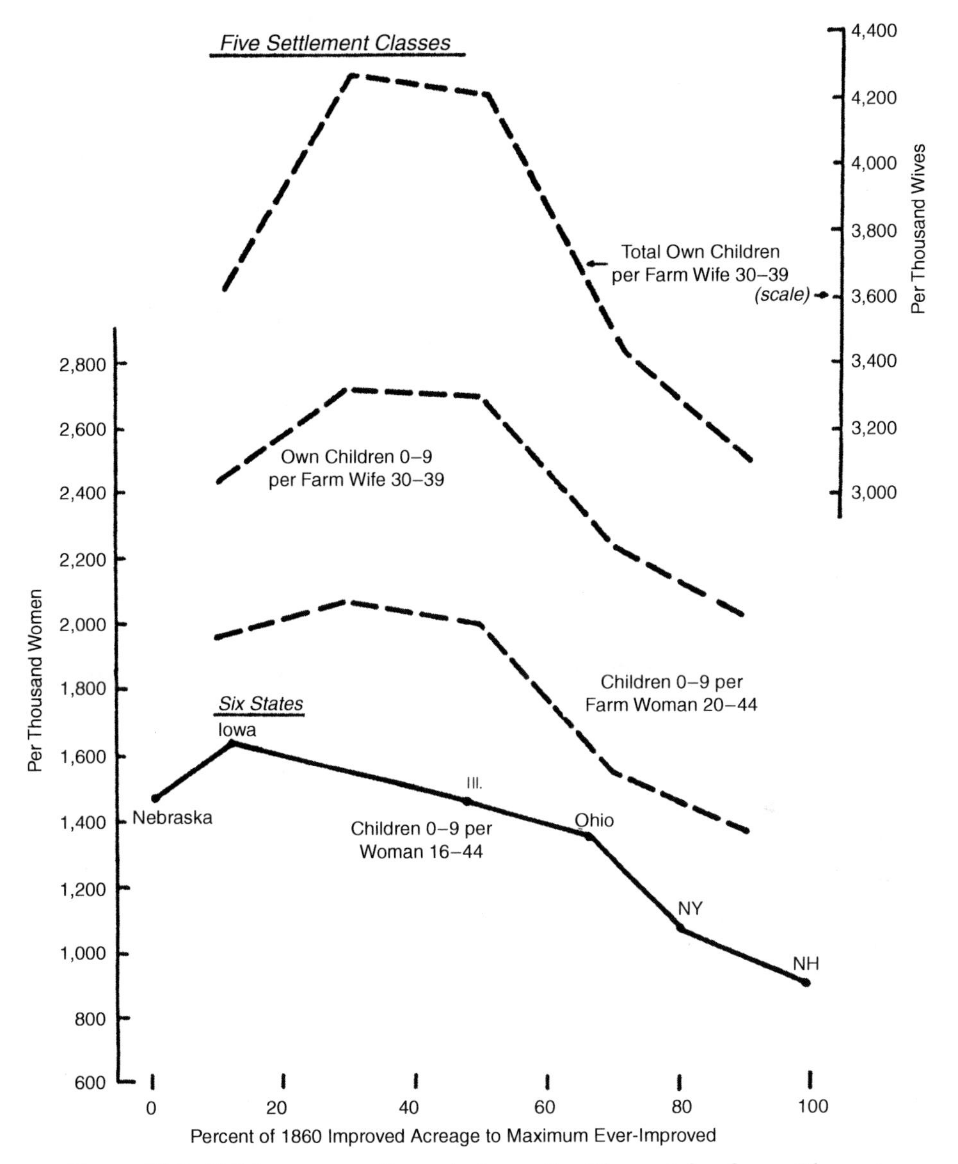

Figure 10.2. Child–woman ratio and stage of settlement for five settlement classes and six states, 1860.
Source: State date from Yasuba (1962, 61, Table II-7); data for the five settlement classes derived from the Bateman–Foust sample of the manuscript censuses.

The households in each settlement class are then combined to obtain measures of average fertility, average farm size and farm value, and so on. In the three broken-line curves of Figure 10.2, the child–woman ratio for farm households in the oldest settlement class, that with 80 to 100 percent of the maximum improved acreage under cultivation, is plotted against the midpoint value of the settlement class (90 percent), and similarly for each of the other four settlement classes. Comparison of the curves in Figure 10.2 indicates that the level of fertility in the farm settlement groups (the broken line curves) is higher than that in the rural population of the six states (the solid line). This is because the lower fertility rural nonfarm population included in the state data is omitted from the farm settlement groups. Also, the denominator of the fertility measure for the state data encompasses a slightly larger age group. But the shape of all three broken line curves is similar to that of the solid-line state curve. Thus, the negative relationship between fertility and stage of settlement observed in published census data for the total rural population (farm plus nonfarm) turns out to be reasonably well replicated in the cross-sectional sample for the farm population alone.

The upper two broken-line curves in Figure 10.2 provide somewhat more refined measures of farm family fertility than the lowest broken-line curve. They relate to the marital fertility of farm wives aged 30–9. The lower curve is a "current" fertility measure, including only children 0 to 9 (those born in the last ten years), and the upper one, a cumulative measure, including all living children. It is clear that the pattern of fertility differences between old and new settlement areas holds up equally well with the more refined fertility measures and that it applies to completed as well as current fertility.[3]

A question is sometimes raised whether the cross-sectional differences between new and old settlement areas in the child–woman ratio are merely due to differences among those areas in the composition of the population by marital status and age. The question implies that there may be no real differences in the reproductive behavior of women in these areas once allowance is made for such differences in the population's composition. The data plotted in the upper two curves of

[3] The cumulative fertility of women aged 30–9 is not fully their completed fertility, but the pattern of differentials shown by the former is likely to be a close approximation to the differentials that their completed fertility will show.

Figure 10.2 resolve the matter. These curves are for farm wives in their 30s; hence, the fertility pattern is, in effect, controlled for marital status and age as well as place of residence. There are clearly real and substantial differences in marital fertility between old and new areas just as there is a real decline as a farm area progresses from its early stage of settlement to an established agricultural area. What is needed is an explanation that can account for these patterns of marital fertility by stage of settlement – both the cross-sectional differences and time series changes. In the following analysis I emphasize the cross-sectional data because the Bateman–Foust sample permits a much more intensive inquiry than would otherwise be possible, but, as will be noted, the argument is equally applicable to the time series data.

THE FERTILITY DECLINE

What caused American farm families in the older areas of settlement to start limiting fertility within marriage? In terms of the fertility determinants discussed in Chapters 8 and 9, there is little reason to think that farm families in older states were privy to knowledge not available to those in newer states about how to control fertility because those in newer states were so often migrants from older states. Hence, the difference among areas in fertility behavior must reflect a greater motivation in older areas to control fertility. Of the two factors that determine motivation, potential family size and desired family size, the first can be discounted because there is little evidence of sizable differences between old and new areas in either natural fertility or child survival. Thus, the lower rates of childbearing in older areas must be due to a lower demand for children that created a greater motivation to limit childbearing.

But why the lower demand for children in older areas? We can begin by eliminating several possible reasons (Easterlin 1976; Easterlin, Condran, and Alter 1978). First, most childbearing households, both in older and newer areas, were free of the burden of aged dependents and therefore of the pressure for limiting family size that old-age dependency might cause. Second, it is doubtful that wives in older areas could earn more if they entered the labor market and that their opportunity cost of childbearing was consequently higher. There is little evidence that educational attainment – often taken as an indicator of wives' opportunity costs in the mainstream economic theory of fertility – was

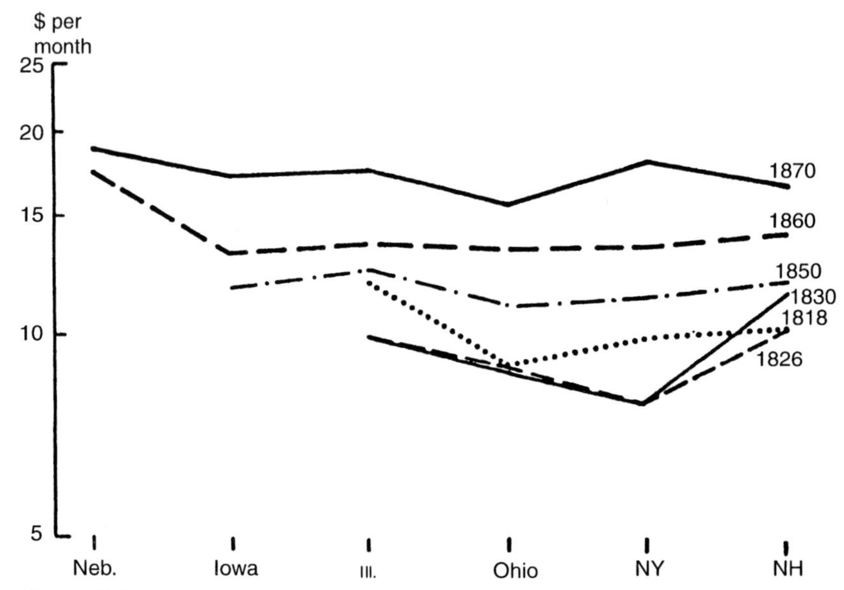

Figure 10.3. Average monthly money earnings with board of farm laborers in specified states, selected dates, 1818–70.

higher in older areas: literacy rates of adults and school attendance rates of children were at fairly similar levels everywhere in the northern states. Moreover, almost no farm wives in older areas actually reported an occupation, as one might expect if women had more rewarding job possibilities there.

Perhaps the most frequently cited explanation for possible differences in the demand for children is that child labor is more valuable in newer areas than in old; hence, lower fertility in older areas was a result of lower returns from children's labor. But the evidence is that the labor of young persons was about equally valuable in old and new areas (Easterlin et al. 1978; Lebergott 1964). Stanley Lebergott's compilation of farm laborers' average monthly earnings (including board) provides a good indicator of the value of young persons' labor, for over 90 percent of farm laborers were males under age 30. In Figure 10.3, wage rates are plotted for the six states of Figure 10.1 for dates ranging from 1818 to 1870.[4] It is striking how level the curves are, especially those for 1850,

[4] Only state data are readily available. Wage rate data at the county level are available for a few states from the manuscript censuses for 1850 and 1860, and these give a picture consistent with the state data.

1860, and 1870, when the coverage (based on the federal censuses) is much more comprehensive. Note, too, that the curves shift upward in roughly parallel fashion, implying that the trend in wage rates was fairly similar among regions. There is some indication that the frontier states proper usually had higher wage rates, but, as we have seen, the highest fertility levels were in the areas somewhat behind the frontier, not at the frontier. For example, of the states in Figure 10.3, it is Iowa and Illinois that have the highest fertility levels in 1860, and their wage rates are much the same as those in Ohio, New York, and New Hampshire.

What about the labor of young females? For girls, the wage rates for domestic help provide a reasonable index of the value of their labor because most of those in domestic service in northern farm areas were under age 30. A plot (not shown) of the wage rates for domestics, like that in Figure 10.3, reveals essentially the same picture, although the curves are more U-shaped because the highest wages occur in New Hampshire and Nebraska.

It may be argued that the picture of money wage rates shown here needs adjustment for price differences among areas. This is true in principle, but there is a question as to the appropriate deflator. The plotted wage rates are for earnings, including board. One can reasonably assume that the real content of board was much the same among regions. If farm hands used their money wages to purchase manufactured items, these may well have been cheaper in places closer to the main sources of production, that is, in the East. If farm hands were trying to build up a nest egg toward the purchase of a farm, as Danhof (1969) suggests, then both those in older and newer areas could take advantage of the lower acreage prices in newer areas. It seems unlikely, therefore, that a real wage rate comparison for the six states would alter the picture shown by the money wage rate data in a way favorable to the child labor hypothesis.

One explanatory factor stressed in other studies that does hold up well is land availability (Forster and Tucker 1972; Leet 1975; Merrick 1978; Van Landingham and Hirschman 2001; Yasuba 1962). Farm family fertility is typically lower in areas where the cultivable land available for settlement has declined. The problem with this explanation, however, is the lack of a theory as to how the pressure of land scarcity affects the demand for children. Why, for example, should a married farm owner in an old area have lower fertility than his twin brother in a new area even though the availability of cultivable land elsewhere in his community has declined? Indeed, it is not certain that land availability is actually the factor operating on fertility because, as has been seen, there is a high degree of correlation among the different economic and demographic variables during settlement. It is to this question of the real determining variable and its effect on the demand for children to which I now turn.

THE "BEQUEST" MODEL

The central idea of the interpretation presented here is captured in the epigraph to this chapter. The idea is not new; it goes back at least to Frederick Le Play and has found expression in studies ranging from that of sociologist Kingsley Davis (1963) and historian James C. Davis (1975) to economists Joseph J. Spengler (1968) and Marc Nerlove (1974). The immediate stimulus here was Philip Greven's valuable description of the transmission of property through four generations in the settlement of colonial Andover (Greven 1970).

Let me start by noting some pertinent features of American farming. First, American farmers were fairly well-to-do for their time, owning a substantial share of the nation's wealth (Goldsmith 1952). Like most propertied persons, they were interested in preserving and increasing their wealth and in transmitting it to the next generation.

Second, American farms were first and foremost family units of organization (Davis, Easterlin, and Parker 1972). One of the pressing concerns of farmers was the "establishment" of their children, that is, to give their offspring a proper start in life. Preferably this might be on their own or a nearby farm. But if this were not possible, then a start in farming in newer areas, or in a nonfarm occupation of equivalent status, was acceptable. Among nonfarm occupations, a career as factory or mill hand tended to be viewed with disfavor. Much more satisfactory was the establishment of offspring in a trade that, like farming, meant proprietorship status, not employee status, although it too necessitated a sizable initial capital outlay.[5]

[5] Some evidence on the limited role of native Americans in factory labor is given in Davis et al. (1972, Chap. v) and Hutchinson (1956). In *Four Generations*, Greven (1970) provides evidence of the increase over time in the entry of sons into trades. Sometimes the cost of establishing a child took the form of outlays on education, as is true today of many middle-class families.

Third, mortality conditions in American farming areas were fairly good compared with those in American cities or Europe and probably had been for a century or more (Davis et al. 1972). By today's standards, infant and child mortality were high. Yet mortality was low enough to guarantee, in conjunction with the well-established fecundity of American women, that, if fertility were unregulated, one could be sure of several surviving heirs for whom provision had to be made. In contrast, mortality under most premodern conditions has often been so high as to cause considerable uncertainty about maintenance of the family line even with uncontrolled fertility.

Finally, American farming is characterized by the institution of multigeniture, that is, division of a decedent's estate equally among the heirs. Although primogeniture came to the colonies with the early settlers from England, it proved to be short lived. The practice in northern farming areas of equal treatment of one's offspring through gift or inheritance appears to have been well established as early as the seventeenth century (Greven 1970; Morris 1959).

Now suppose we translate a farmer's concern for "establishing" his children into the specific assumption that he seeks to provide a start in life for each of his offspring at least as good as that which his father gave to him. He might, of course, aspire to improve on his own experience, but for the present purpose it will suffice to suppose that he sets a target equal to that of his own experience. Thus, if he started off with $1,000 provided by his father, he wants to give each of his children $1,000.[6] If he cannot do as well as this for his children, and their socioeconomic status is therefore subject to potential deterioration, he will be unhappy. If he is able to reach his target, he will feel satisfied, and, if he surpasses it, he will be even happier. But the impact on his subjective feelings of a shortfall versus excess of a given amount is asymmetrical. What motivates him most is concern about loss of status for his children; if his children end up better than he did that is all to the good, but it is not as critical as avoiding a shortfall.

Note that the provision for one's children does not necessarily take the form of land, whether at home, nearby, or far away. What is sought is equal treatment of offspring in terms of money value. It is certainly true

[6] Leibenstein (1974a) has a theory in which targets play a critical role. One of the first applications of notions of this sort to fertility behavior is Banks (1954).

that a foremost concern of the farmer is to see his farm kept in the family and, unless his holdings are extensive, maintained physically intact, not subdivided among his heirs; hence, the farm as such goes only to one child. This, however, can be reconciled with equal treatment for each child through various devices, for example, by mortgaging the farm and sharing the proceeds among those not succeeding to the farm (Gagan 1981).

Given, then, a father's target of $X for each child, equal to the $X his own father gave him, the critical question shaping a farmer's freedom to have children is the prospective growth in his initial capital. If over the course of one's lifetime as a farmer, $X can be multiplied into $NX, then one will be able to provide for N children. The greater the prospective growth in one's capital, the greater the number of children one can afford. If, however, the outlook is for "hard times," then as additional offspring appear, one will begin to worry more and more about one's ability to establish them suitably.

We can see now why twin brothers, one in an old area and one in a new area, with an equal start in life, might have different numbers of offspring. The brother in the new area, where returns are high, can look forward to substantial multiplication of his capital and has little concern about providing for his offspring; the one in the old area anticipates much slower growth in capital and may even be worried about his ability "to keep his capital intact." Hence, as his family grows, the brother in the old area will become increasingly concerned about providing for the children and feel pressure to prevent further additions.

It is, then, the prospective "increase of capital," an everpresent concern of farmers, that chiefly governs the changing size of farm families. The less the prospective growth of capital, the more will a farmer feel pressure to start limiting family size.

There are ample indications of lower returns in eastern compared with western areas in the mid-nineteenth century, as, indeed, economic theory would predict, because higher returns in the West were necessary to induce the required redistribution of farming to that area. Danhof, generalizing from his reading of the literary evidence on the American North around midcentury, points out that

> the amounts of capital required to make a beginning [in the older farming areas] were little different from those necessary for the establishment of a farm in the

> newer regions. . . . The possession of capital was scarcely the determining factor in the choice between East and West. More important were the modest returns that seemed to be in prospect [in the older areas]. . . .[7]

Elsewhere, he refers to "Eastern farmers operating fully capitalized farms, enjoying no increase in the values of their land but suffering from shrinking prices, higher costs and declining [land] fertility. . . ."[8] Neil McNall's study of the Genesee Valley in New York documents the historical evolution of an area from one of bright promise when it was being settled at the start of the nineteenth century to one of struggle for adequate returns by midcentury (McNall 1952; see also Ellis 1946). The competition engendered by the opening up of new areas in the West was in part responsible for the dimming outlook in the East. The abandonment of farms in some eastern areas and the need in other eastern areas to take up new lines of activity such as dairying and market gardens attest to the pressures that were being felt in the East.

If returns were higher in western farming areas, one may ask why eastern farmers did not move en masse to the West. Some eastern farmers of course did move, but others did not. For those who stayed behind, there were "nonpecuniary advantages" to compensate for the dimmer economic outlook such as ties to parents, relatives, and friends in the community. This does not necessarily mean that there were differences in tastes between those who moved and those who stayed behind. Rather, the question of who moved probably depended primarily on birth order. Older sons may frequently have reached adulthood while their fathers still felt in the prime of life; hence, they went west while the family farm, together with responsibility for the parents in their old age, went to younger sons.[9]

Those remaining in the East might seek to raise their returns by diversifying their capital through purchases of western lands, investment in factory industry, and so on. There were farmers who did engage in these wider investment activities, particularly in regard to farm mortgages and transport investments. But one can imagine that, for many farmers,

[7] Danhof (1969, 113).

[8] Ibid., p. 121.

[9] One of the few studies providing evidence on farm succession practices is Tarver (1952, 266–71). See also the epigraph to this chapter.

there was considerable hesitation to strike out very far in these new directions because their knowledge and experience related primarily to local farming conditions. The personal wealth data in the Bateman–Foust sample indicate that, for the great majority of eastern farmers, their own farm was the overwhelming source of their wealth. In the most settled region in 1860, less than one farmer in four had total (real plus personal) property holdings worth more than 40 percent above the value of his farm. This proportion remains almost the same, rising only slightly as one moves westward to less settled regions. (Not surprisingly, the frontier area is something of an exception – two farmers out of five had property holdings worth more than 40 percent above the value of their farm.) Thus, the lower level of farm family fertility in the East, a phenomenon reflecting the behavior of the mass of the population, was shaped primarily by persons who depended on their own farms for their livelihood.

How widespread was the practice of providing a start in life for one's children? Greven's careful study of the transmission of property in colonial Andover indicates that the practice was extensive in the seventeenth and eighteenth centuries. Indeed, he makes the point that the lure of such a nest egg was an important means of parents' control over their children's behavior and fidelity. We have no studies comparable to Greven's for the nineteenth century – a research gap that badly needs to be filled – but the literature contains frequent testimony of farmers' concerns for establishing their children. A typical example is provided by a farmer in the 1850s who, in describing the situation in Connecticut at that time, refers to "many hard working men ... in middle life [who] find themselves in possession of good homesteads *prepared to educate and establish their children....*"[10] For the late nineteenth and early twentieth centuries, the principal study that I have been able to locate is W. J. Spillman's survey around 1920 of how 2,112 farmers in four Midwestern states had acquired their farms (Spillman 1919). Analysis of Spillman's data suggests a maximum estimate of 36 percent who may have acquired farms

[10] As quoted in Danhof (1969), *Change in Agriculture*, p. 111 (italics added). References to the concern for providing for one's children appear also in Bogue (1994) pp. 51, 185, 193, 266.

without the help of families or close relatives.[11] By inference, family assistance was still quite common even at this time.

Dov Friedlander (1969) has advanced the hypothesis that "industrialization" mitigates pressures for fertility reduction in farm areas. Following a line of inquiry opened up by Kingsley Davis (1963), Friedlander argues that out-migration opportunities due to industrialization serve, in effect, as an escape valve, alleviating pressures for fertility reduction that would arise if economic opportunities for children were limited to those in the immediate vicinity. But in the United States fertility declined first and most markedly in the New England farm areas despite the rural out-migration opportunities afforded both by industrialization there and by farming in newer areas. My theory makes clear the reason for this. A farmer felt obligated to give a child a proper start in life, whether the child was staying at home or making his fortune elsewhere. Thus, the fact that one's children might eventually migrate to urban areas or the frontier in no way relieved parents of the costs of providing for children. In consequence, fertility declined despite ample opportunities for out-migration.

SUMMARY AND DISCUSSION

The westward spread of farm settlement in the northern United States was characterized by repetitive economic and demographic changes. Of particular note is the pattern of farm population growth. Area after area went through a transition from initially high growth to zero or negative growth. Underlying this movement were repeated trends in two components of population change: a shift from in-migration to out-migration, and, starting at an early date in the settlement process, a

[11] This figure is the proportion for those other than Spillman's "FO" group obtaining their farms by purchase (excluding "purchase from close relatives," which Spillman takes to mean "easy terms"). The FO group refers to persons who went directly from unpaid family labor to farm ownership status. These persons typically would have needed family help to purchase a farm. Similarly, it is quite likely that many of those in his other groups who purchased farms had family help, which accounts for the description of the 36-percent figure in the text as a maximum estimate. Spillman reports that about one-third of his sample acquired farms by inheritance, but this refers only to the direct transmission of the family farm.

steady decline in fertility from a level that was initially quite high to one approaching replacement. This "adjustment" of population to the agricultural opportunities offered by an area, including the reduction in fertility, dates from a very early time in American history. It started in parts of New England in the eighteenth century and continued in areas to the west throughout the nineteenth century despite the abundant agricultural opportunities in newer areas. This voluntary adjustment of fertility and thereby population growth to the economic environment demands explanation.

Several possible causes of the fertility decline have been touched on briefly: the composition of the population by such factors as age and marital status, the burden of aged dependents, schooling and literacy, wives' off-farm working opportunities, mortality conditions, and the value of child labor. These were found to be of limited explanatory value or to fit the evidence not at all. The one factor from previous studies that stands up best is "land availability" or farm population density, that is, high family fertility going with high land availability and low population density, and conversely for low fertility. But a theory that provides a plausible explanation of the mechanisms by which land availability exerts its effect is lacking.

The explanation of the fertility decline suggested here centers on decreasing demand for children owing to farmers' concern for giving their children a "proper" start in life. It takes as given the practice of multigeniture and reasonable survival prospects of infants and children, both of which were true of the nineteenth-century United States. If one assumes that a farmer wishes to provide for each of his children as well as he himself was provided for, then the number of children he can "afford" will depend on how much he can multiply his capital during the course of his lifetime. As an area is initially settled, farmers anticipate high returns and a rapid increase of their capital, which means relatively little problem in giving their offspring a proper start in life. As an area ages, the prospective rate of return declines (in part because of the opening up of newer areas), and the outlook for continuing to increase one's capital at the same rate as at an earlier settlement stage diminishes correspondingly. Hence, as the number of his offspring grows, a farmer in an older area will become increasingly concerned about his ability to give his children a proper start in life and will feel pressure to prevent further additions. I theorize that it is this pressure, stemming from the diminished prospect of maintaining a high rate of increase of one's capital, that is the basic source of the farm family fertility decline.

This theory lends itself to a broader picture of the relationship between economic and demographic variables during settlement of a farm area. Economic factors would be expected to affect migration as well as fertility, and changes in demographic variables, in turn, might have feedback effects on economic conditions. The principal interactions between economic and demographic factors may be conceived as follows.

First, the reasoning about the dependence of fertility on the prospective "increase of capital" can be applied also to migration; that is, the prospect of high returns causes in-migration; low returns, out-migration. If, for simplicity, one assumes that low farm values imply high prospective returns, and conversely for high farm values, then both fertility and migration may be taken to vary inversely with the value of farm acreage. Suppose, further, that farm value per acre is taken to vary directly with farm population density as measured by the ratio of farm population to potentially cultivable land in a given area. Then, we can construct the following picture of economic and demographic interactions during settlement.

Let me start with an area in which a given amount of potentially cultivable land is being opened up for settlement. Both population density and farm value per acre are low. Cheap acreage induces in-migration and encourages high fertility among new settlers because of the good prospects for multiplication of one's capital. Given the relatively low death rate, high in-migration and high fertility generate an initially high rate of population growth. This, in turn, leads to a rapid rise in population density, driving up farm acreage values. The rise in acreage values, however, reacts adversely upon the rate of population growth, slowing it down, by lowering fertility and gradually transforming in-migration to out-migration. As the rate of population growth and increase in density slow down, the rise in farm values moderates, thereby slowing down the declines in fertility, migration, and population change. This goes on, back and forth, until total population, fertility, net migration, and farm acreage values stabilize at a level commensurate with the area's potential. Although this is a highly simplified account, it probably captures the principal mechanisms that have produced the closely linked patterns of economic and demographic change recurrent in state after state, as shown in Figure 10.1.[12]

This model explicitly brings out the manner in which rapid population growth in a farm area sets in motion reactions that eventually bring population growth to a halt. As the cultivable land fills up and population density rises, farm values increase and prospective returns fall. The consequences of this for population growth are twofold. First, the deteriorating rate of return discourages further in-migration and eventually leads to out-migration. Second, the dimming outlook for increasing one's capital at the same rate as in the early settlement stage creates growing concern among farmers about the possibility of providing a proper start in life for one's children and leads to the spread of family limitation. As a result, the rate of population growth declines. But as long as population growth is positive, upward pressure on farm values continues, though at a decreasing rate, and this growth in farm values eventually brings population growth to an end. Thus, rapid population growth triggers economic mechanisms that induce fertility decline and the eventual adjustment of population size to the economic potential of an area.

[12] Morton Owen Schapiro (1986) develops and tests this model rigorously.

11

America's Baby Boom and Bust, 1940–1980: Causes and Consequences

The period around 1960 marked a turning point in many aspects of American experience. A precipitous decline in fertility rates began. There was also a marked shift in female labor force participation characterized by a more rapid increase of young women's rates and a slowdown for older. On the social scene, there was an acceleration in divorce, a rise in suicide rates among the young, and an upturn in crime rates. In the political arena, there was growing alienation from the established system.

These developments contrast sharply with those during most of the previous two decades. After World War II there was a large and protracted baby boom. Labor force participation among older women rose at an unprecedented pace, whereas younger women's rates were flat. The historical uptrend in divorce slowed markedly, and suicide, crime, and political alienation were either constant or slightly declining.

I think these seemingly disparate developments were in part (and I stress in part) the result of a new relationship between population and the economy that emerged after 1940. This relationship centered on shifts in the size of the younger relative to the older working age population that produced pronounced reversals in the relative economic condition of the two groups. In this chapter, I take up first the factors responsible for the new pattern after 1940 and then the manner in which twists in age structure produced such startling shifts in socioeconomic

Reprinted with permission in revised form from "What Will 1984 Be Like? Socioeconomic Implications of the Recent Twists in Age Structure," *Demography* 15, 4 (November 1978): 397–432.

conditions.[1] My interest is not in year-to-year fluctuations but in the contrast between the longer-term movements in the two decades before and after 1960. I focus on this period because it has been the subject of my own research. This analysis has recently been extended to the period since 1980 in elegant fashion by Diane Macunovich (2002).

THE BREAK WITH PAST EXPERIENCE

Let me start with the assertion that the 1940s marked a new age in the relation between population and the economy. Table 11.1 contrasts the essential features of the pre– and post–World War II periods. The main point is that a reversal occurred in the roles of aggregate demand and labor supply. Before World War II and stretching back for a century or more, swings in labor supply and, thereby, population arose chiefly from immigration and occurred usually only in response to corresponding swings in aggregate demand (Abramovitz 1961, 1968; Easterlin 1968b; Kuznets 1958, 1961; Chapter 5 herein). After World War II, sizable swings in labor supply involving concurrent changes in the proportion of young to old in the working age population occurred as an echo of prior movements in the birth rate. Aggregate demand fluctuated fairly mildly compared with the past as a result of government management. Thus, after World War II changes in the supply of labor occurred largely independently of aggregate demand. Before World War II, swings in aggregate demand were the active factor, and labor supply was passive; subsequently, the opposite was the case.

What was responsible for this new era in the relation between longer-term economic and demographic swings? Three causes can be given.

First, severely restrictive immigration legislation of the 1920s meant a sharp curtailment in the foreign labor reserve that had traditionally supplied the demands of major economic booms. Thus, in the 1940s and 1950s, when labor force growth from native sources was at an all-time low, a massive influx of European immigrants to satisfy the labor demand of a major economic boom did not occur as in the past. In effect, the role that immigration had played in buffering the favorable impact of economic booms on the native population was eliminated by restrictive legislation.

[1] The analysis here is developed more fully in Easterlin (1987).

Table 11.1. Contrasting movements in aggregate demand and labor supply before and after World War II

	Before World War II	After World War II
Aggregate demand	Active role: Private investment booms initiate a major swing in aggregate demand independently of labor supply conditions.	Passive role: Relatively high and sustained growth in aggregate demand maintained by monetary-fiscal policy.
Labor supply	Passive role: Swings in labor supply occur because of immigration movements induced by aggregate demand swing.	Active role: Swings in labor supply and in proportion of young to old in the working age population occur independently of aggregate demand as a lagged effect of birth rate movements.

Second, the Employment Act of 1946 committed the federal government to maintaining a high and growing level of aggregate demand through monetary and fiscal policies. Also, the substantial rise in the government's share of GDP after World War II compared with its share before that time helped to stabilize aggregate demand. Between 1942 and 1974, the annual unemployment rate rose above 6 percent in only two years, and even then by less than 1 percentage point. Compared with any prior thirty-year period, this was an unprecedented stretch of relatively uninterrupted growth in labor demand.

Finally, and most important for the present purpose, the declining birth rate of the 1920s and 1930s and the rising birth rate of the 1940s and 1950s caused, with about a twenty-year lag, first a growing scarcity of younger workers and then a growing abundance. Between 1940 and 1960 there was a noticeable interruption in the pre-1940 growth of the population aged 15 to 29, echoing the low birth rates of the 1920s and 1930s. After 1960, growth resumed at a more rapid rate than in the pre-1940 period, reflecting the sharp upsurge in fertility of the 1940s and 1950s. This pronounced fluctuation in the growth of the younger age group was not matched by those in older ages. As a result, the proportion of younger to older working age population fluctuated sharply in the period after 1940. Through the late 1950s, younger persons were becoming relatively scarce; thereafter, there was a growing abundance of younger persons.

These shifts in age structure – in the proportion of young to old in the working age population – under conditions of high and sustained growth in aggregate demand and restricted immigration had major ramifications.

EFFECT OF CHANGING AGE STRUCTURE ON THE RELATIVE ECONOMIC POSITION OF YOUNG MALES

Consider first the effect of these age structure shifts on the relative economic condition of young males. To make the argument as clear as possible, I make some very simple assumptions.

The essence of the reasoning is outlined in Table 11.2. Disregarding females (to whom I will return shortly), suppose that the labor supply consists of only two types of labor, younger and older males, as in the upper panel. Younger males are a relatively inexperienced and low-skilled group that is fairly new in the labor market with rather tentative job commitments. This group, a "career-entry" group, is engaged in a considerable amount of job search with consequently high job turnover. Older males are an experienced, skilled group that occupies higher level career jobs and has relatively low job turnover. The degree of substitutability between these two groups is low. Both groups are fully in the labor force; that is, their labor force participation rates are close to 100 percent.

Now, assume that the growth in the economy's aggregate demand for labor comprises some normal division between younger and older workers. (One need not assume that the demand for each group grows equally but only that for each group the rate of growth in demand remains constant over time.) Suppose, now, that every two decades or so a substantial shift occurs in the relative supply of younger versus older workers, reflecting corresponding changes in the working age population. In one period, younger workers are relatively scarce; in the next, they are relatively abundant.

Given the steady growth in demand for both groups, these changes in the supply of labor will create imbalances in the labor market for younger and older workers. What will be the consequences of these imbalances? As shown in the upper panel of Table 11.2, a scarcity of younger workers will favorably affect their relative wages, unemployment

Table 11.2. Ceteris paribus effects of shifts in scarcity of younger adults relative to older ones

Assumption A: Working age population comprises only younger and older males

Independent variables
- Labor demand: growing at trend rates for both groups
- Labor supply: large shifts in younger versus older males due to corresponding shifts in the working age population

Adjustments in dependent variables	*If scarcity of young*		*If abundance of young*	
	younger males	older males	younger males	older males
Wages	+	−	−	+
Unemployment	−	+	+	−
Occupational mobility	+	−	−	+

Assumption B: Working age population comprises younger and older males and females

Independent variables
- Labor demand: growing at trend rates for all four groups
- Labor supply: large shifts in younger versus older persons due to corresponding shifts in the working age population

	If scarcity of young		*If abundance of young*	
	younger males	older males (same as for Assumption A)	younger males	older males
	younger females	older females	younger females	older females
Wages	(+)	(−)	(−)	(+)
Unemployment rates	(−)	(+)	(+)	(−)
Labor force participation rates	−	+	+	−
	younger males and females		younger males and females	
Marriage	+		−	
Fertility	+		−	

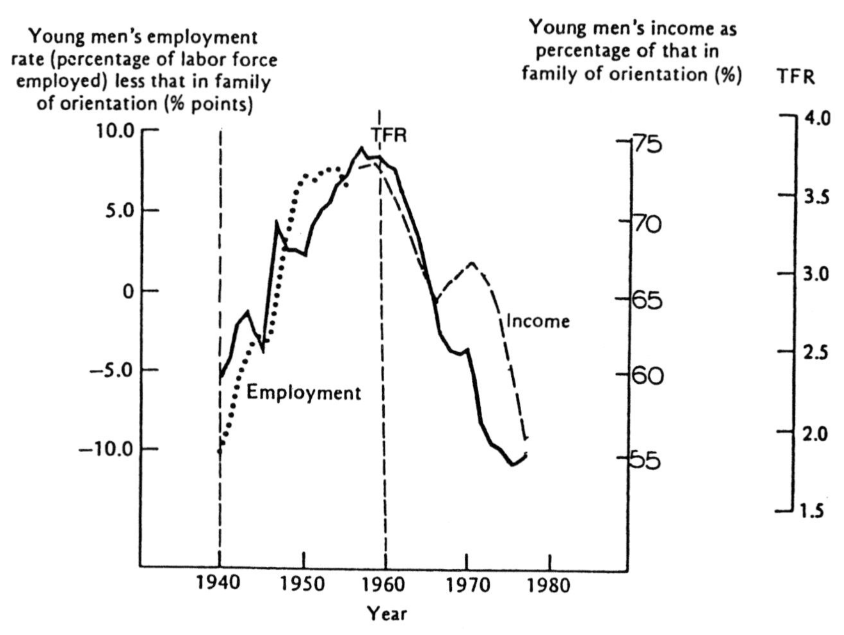

Figure 11.1. Total fertility rate (TFR), 1940–77; relative employment experience of young adult males, 1940–55; and relative income experience of young adult males, 1957–77.

rates, and upward mobility. The opposite would be true when there is an abundance of younger workers. There would also tend to be some substitution between older and younger workers, but such possibilities are fairly limited. (There might also be feedback effects from the labor supply side to aggregate demand, affecting both the size and composition of aggregate demand.) Thus, in periods when young males are scarce, their relative economic position would improve; when young males are abundant, their relative economic position would deteriorate.

A variety of evidence indicates that this was, in fact, the case. The dotted and broken lines of Figure 11.1 give some illustrative measures based on the limited data available of the circumstances of young males relative to that of older (that is, relative to their fathers in their "family of orientation"). Through the mid-1950s, the measure is for relative employment; thereafter, it is for relative income. These measures show that the relative economic position of young males after 1940 tended to vary directly with their relative scarcity (see also Easterlin 1968b, 114–18;

Easterlin 1973; Wachter 1976, 1977). Young males were relatively better off when in scarce supply and were relatively worse off when in abundance. (The TFR curve in Figure 11.1 is discussed below.)

EFFECT OF CHANGING AGE STRUCTURE ON FERTILITY AND FEMALE LABOR FORCE PARTICIPATION

Next, let us add to the analysis the effects of age structure on fertility and female labor force participation. The working age population is now taken to consist of four groups: younger and older males and younger and older females. Three additional assumptions are made.

First, there is a traditional division between male and female roles; that is, males are the primary "breadwinners" and have labor force participation rates close to 100 percent whereas females' attachment to the labor market is less permanent (participation rates are substantially below 100) and their concerns encompass not only the labor market but also childbearing, childrearing, and care of the home. This assumption implies no judgment about the desirability of these disparate sex roles; I view it simply as a reasonable assumption about reality at that time.

Second, there are three classes of jobs: (a) "career jobs," involving considerable experience and skill that are typically filled by older males because of their continuing labor force attachment and accumulated experience; (b) "career-entry jobs" that are typically held by younger males; and (c) "noncareer jobs," which are typically held by women. As a result, only limited substitution is possible between younger and older males and between women and men, but a high degree of substitution is possible between older and younger women.

Third, marriage and childbearing vary directly with the income of younger relative to older men. The reasoning is that the *relative* income of younger men may be taken as a rough index of the primary breadwinner's ability to support a young household's material aspirations. These aspirations are formed by the material environment that the spouses experienced as they grew up, which depends, in turn, largely on their parents' incomes. Hence, when young males' income is high relative to older males', it means that they may more easily support the material aspirations that they and their potential spouses formed in the income environment of their families of origin. Young people will then feel freer to marry and have children.

Now, let us consider the effect of imbalances in the labor market arising from sizable shifts in the age distribution of the working age population (Table 11.2, lower panel). As before, it is assumed that the growth of labor demand for all labor force groups (this time four) is at constant, though not identical, rates. One might also suppose there is a normal trend increment in labor force participation rates of younger and older females. Suppose, now, that there is a scarcity of younger workers as a result of a corresponding change in the working age population. In the labor market for younger and older males, the adjustments would be the same as those in the upper panel of Table 11.2; that is, younger males would experience relatively favorable changes in wages, unemployment rates, and upward mobility. Now, however, one must consider additionally the implications of the improved relative income of young males for the situation of females. First, it would be easier for young men and women to marry and start families. This would, in turn, dampen and perhaps eliminate the normal increment in labor force participation of young females as the proportion of single young women declined and those married and with young children rose. The scarcity of younger women would tend to have favorable effects on their relative wages and unemployment rates, but, because there is a high degree of substitution between older and younger women, these effects would be relatively moderate. This is the reason for the parentheses in the lines for these variables in the bottom panel of Table 11.2. The more important effect would be the replacement of younger by older females in supplying labor market needs. This means that a less-than-normal increment in participation rates for younger females would be compensated by a more-than-normal increase in the rates for older females.[2] The entry of older women into the labor market might be further stimulated by the situation of older males, whose relative income situation, as shown in Table 11.2, is unfavorable. If we compare in simple price-quantity terms the labor market adjustments of males and females, for males the

[2] Studies noting a link between the differential changes in participation rates of younger and older women and the relative scarcity of young persons in the post–World War II period are Bancroft (1958), Oppenheimer (1970), United Nations (1962), and Wachter (1972).

scarcity of young persons induces an adjustment primarily in terms of relative income, and for females, primarily in terms of relative quantities via differential change in labor force participation rates.

The analysis also suggests that a birth cohort carries its fortunes, good or bad, throughout its life cycle. As a scarce cohort ages, its relatively favorable supply conditions mean that it carries with it relatively favorable wage and employment conditions; conversely, an abundant cohort continues to suffer relatively unfavorable labor market conditions.

Admittedly, this is a highly simplified view of the makeup of the labor supply and the causal factors at work. One might, for example, distinguish within the group of younger males a "noncareer" group of disadvantaged workers, and within females a "career" group of college graduates. I believe, however, that this view, simple as it is, captures an important part of the forces shaping post–World War II experience. Consider the patterns of fertility and female labor force participation at that time. Starting around 1940, there was a marked break with previous experience. Between 1940 and 1960, the upward trend in participation rates of young women was interrupted, and their fertility rose markedly (Figure 11.2, left panel). Participation rates of older women, which had previously shown only mild increases, shot up dramatically (right panel). After 1960, there was a reversal in this age pattern of participation rates; rates for younger women rose sharply, whereas those for older women increased at a slower pace than before or not at all. At the same time, a sharp downturn in fertility occurred among younger women.

Referring back to the lower panel of Table 11.2, one finds that the analytical model just sketched generates behavior of just this type: an inverse association between the growth in labor force participation rates of younger versus older women, an inverse association between the growth in labor force participation rates of younger women and their fertility, and a positive association between the growth in labor force participation of older women and the fertility of younger women. But fertility is not causing participation rate change or vice versa. Rather, all of these developments flow from the imbalance in the labor markets of younger versus older workers owing to shifts in the relative supplies of the two groups.

I am not claiming that the model completely explains the magnitudes of change observed; it clearly neglects, for example, the determinants of the general upward trend in labor force participation rates of females as

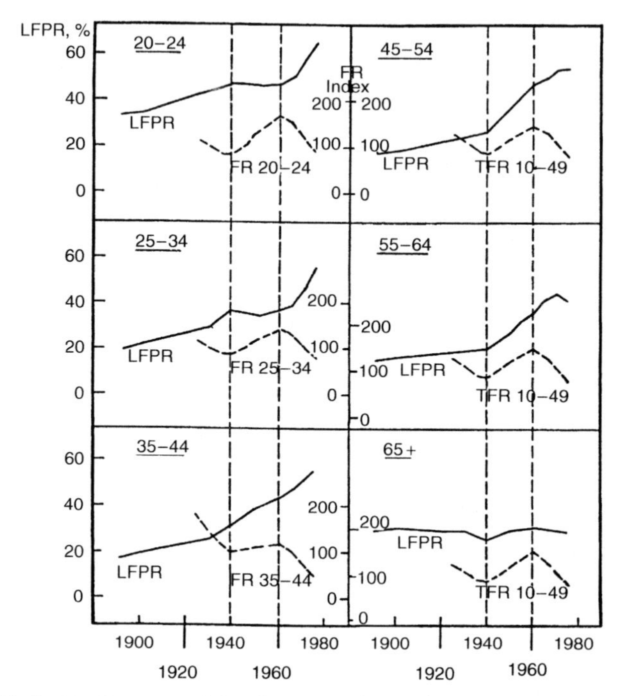

Figure 11.2. Labor force participation rates (LFPR) of females aged 20+ by age group, decennially, 1890–1950; quinquennially, 1950–75; and index (1940–45 = 100) of fertility rates for specified age groups, quinquennial averages, 1921–25 to 1971–75.

a whole. It does capture, however, the essential outlines of the longer-term swings in the four decades after 1940. For some variables, it may even do well on magnitudes, as is suggested by Figure 11.1, in which the total fertility rate shows a clear parallel with relative income and its proxy based on the unemployment rate.

EFFECT OF CHANGING AGE STRUCTURE ON SOCIAL VARIABLES

Let me turn briefly to the social and political effects of these post-1940 shifts in age structure. The theoretical underpinning for such effects derives from relative income or relative deprivation models of the type pioneered in economics by Duesenberry (1949) and Modigliani (1949) and in sociology and psychology by Durkheim (1951) and Stouffer et al. (1949). Favorable turns in a cohort's relative status moderate tendencies

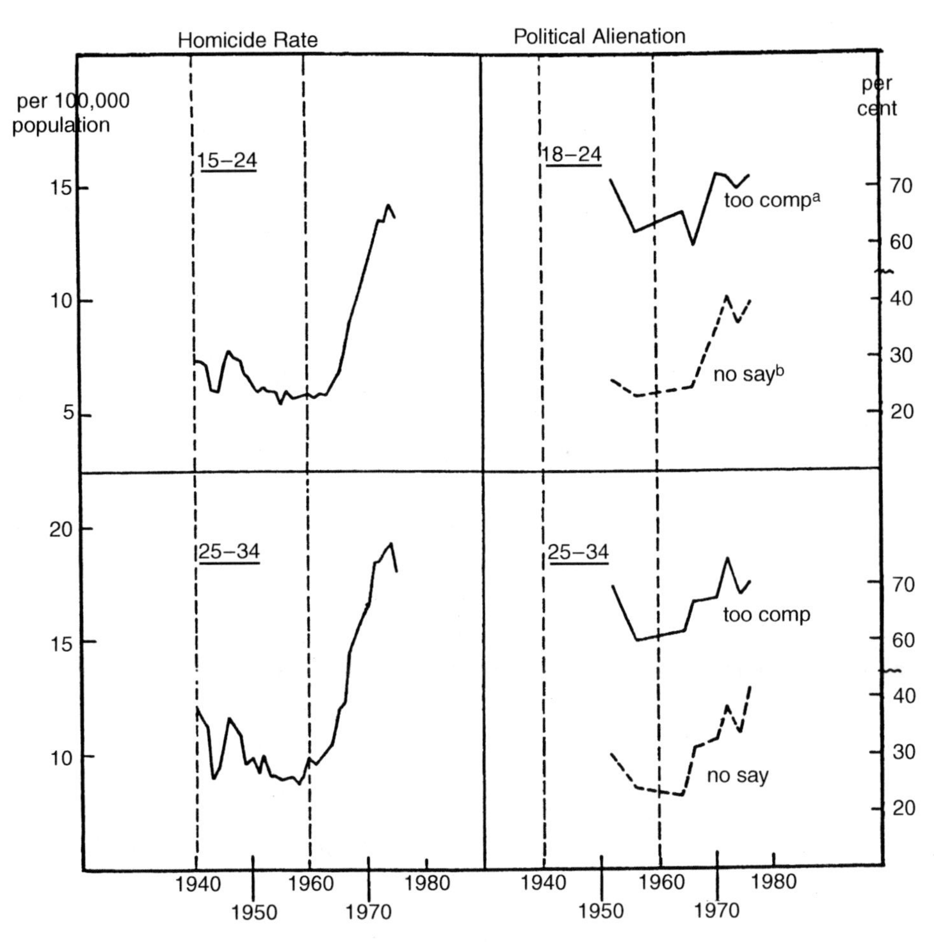

[a]too comp = % agreeing with the statement "Sometimes politics and government seem so complicated that a person like me can't really understand what's going on."
[b]no say = % agreeing with the statement "People like me don't have any say about what the government does."

Figure 11.3. Homicide and political alienation among the young, 1940–77.

toward divorce, suicide, crime, and alienation; adverse changes aggravate these conditions.

The empirical evidence is consistent with such effects. For the marriage cohorts that produced the baby boom, divorce was considerably below the rate expected on the basis of past trends; for subsequent marriage cohorts, as their fertility turned downward, divorce rose above normal trend rates (Preston and McDonald 1979). Suicide rates among the young similarly moved inversely to fertility (O'Connell 1975).

Such correlations of divorce and suicide with fertility do not imply causality. I have already argued that the inverse correlation between the growth in labor force participation of younger females and their fertility is due not to a cause–effect relation between the two but to a common response to the same cause: relative income. The Preston–McDonald and O'Connell studies suggest that the same is true for the correlations they observe. Both advance a relative income hypothesis (though in somewhat different form) and test for its explanatory power. The results are positive, for a deterioration in relative income of the young makes for more frequent divorce and a rise in suicide among young males; an improvement has the opposite effect.[3]

Crime rates and political alienation also change in a manner consistent with a relative status model. Figure 11.3 presents homicide rates, which are taken here as representative more generally of crime rates, and two measures of political alienation among the young. Although the series are short and not adjusted for trends, there is a common pattern – a suggestion of slight improvement to around 1960 (a downward movement of the curves) and a noticeable deterioration thereafter (an upward movement). I am not claiming that age structure and "relative income" are the whole story of these post-1940 changes in crime rates and political alienation. But these are variables that in theory should reflect relative status influences, and there is a hint in the evidence that this is the case.

ALTERNATIVE HYPOTHESES

What of competing interpretations of this period? The dramatic decline after 1960 in the fertility of young women and the rapid rise in their labor force participation excited much scholarly discussion. Among the reasons given for these developments, three are mentioned most frequently: exceptional employment opportunities for young women,

[3] Simon (1968, 1969, 1975) develops similar relative income models to explain fertility and suicide. See also Ahlburg (1983), Ahlburg and Schapiro (1984), and Schapiro and Ahlburg (1986).

new techniques for preventing conception, and less traditional views of women's roles arising from the women's liberation movement.

With regard to employment opportunities for young women, the argument is that these expanded rapidly after 1960, thereby encouraging substitution of work in the marketplace for childbearing and work at home (Butz and Ward 1977). The basic question, however, is not whether employment opportunities of young women expanded after 1960 but whether the labor market for young women was better after 1960, when young women were increasingly plentiful in the population, than before 1960, when they were increasingly scarce. I believe most labor market students would argue, as I would, that the post–World War II labor market for young women was, like that for young men, exceptionally good, and that young women opted for marriage and childbearing, not because of inadequate employment opportunities, but in the face of very good opportunities. The economy's occupational structure did not change in a way favoring women after 1960, as compared with before, and changes after the late 1940s in the unemployment rates of females aged 20 to 24 imply a stronger labor market before 1960 than after (see Easterlin 1987, Chap. 2).

Interpretations of the post-1960 shift of young females from home to workplace that stress the women's movement or the development and adoption of new fertility control measures are, at least, more consistent with the facts. However, the factors cited in these "explanations" may themselves be partly the effects of the twist in age structure operating via a relative income mechanism. With regard to fertility control, after 1960, with the growing abundance of young workers and the relative deterioration in their labor market position, families felt greater pressure to adopt available fertility control methods – old or new – to restrict births. The rapid spread of new measures of fertility control was thus, in part, induced by the pressures on young adults arising from their labor market conditions.

The women's movement is said to have caused the acceleration in the growth of young women's labor force participation rates after 1960 by shifting women's attitudes in a direction favorable to work and a career. But empirical investigation by Karen Mason and her collaborators (1976) suggests that a favorable turn in women's attitudes toward work in the marketplace was an effect, not a cause, of the rise in labor force participation. Because the rise in labor force participation was, in turn, partly ascribable to the relative income mechanism just described, changing age structure turns out to be one of the forces furthering the women's movement.

A more general objection to these two explanations, the one centering on fertility control and the other, on the women's movement, is that they deal only with experience after 1960. A basic tenet of my approach is that explanations of experience after 1960 should apply as well to the contrasting experience of the pre-1960 period. Neither of these views can offer any explanation of the pre-1960 baby boom. Indeed, so far as fertility control possibilities are concerned, the baby boom occurred despite what must have been a major advance in contraceptive knowledge among young persons as a result of information disseminated to the armed forces in World War II and the Korean War.

Moreover, the behavior that the fertility control and women's movement explanations seek to interpret, namely, childbearing and young women's labor force participation, is much narrower than the behavior analyzed here. The relative income interpretation I am suggesting seems to fit not only these developments but a much wider range of behavioral changes, including divorce, suicide, homicide, and political alienation. These other variables are ones that theory would lead one to expect would fit a relative deprivation-type model, and they do. That the present interpretation is consistent with a wider range of socioeconomic data, and that it fits pre-1960 as well as post-1960 experience, tends to strengthen one's confidence in it.

I am not claiming that age structure and relative income are the be-all and end-all in the explanation of these and other developments of the 1940–80 period. The women's movement may have a lasting effect on females' roles through institutionalizing the attitude changes that have occurred, and greater resort to fertility control has not necessarily been wholly induced. It is quite possible that these developments have exerted and will exert an independent effect on behavior. Other factors, such as the Vietnam War, have doubtlessly influenced the movements of the variables surveyed here. I am arguing only that the evidence is consistent with the view that age structure and relative income have been much more important and pervasive influences in socioeconomic change from 1940 to 1980 than has heretofore been recognized.

12

Preferences and Prices in Choice of Career: The Switch to Business

In the early 1970s I voted, along with most of my economics colleagues at the University of Pennsylvania, for moving the economics department from its historic location in the Wharton School of Finance and Commerce to the newly established liberal arts college. How poorly we read our economic future! Then, as now, Penn was on a "revenue center" budget system in which a school's financial fate was driven by undergraduate enrollment. Over the next decade, the department watched helplessly as shifting enrollments endowed the business school with large profits while liberal arts became the university's loss center. It is not surprising that Penn's finance department, along with comparable departments in many other business schools, came to be a magnet for many of the most promising newly minted economists.

This anecdote exemplifies how even the personal lives of economists remain at the whim of forces only dimly perceived. From 1972 to 1987, among American colleges and universities, business enrollments soared as a proportion of total undergraduate enrollment. Except for incidental discussion in Ehrenberg (1991), this remarkable development has been almost wholly neglected in the economics literature despite its manifest impact on the functioning of institutions of higher education and the economy's labor supply. This chapter assembles and evaluates some pertinent evidence on reasons for this growth in the context more

Reprinted with permission in revised form from "Preferences and Prices in Choice of Career: The Switch to Business, 1972–87," *Journal of Economic Behavior and Organization* 27, 1 (June 1995): 1–34. © 1995 by Elsevier Science. The data sources for Chapter 12 are given in Appendix A of this article.

generally of the literature and evidence on occupational choice and choice of major by undergraduates.

Reading the empirical literature on occupational choice, one comes away with the impression that relative rates of return, or "prices," are the dominant, if not the sole, determinant of choice of career (see the seminal work of Richard Freeman 1971, 1975, 1976 and articles cited therein; also Boskin 1974; Falaris 1984; Fogel and Mitchell 1973; Siow 1984; Zabalza 1979; and Zarkin 1985). In theory, a wide variety of factors are potentially at work (Freeman 1971, Chap. 1 provides a good overview); in practice, all but prices are assumed away. Typical statements are as follows: "Abstracting for the moment from any differential nonpecuniary costs and benefits among occupations ... " (Boskin 1974, 390, n. 3); "[n]on-pecuniary preferences are assumed to be equal as far as each occupation is concerned" (Zabalza 1979, 132); and "it is implicitly assumed that these factors (the nonpecuniary returns arising from the choice of a major and training costs in each major) are constant across majors or, alternatively, that the background factors control for these differences ... " (Berger 1988, 419). The trend in this literature is toward experimenting with more sophisticated measures of prices rather than investigating nonprice determinants.

The neglect of influences other than prices is less true of the more limited empirical literature on choice of undergraduate major. To be sure, there are studies that follow the tradition of the literature on occupational choice, on rates of return (Berger 1988; Cebula and Lopes 1982; Koch 1972 and ensuing discussion by Bell 1975; Ross 1975; and Koch 1975). But there are, in addition, studies that explicitly consider that factors such as the abilities and "interests" of individuals may also play a part in choice of major (Ehrenberg 1991; Fiorito and Dauffenbach 1982; Gambetta 1987; Gordon 1973, Chap. 1; Polachek 1978). Indeed, the emphasis in the psychological literature is almost wholly on such factors (see the survey in Furnham and Stacey 1991, Chap. 4). If, for example, "peripheral" studies in primary and secondary schools, such as the creative arts, are the victim of budget cuts, then fewer young people are likely to develop artistic interests and abilities and, on reaching college age, opt for artistic careers. Again, if society makes politicians the butt of contemptuous jokes and extols money making, the occupational preferences of the young are likely to be correspondingly affected. In a microlevel study similar to the present one in posing the issue of market versus nonmarket influences, Fiorito and Dauffenbach (1982, 100) conclude that "[t]he results for the interest and ability variables suggest that greater attention must be given to these factors in empirical studies of curriculum choice."

In terms of simple demand-supply analysis of the labor market, the traditional rate of return approach implicitly stresses the importance of a differential increase in demand that raises returns to a given occupation and thereby attracts more entrants via movement along a given labor supply curve. In contrast, changes in abilities or interests favoring a given occupation would result in greater numbers willing to work at a given wage. Given demand, the resulting rightward shift of the labor supply curve would not only increase the number of entrants to the occupation but cause a relative decline in returns to that occupation.

It is hard to understand why there should be a gulf between the literature on occupational choice and that on choice of undergraduate major. For most college students, choice of major is geared to a career objective, and most students, on entering college, already have a career in mind. Annual surveys going back to the 1960s repeatedly find that only about 10 percent of entering freshmen are undecided when asked about career plans (Dey, Astin, and Kom 1991). Most of those who plan business careers choose a business major; teaching, an education major; law, a history or political science major; architecture, a fine arts major; engineering, an engineering major; medicine, a biology major; and so on. For most students, choice of major and choice of career obviously reflect the same basic determinants. If abilities and interests as well as prices are relevant to choice of major, shouldn't they also be relevant to choice of career?

This chapter aims to make a start on this issue by exploring with time series data the role of preferences, as well as prices, in the switch to business careers. In the last few decades, serious analysis of preferences has started to gain a respected, if marginal, foothold in the economics literature, reflecting the impact of work by scholars such as Elster, Hirschman, and Sen. For the most part, however, this work has been conceptual, or, if empirical, confined to a single date (see, for example, the interesting new compilation of studies in Koford and Miller 1991). What has been lacking has been empirical implementation of concepts and, particularly, the demonstration of the empirical relevance of preferences to the explanation of change over time. This study seeks to contribute toward supplying this need, using for the empirical analysis of preferences survey data on life goals gathered in nationally representative surveys of about 200,000 college freshmen conducted annually since the mid-1960s (Dey et al. 1991). The conceptual roots of these data lie in psychology (see Astin 1977, 47). No doubt it would be preferable to use data that build more directly on economic theory. But such data do not exist, and there is a need to see what can be done with the data at hand, imperfect though they may be. A previous study in which I participated analyzed these reports on life goals in detail (Easterlin and Crimmins 1991). It is important to note that the trends in the freshmen survey data are very consistent with those in a completely independent representative national survey of high school seniors conducted since the mid-1970s, the so-called Monitoring the Future survey. The latter provides valuable additional information that is used here on the state of mind of young people and their views about the future.

The first section of this chapter documents the rise in business majors and demonstrates that freshmen major and career plans are closely replicated in graduation rates by field four years later. The second section looks at prices, not only for business, but for engineering and education graduates as well. The third section considers the role of changing preferences in the switch to business majors. The fourth section investigates the mechanisms generating preference change among the young, including whether such changes merely mirror changing economic conditions. The fifth deals with the decline in business enrollments after 1987.

The principal conclusion of the analysis is that, although prices have influenced the switch to business careers, an important force has also been shifting preferences, specifically, a change in life goals of the young. This shift in life goals is not due to greater economic insecurity among the young or an adverse turn in their expectations about job prospects engendered by the state of the economy. Rather, the evidence indicates that, during the study period, the attitudes of the young became more positive about their future. Instead, the shift in young people's life goals reflects with a lag changing attitudes of parents and other adults influential in the socialization experience of the young. The changing attitudes of parents and other adults are themselves largely determined by changing macroeconomic conditions. In this sense, the state of the economy does ultimately influence the young, but only with a lag and via their socialization experience.

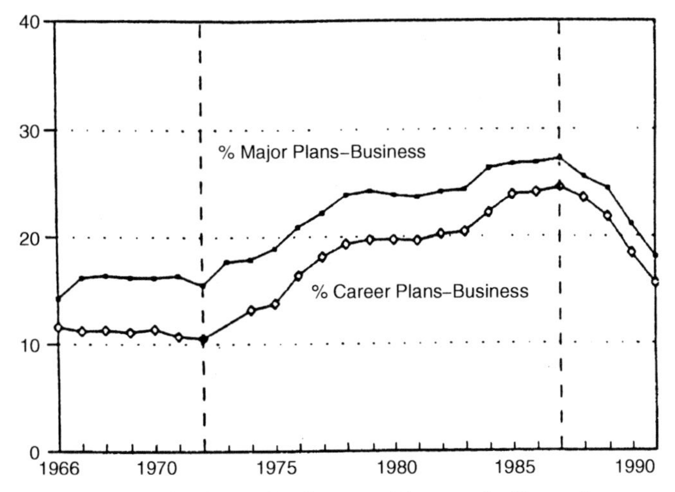

Figure 12.1. Percent of college freshmen with a probable major or career in business, 1966–91.

THE RISE OF BUSINESS ENROLLMENTS

Major and career plans of successive classes of college freshmen since 1966 tell a highly consistent story. After a period of stability in the late 1960s and early 1970s, the percentage of freshmen opting for a business career rose sharply from about 11 percent in 1972 to an all-time high of 25 percent in 1987 (Figure 12.1).[1] Between 1979 and 1983, there was a leveling off. After 1987, the proportion wishing to enter business declined abruptly, returning to near its mid-1970s level. Although the analysis here focuses chiefly on the upsurge in business enrollments, the decline will be looked at more closely in the section titled "The Recent Decline in Business Enrollments".

Trends in the statements of freshmen on probable business major and career gathered in annual surveys administered at the start of their freshman year predict with high accuracy the proportions graduating four years later. The rise after 1972 in the percentage planning to major in business is matched by a rise after 1976 of similar magnitude in the proportion of business graduates (Figure 12.2). By and large, switching

[1] Business majors include those in accounting, business administration, finance, marketing, management, secretarial studies, and other business. Business careers include accountant or actuary, management, business owner or proprietor, and sales representative or buyer. See Dey et al. (1991, 189–90).

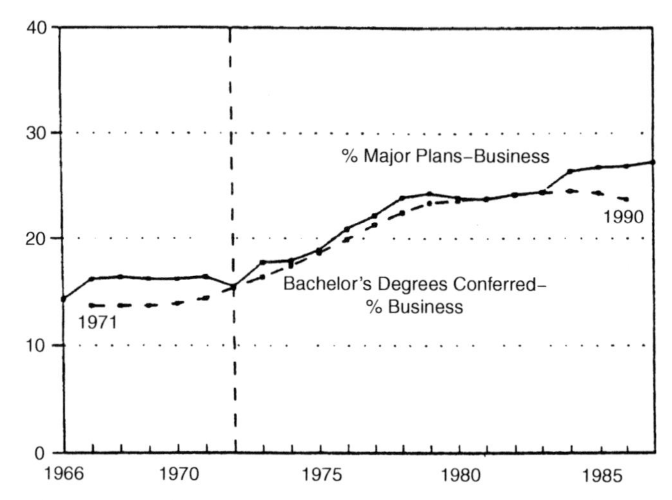

Figure 12.2. Percent of college freshmen with a probable major in business, 1966–87, and business share of all bachelor's degrees four years later.

into and out of business school during the college career appears largely to balance out, and plans and behavior, on average, go hand in hand. This result, the consistency of freshman survey data with entirely independent data on graduation, gives additional support to the validity of the survey data. After 1987, however, the share of business graduates falls increasingly short of business majors four years earlier. The reason for this is discussed in the Section titled "The Recent Decline in Business Enrollment."

PRICES AND CHOICE OF CAREER

Do changing relative returns of different occupations influence choice of career? In investigating this, it is helpful first to add engineering and teaching to the analysis, the two fields that along with business account for the predominant share of undergraduate professional school enrollment. These fields are also of interest because systematic economic analysis of career choices of college students refers almost entirely to professional jobs such as these, not to business occupations.

The proportion of freshmen planning an engineering career rose from 1974 to 1982 and declined to 1987; since then, it has leveled off (Figure 12.3). In engineering, as in business, movements in career plans closely foreshadow changes in bachelor's degree graduates four years later. Moreover, freshmen career plans for engineering appear to track

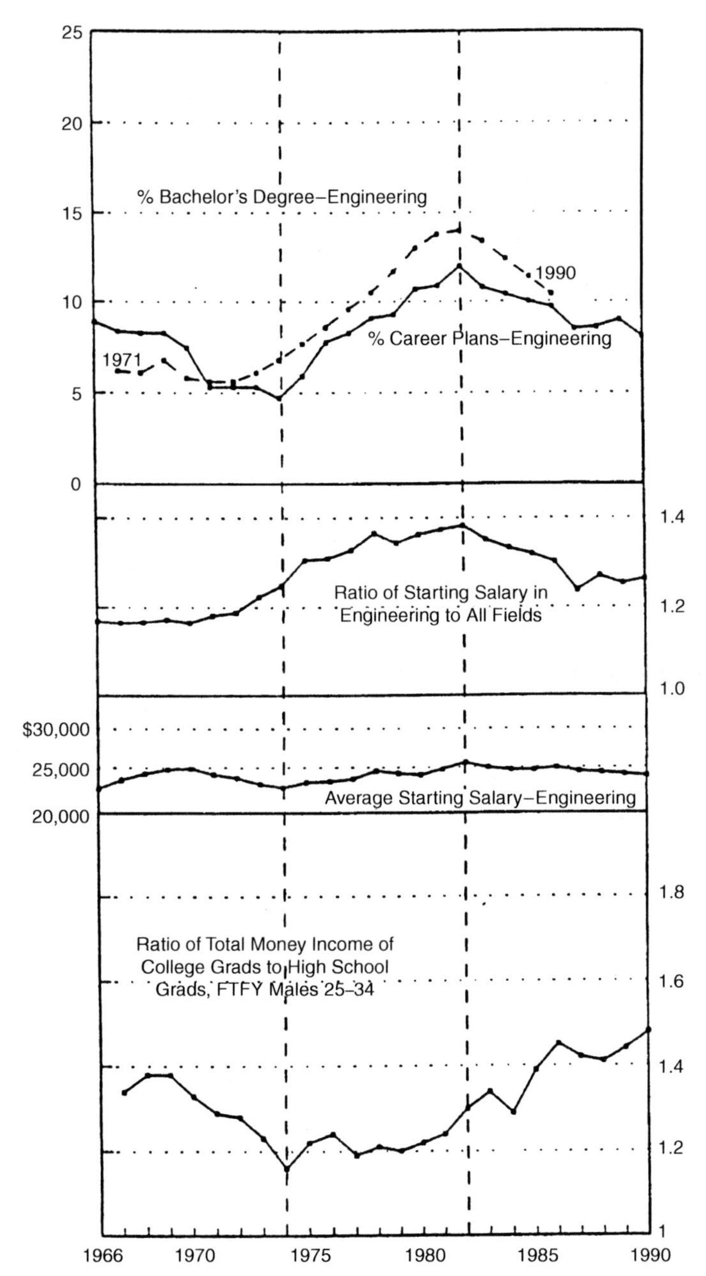

Figure 12.3. Percent of college freshmen with a probable career in engineering and indicators of returns to engineering or college education, 1966–90.

relative starting salaries in engineering closely.[2] When relative starting salaries swing upward, so too does the share of freshmen planning an engineering career. There is also fair similarity between engineering career plans and the absolute level of engineering salaries. However, the magnitude of change in relative starting salaries is greater than that in the absolute level, ranging from under 20 to almost 40 percent above the average for all fields. In contrast, absolute salaries vary over time only by about $2,000 on a base of nearly $25,000, or less than 10 percent. This suggests that relative salaries are the more plausible determinant of career plans, as theory would lead one to expect.

An alternative "returns" argument is that, if the income of college graduates falls relative to that of high school graduates, then, among those entering college, the proportion opting for majors with higher payoffs like engineering will rise (Freeman 1976).[3] If one judges from the earnings of male college graduates relative to high school graduates aged 25–34, this does not appear to be true for engineers (Figure 12.3, bottom panel).

If teaching is considered, the percentage planning careers as elementary and secondary school teachers slides downward through 1982 and then rises through 1988, after which it levels off (Figure 12.4). Again, the movement in career plans anticipates that in proportions graduating. And once again the market response argument appears to hold: relative starting salaries of teachers move together with plans to enter the field. Relative earnings of college versus high school graduates – in this case, for females – again looks like a less promising explanatory variable (Figure 12.4, bottom panel).

In the light of results like these, those for business are disappointing. Starting salaries provide no evidence that the striking rise in plans for business careers is due to markedly better financial opportunities in business (Figure 12.5; see also Ehrenberg 1991, 849). From 1973 to 1987, although the proportion planning a business career more than doubled,

[2] Relative starting salaries are measured using the average for all fields as a base because the analysis seeks to explain the proportion of engineering majors or graduates to those in all fields.

[3] So far as modeling is concerned, Freeman's work focuses on total college enrollment, but the text includes substantial discussion of major and career choice as a response to the relative market prospects of college versus high school graduates (Freeman 1976, 39–42).

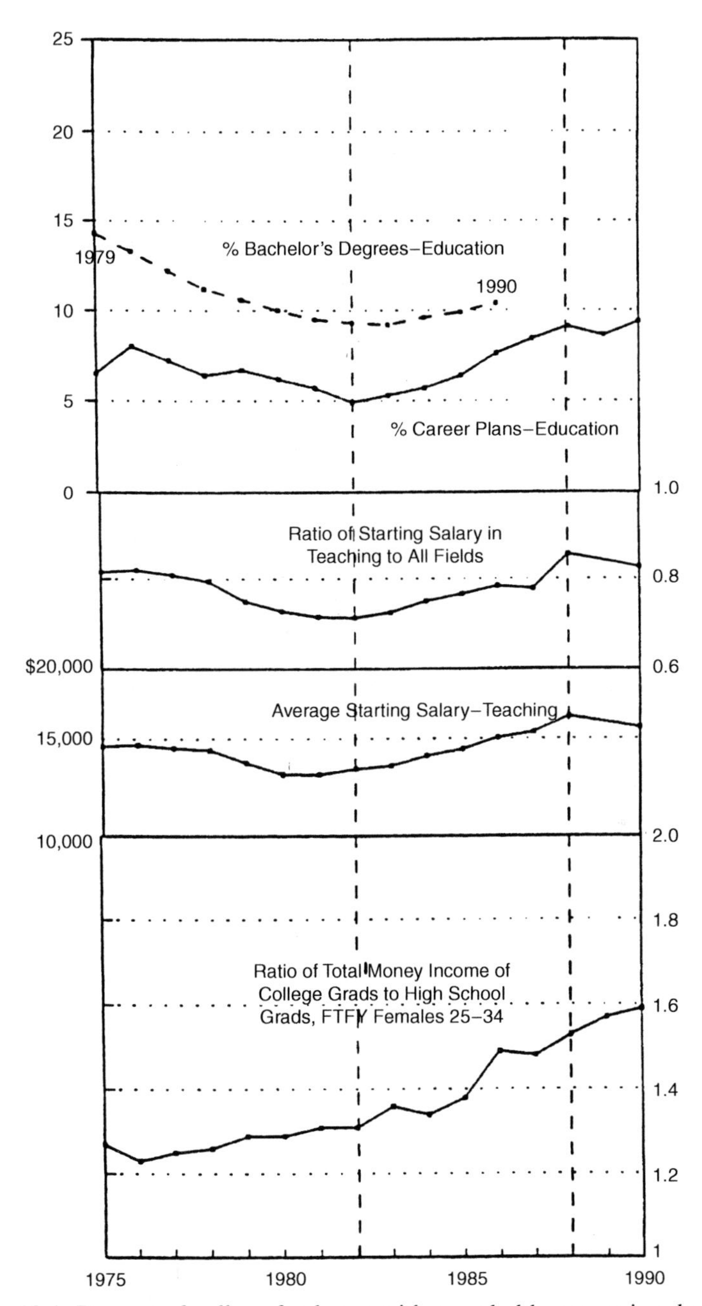

Figure 12.4. Percent of college freshmen with a probable career in education and indicators of returns to teaching or college education, 1975–90.

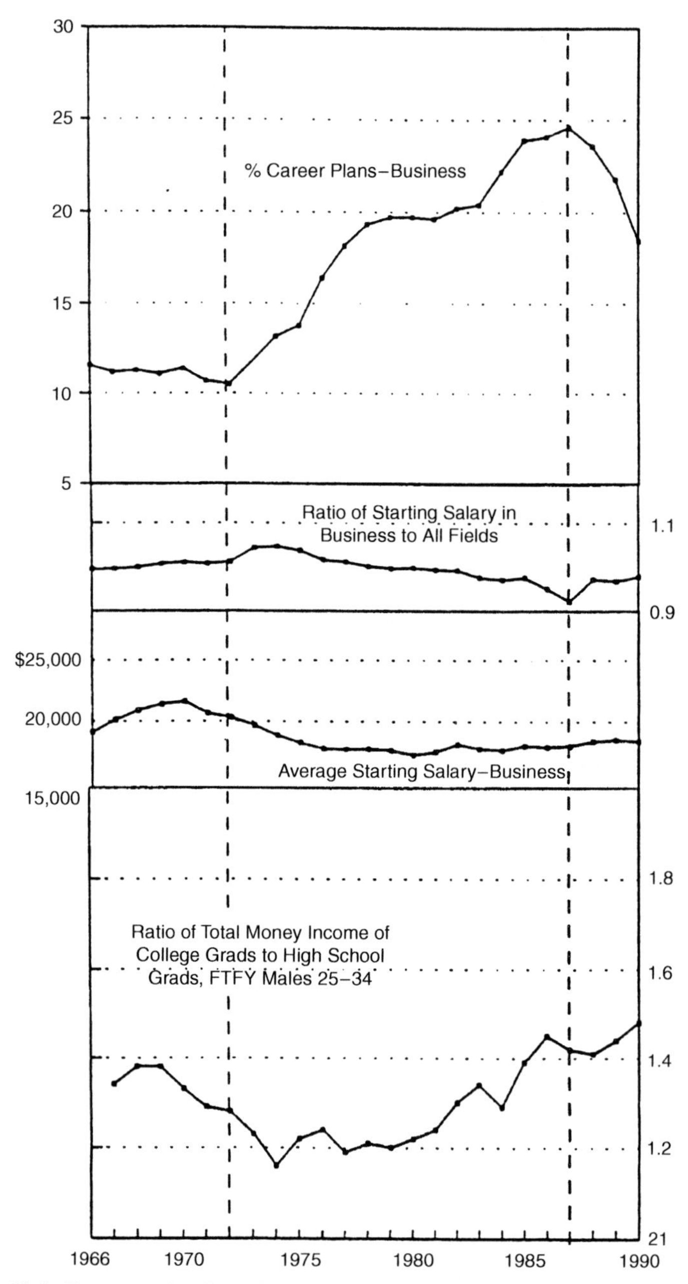

Figure 12.5. Percent of college freshmen with a probable career in business and indicators of returns to business or college education, 1966–90.

relative starting salaries in business edged downward. This movement in relative wages is consistent with a supply-side effect arising from a shift in preferences rather than a change in demand. Nor does the more general argument of the causal role of relative returns to college versus high school education seem to apply: relative returns are essentially unchanged from 1972 to 1982, whereas business enrollments rise rapidly (Figure 12.5, bottom panel).

Another possibility, that undergraduate business enrollments are due to the distant allure of high M.B.A. salaries, does not hold up either. Enrollments for M.B.A. degrees do soar like undergraduate business enrollments, although they are never as much as one-third as large. This increase occurs even though the ratio of M.B.A. to bachelor starting salaries is virtually constant throughout the period under study.[4]

Those entering business may be attracted by the prospect of exceptionally high executive salaries despite the low probability of realizing them. To explain changes in career plans by this argument, however, one would have to point to progressively improving prospects of exceptionally high returns from 1972 to 1987. This case might most plausibly be made for the period from 1982 to 1987, when the stock market boomed. But the major part of the switch to business occurred before 1982.[5]

Yet another possibility is that young people moving into business are responding to improved relative employment opportunities rather than incomes per se (Freeman 1976, 1980). But one indicator of relative employment opportunities, the business share of college jobs (those occupations in which college graduates account for the predominant share of jobs held), is virtually constant in the period after 1972 (Table 12.1). Perhaps instead of actual trends in business employment, young people's assessment of employment prospects is based on the expert projections of the Bureau of Labor Statistics (BLS) embodied in its widely distributed biennial *Occupational Outlook Handbook*. But the projections also fail to explain the shift to business. In projections published from 1971 through 1991, BLS forecasters have repeatedly foreseen an adverse outlook for business jobs relative to college jobs generally (Table 12.2).

4 M.B.A. salaries are given in Connell (1991).

5 Mohrman (1987) touches on another possible "price" factor, federal student aid policies, especially the shift from grants to loans, but says that the evidence that this influenced choice of major is ambiguous.

Table 12.1. Business jobs as share of all college jobs, 1968–92

Year	Percent business	Year	Percent business
1968	46.1	1981	43.6
1969	45.4	1982	43.2
1970	45.9	1983	40.2
1971	44.8	1984	40.8
1972	42.0	1985	42.2
1973	43.3	1986	41.9
1974	43.5	1987	42.1
1975	42.5	1988	42.7
1976	42.2	1989	43.5
1977	42.5	1990	42.8
1978	43.8	1991	43.1
1979	42.8	1992	42.6
1980	42.7		

Source: CPS public use tapes.

Table 12.2. Projected change in business jobs as share of all college jobs, 1969–91

(1)	(2) Projection period	(3)	(4) Percent business	(5)	(6)
Publication date of projection	Base year	Projection year	Base year	Projection year	Change (5)–(4) % points
1969	1960	1975	48.6	41.1	−7.5
1971	1970	1980	42.5	38.0	−4.5
1973	1972	1980	41.2	40.1	−1.1
1973	1972	1985	41.2	38.0	−3.2
1976	1974	1985	41.9	40.4	−1.5
1981	1978	1990	36.1	34.5	−1.6
1983	1982	1995	36.6	36.0	−0.6
1985[a]	1984	1995	46.9	46.9	0
1987[a]	1986	2000	44.0	44.2	0.2
1989[a]	1988	2000	45.1	44.8	−0.3
1991[a]	1990	2005	44.2	43.2	−1.0

[a] New occupational classification.

Source: Bureau of Labor Statistics, Bulletin 1606, 1737; Monthly Labor Review, Dec. 1973, Nov. 1976, Aug. 1981, Aug. 1983, Nov. 1985, Sept. 1987, Nov. 1989, Nov. 1991.

The analysis here uses starting salary and employment data to gauge market prospects much like those in Richard Freeman's original work (1971, 1976). These are the simplest and most readily available data, those to which college freshmen are most likely to be privy through sources such as the *Occupational Outlook Handbook*, the publications of the College Placement Council, and their career guidance offices, which carry such publications. Economic theory suggests that life cycle income would be a better measure of the financial value of a career than starting salary. Certainly, differentials by career in life cycle income may not be the same as those in starting salaries. However, this does not preclude the possibility that changes in relative starting salaries may be taken by young people as signaling changes in the life cycle returns from different careers. As has been seen, the movements in relative starting salaries are, in fact, consistent with an economic interpretation that sees wages in engineering and teaching as dominated by differential demand changes. But starting salaries in business suggest a differential supply influence such as a favorable shift in preferences.

For economists reluctant to see an explanation for business in which rate of return is not the dominant player, the next step would no doubt be to seek a "better" measure of returns. One problem with this is that, unlike starting salaries, annual time series for measures such as life cycle income by career are not available.[6] If economists do not have such measures at hand, there is some doubt that young people do and that their choices are geared to such measures. For those willing to tolerate the possibility of a supply-side explanation for business, the issue becomes one of whether there is evidence supporting the inference of preference change. The next section shows that there is.

PREFERENCES AND CHOICE OF CAREER

The view that the switch to business is preference driven comes across most clearly in the writings of the scholars who have been conducting the freshmen surveys used here. Repeatedly they point to the rise of

[6] The biennial *Occupational Outlook Handbook*, especially recent issues, sometimes includes for an occupation median earnings information or earnings by various experience categories. But there was a hiatus in the coverage of managerial occupations, and hence in earnings relating thereto, from the issue of 1972–3 to that of 1980–1, the period when much of the growth in business enrollments occurred.

business majors as being associated with a marked increase in the proportion of undergraduates who, when asked about the importance to them personally of "being very well off financially" respond "essential" or "very important," the top two-out-of-four response categories (see, e.g., Astin 1985a,b). Since the early 1970s, among young people this particular life goal out of a list of eighteen has risen in importance much more than any other (Easterlin and Crimmins 1991).

Other things being equal, the rise in interest in money would be expected particularly to favor business because those with a strong interest in making money, compared with freshmen generally, disproportionately prefer business as career. Microlevel support for a positive association between the desire to make money and choice of a business major (and only this major) is provided by Polachek's multivariate study (Polachek 1978). In an analysis of choices among eight major fields, only business was significantly related to a money-making variable virtually identical to that used here. The reason interest in making money especially affects business is probably due to a matching of student abilities with the ability requirements of different fields. Among college students generally, those in business have typically ranked relatively low in ability. In 1974–5, for example, SAT scores of entering freshmen in business were below most fields except education (Astin 1985a, 121). To the growing number of students with modest abilities but a strong interest in making money, professional fields offering good incomes, such as engineering, medicine, and law, doubtless seem a difficult undertaking compared with business, which accounts for the strong differential preference for business among those for whom making money is high among their life goals.

When data on the importance of making money are put together with business career plans, one finds a marked increase in both series from the early 1970s to 1987 (Figure 12.6). This is consistent with the notion that changes in life goals of entering students were leading to a reassessment of the relative attractiveness of different fields in favor of business. As previously mentioned, the change in relative starting salaries in business – a mild downward movement (Figure 12.5) – is also consistent with the notion that the relative supply of entrants to the occupation was expanding rather than that demand was disproportionately increasing. After 1987, however, the life goal and career plans series diverge considerably.

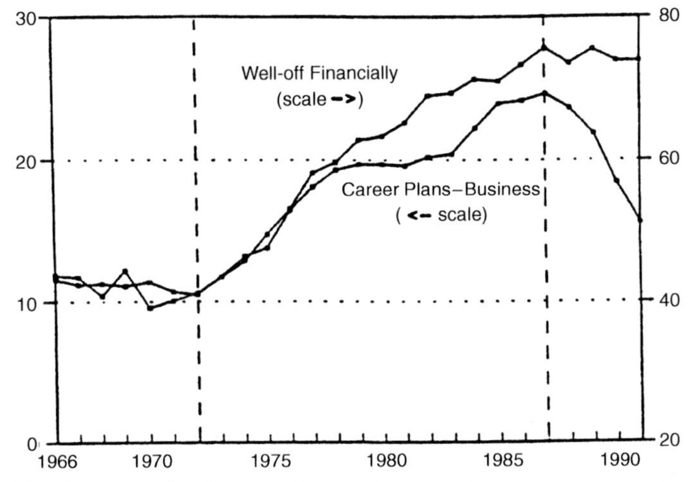

Figure 12.6. Percent of college freshmen planning a business career and percent that consider being well-off financially essential or important, 1966–91.

THE MECHANISMS OF PREFERENCE CHANGE

If changing life goals played a major role in the switch to business through 1987, the question naturally arises, What caused preferences to change? The dominant view in economics on the causes of preference change contrasts sharply with that in sociology. To many economists, preference data of the type used here merely mirror current market conditions. In contrast, sociologists and social psychologists see the preferences of young persons on reaching adulthood as molded in substantial part by their prior life cycle experience (Bachman, O'Malley, and Johnston 1978; Rosenberg 1979). In this section, an attempt is made to explore both views empirically.

On the economists' mirror-image side, there is a ready-to-hand example from the economics literature relating specifically to the series used here. Along with several other indicators, Freeman cites data for 1970 and 1974 on interest in money making identical to those used here as evidence of a "major change in the mood on campuses" (p. 43). He sees this change in mood as a response to the depressed college labor market and a consequent growth in economic insecurity among those going to college. Although no test is specifically presented, the prime mover is presumably declining returns of college relative to high school graduates. As has been seen, however, the timing of the change in college graduates' relative earnings does not correspond to that in the switch to business (Figure 12.5), nor does it fit with the timing of the rise in the importance of money making among college freshmen. (Compare the bottom panels of Figures 12.3 and 12.4 with Figure 12.6.)

Of even greater relevance is that the shift in mood in favor of money making was common to *all* youth, not just the college population. This is apparent from surveys of high school seniors that first appeared in the year Freeman's book was published and hence were not available to him. Since 1976, the increased importance of money among high school seniors who do not expect to go to college is virtually the same as that for those who do (Table 12.3, line 1). Indeed, the similarities between the noncollege and college-bound groups in attitudes relevant to labor market behavior are considerable. Job expectations at age 30 and preferred job characteristics both change similarly for those who do and do not plan to attend college (lines 2 and 3). It seems unlikely that such similar changes for the two groups would have anything to do with the relative returns from college compared with high school education.

Ehrenberg (1991, 853) speculates that the shift toward business is due to an increased proportion among college entrants of lower "quality" students whose interests are more pragmatic. The implication is that interest in money making, and hence in business careers, is greater among high school students who come from lower-income backgrounds. Yet, as Table 12.3 shows, interest in money making is very similar for those who plan to go to college and those who do not (those from lower-income backgrounds). This implies that a change in the composition of college students of the type suggested by Ehrenberg cannot account for the striking increase in business majors. Rather, it is the shift in life goals in favor of money making occurring irrespective of socioeconomic background that accounts for the rise.

A direct implication is that an acceptable explanation of the change in life goals must account for why young people generally, not just college students, became increasingly concerned with making money. This suggests as an alternative mirror-image hypothesis that the increased emphasis on money making reflects a worsening labor market for the young as a whole rather than differential returns to college compared with high school graduates. To investigate this, one has available not only the usual macrolevel labor market indicators but evidence directly from the Monitoring the Future surveys of high school students' work experience, longer-term job plans, and feelings of economic insecurity.

Table 12.3. Life goals, job preferences, and job expectations of high school seniors by plans to attend four-year college, 1976 and 1987 (percent)

	1976		1987		Change, 1976–87	
	College plans	No college plans	College plans	No college plans	College plans	No college plans
1. Life goals: having lots of money	43.1	45.0	62.6	64.6	19.5	19.4
2. Preferred job characteristics: a job that provides you with a chance to earn a good deal of money	40.8	51.3	55.0	64.3	14.2	13.0
3. Job expectations, age 30: business	10.6	6.4	23.0	14.2	12.4	7.8

The questions read as follows with the response categories in parentheses (the categories used above are italicized where appropriate).
(A) How important is each of the following to you in your life? (Not important, Somewhat important, *Quite important, Extremely important*).
(B) Different people may look for different things in their work. Below is a list of some of these things. Please read each one of these things. Then indicate how important this thing is for you (Not important, A little important, Pretty important, *Very important*).
(C) What kind of work do you think you will be doing when you are 30 years old? Response categories include 14 occupational categories and full-time homemaker or housewife. Business jobs are the sum of three response categories: owner of small business, sales representative, and manager or administrator.

Macrolevel data provide little support for the economic insecurity hypothesis. The rise in interest in making money does not occur more rapidly in recession than expansion periods (Easterlin and Crimmins 1991, 522). Also, neither the unemployment rate among 20–24-year-olds nor the rate of consumer inflation has a pattern similar to that for interest in money making (Easterlin and Crimmins 1991). Trends and fluctuations in unemployment rates for all workers and 16–19-year-olds in this period are virtually identical to those in the rate for 20–24-year-olds.

It is possible, however, that these macroeconomic series do not correctly capture the immediate economic circumstances influencing teenagers' attitudes. Perhaps more directly pertinent is the job situation of teenagers themselves, about three-fourths of whom do some work for pay during the school year. If there were a trend toward poorer labor market experience among teenagers and consequently greater concern about finding and keeping jobs, then increased emphasis on material success might result. However, there is little evidence of adverse trends in teenagers' labor market experience, for the proportions working, average weekly hours, and concerns about getting or losing high school jobs are about the same at the end of the period as at the beginning (Easterlin and Crimmins 1991, p. 523). There is a modest decline in real weekly earnings before 1981, but thereafter the trend is flat.

One might discount teenagers' job experience as a significant factor in shaping their longer-term outlook on the grounds that such jobs have little bearing on their adult occupations. Teenagers themselves clearly downplay the relevance of these jobs to their future. In 1986, when asked whether their high school work was "a good stepping stone toward the kind of work you want in the long run," 56 percent said "not at all," and another 16 percent only said "a little" (Bachman et al., various dates, 1987, 165).

More to the point, perhaps, are their responses to questions about the kind of work they expect to be doing when they are 30 years old, and, in particular, their certainty about actually getting this work. If deteriorating economic conditions bred uncertainty about being able to get jobs in the future, one might expect it to show up in responses to such queries. But, in fact, teenagers in 1986 expected better jobs than did those in 1976, and they felt more certain about getting such jobs and that their choice of job was a good one (Bachman et al. 1987). There

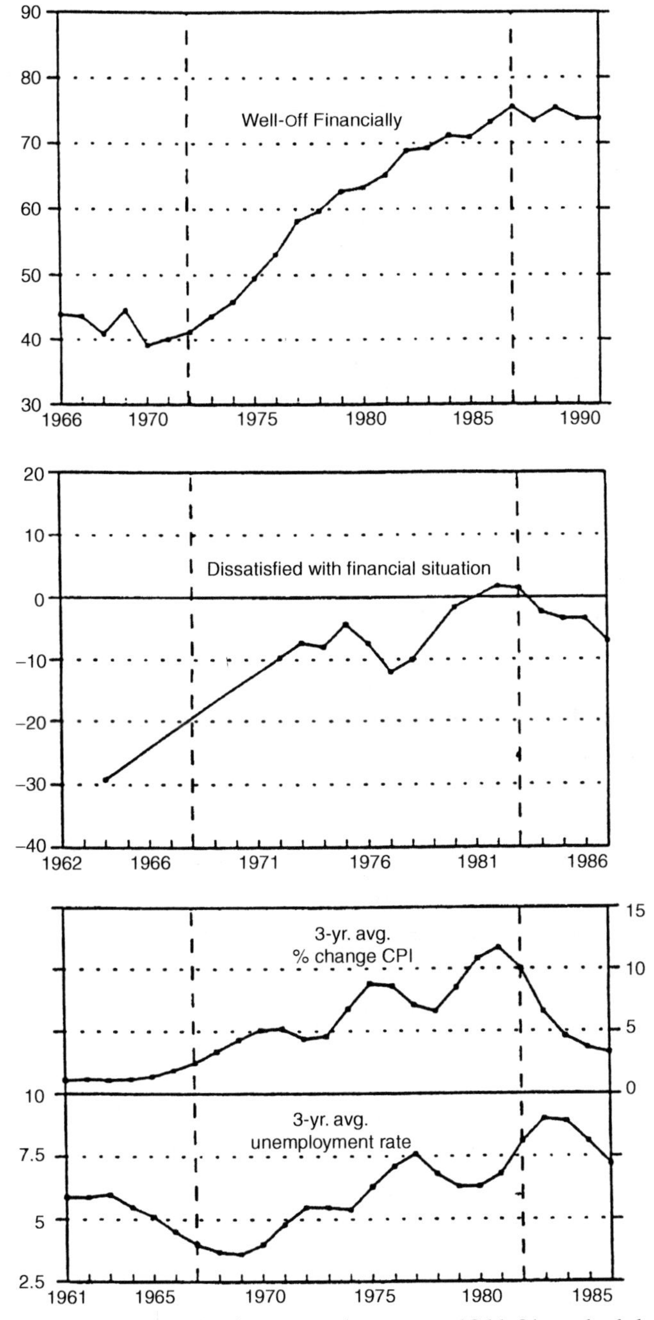

Figure 12.7. Freshmen aspirations to make money, 1966–91, and adults' dissatisfaction with their financial situation five years earlier and economic conditions five years earlier.

is little in the high school senior survey data to suggest that the rising importance of money making among high school seniors reflects greater worry about their own economic future. Nor is there evidence that they have become more worried about the nation's economic prospects. The proportion saying that they worry sometimes or often about the nation's economic problems was down from 68 percent in 1976 to 61 percent in 1986 (Bachman et al., various dates, 1980a, 169; 1987, 177).

One cannot rule out the possibility that data might yet be found to support the mirror-image hypothesis. But a fair number of series that might plausibly be expected to support the hypothesis fail to provide the expected evidence. It seems appropriate, therefore, to turn to the sociological approach to explain preference change.

To social scientists other than economists, the life goals of young people on reaching adulthood reflect in large part a long socialization process in their families of origin and other institutions that shape attitudes, intentionally or unintentionally, although current conditions may play a part too. Consistent with this, over three-fourths of high school seniors say that their ideas of what values are important in life are very or mostly similar to those of their parents (Bachman et al., 1988, 176). Hence, if young people come to adulthood more oriented toward making money, one would expect that this is because there has been greater emphasis on the importance of money in their homes, schools, and other institutions of socialization as they grew up – in short, that the adults with whom they came in contact were increasingly concerned about money.

Is there any evidence that attitudes of adults changed in a way consistent with the shift in values of the young? The answer, again based on survey evidence, is yes, but the shift in adult attitudes leads that in the life goals of the young. Starting in the latter part of the 1960s and continuing with only mild deviations into the early 1980s, the dissatisfaction of adults with their financial situation grew sharply; through the rest of the 1980s there was a mild reversal (Figure 12.7).[7] This suggests that,

[7] Several attitudinal series like that used here show a marked adverse turn starting in the 1960s (Converse et al. 1980, Ch. 6, 7; Levy 1985). Most of these series are oriented primarily toward tapping short-term changes relevant to business cycle behavior. The series in Figure 12.7 (SATFIN) shows less business cycle volatility and presumably better reflects longer-term swings in attitudes. The specific question asked is as follows: "We are interested in how people are getting along financially these days. So far as you and your family are concerned, would you say that you are pretty well satisfied with your present

from the late 1960s on, as parents became increasingly concerned with their own financial situation, they passed this concern on to their children, presumably via greater emphasis on the importance of making money. It seems plausible that school teachers and adults in other value-shaping institutions shared the concerns of parents with similar consequences for the life goals of the young. The shift in life goals of the young lags that in the attitudes of adults by about five years, which is consistent with the notion that the cause-effect mechanism is via a gradual socialization process (Figure 12.7; compare the dates in the top two panels).

As has been seen, attitudinal data for the young give no evidence of heightened economic insecurity, thus suggesting that older adults' influence on the young is via the preferences of the young as reflected in their life goals not via depressed income expectations of the young. But this leads, in turn, to the question of how to reconcile the increased financial concerns of older adults with the fact that young people's economic insecurity does not increase at the same time. The most likely answer is that young people felt more confident about their economic prospects because they responded to the shift in their life goals by reorienting themselves toward pursuits that would increase their earnings capacity. Evidence of this growth in confidence among the young appears in both college freshmen's ratings of their self-confidence and in high school seniors' responses to questions about how good they think they would be in each of several roles: worker, parent, and spouse (Astin et al. 1987, 84; Bachman et al., various dates, 1980, 104–5; Bachman et al. 1986, 107–8).

The view of the socialization process suggested here sees parents (and, more generally, adults) as influencing career choices of the young primarily through their effect on fairly broad life goals, rather than

financial situation, more or less satisfied, or not satisfied at all?" The measure used in Figure 12.7 is the excess of the percentage not satisfied over the percentage pretty well satisfied.

The most studied measure of consumer attitudes is probably the University of Michigan index of consumer sentiment (ICS). Like SATFIN, ICS shows an adverse trend from the mid-1960s to the early 1980s. Thereafter, however, ICS bounces back to near its 1960s level; in contrast, the upswing in SATFIN is much smaller. The index of consumer sentiment is designed particularly with a view to forecasting short-term changes in spending on consumer durables, and the underlying questions on changes in consumer financial status have a time horizon of only a year. In contrast the question used here assesses one's financial status without such a constraint.

specific career choices. An alternative socialization argument, based on a direct linkage of parents' to children's occupations, is that career choices in the children's cohort largely reflect those in the parental cohort. In this view, a shift toward business between 1972 and 1987 among young persons would be due to a corresponding shift toward business among their parents. However, such a shift did not occur among the parents. The parents of young people entering college around 1972 typically graduated in the late 1940s, many of them as beneficiaries of the World War II G. I. Bill. The parents of young people entering college around 1987 mostly graduated in the late 1950s and early 1960s. Between the late 1940s and early 1960s, the proportion of college bachelors' degrees accounted for by business trended slightly downward (Adkins 1975). This contrasts with the sharp uptrend in business degree graduates in the children's cohorts.

If the growing interest in money among the young reflects, with a lag, an increase in such concerns among older adults, how then is one to explain the shift in concerns of older adults? Here, the most obvious explanation is the deteriorating state of the economy. A link between adults' attitudes and the economy is suggested particularly by work on the most widely studied attitudinal series, the index of consumer sentiment. In this work the inflation and unemployment rates are invariably found to be important determinants of consumer sentiment (Throop 1992). In the present data there is, in fact, fair consistency between these macroeconomic magnitudes and adults' feelings of financial security (Figure 12.7, bottom two panels). In the latter part of the 1960s, the rate of inflation began to rise. In the 1970s and on into the early 1980s, unemployment problems added to inflation concerns, and "stagflation" reared its ugly head. Finally, from the early 1980s until the recession that started in 1989, unemployment and inflation rates moderated. This pattern is reasonably consistent with the longer-term movements in adults' assessments of their financial security. The similarity in timing between macroeconomic conditions and attitudes of adults suggests that the mirror-image hypothesis does apply to older adults.[8] But the attitudes of older adults shape those of youth only with a lag. Thus, although

[8] The middle and bottom panels of Figure 12.7 end around 1987. The worsening of macroeconomic conditions after 1989 was accompanied by a new upturn in older adults' dissatisfaction with their financial situation.

changing macroeconomic conditions appear, at bottom, to be the prime mover in young persons' increased interest in money making, it is not directly via the mirror-image mechanism but with a lag through changes in life goals growing out of their socialization experience.

THE RECENT DECLINE IN BUSINESS ENROLLMENTS

Since 1987, there has been a marked decline in business enrollments. It is doubtful that this can be attributed to a relative worsening of the market for business graduates, which shows a modest boom and bust pattern over the ensuing few years. Nor does it seem that a turnaround in the life goals of freshmen could account for the diminished entry into business. The importance to freshmen of making money did decline slightly after 1987, following with a lag a decline in adults' dissatisfaction with their financial circumstances (Figure 12.7). But the slight decline in emphasis on money making is nothing like the drop in the proportion planning to follow a business career.

Why, then, the dramatic turning away from business? One possible explanation is an exogenous shock to preferences caused by an upsurge in antibusiness sentiment. In commenting on the sharp drop in business enrollments, those responsible for the freshman surveys observe that "continuing revelations about scandals in Wall Street, defense contracting, and the savings and loan industry may be having a negative effect on the field of business" (Astin, Kom, and Berz 1990, 6).

Empirical evidence provides support for the "scandals hypothesis." In the period from 1967 to 1984, only one business scandal was important enough to make the annual chronology of U.S. history in the *World Almanac*, and that occurred in 1976. Between 1985 and 1991, five business scandals were listed, including an entry that refers to 1986 as "the most scandalous year in Wall Street history" (*World Almanac and Book of Facts* 1993, 525–9). If one assumes that the impact of scandals is cumulative, a time series like that below can be generated showing business scandals over the five years preceding the year specified:

1985	0	1989	4
1986	1	1990	5
1987	2	1991	5
1988	3	1992	4

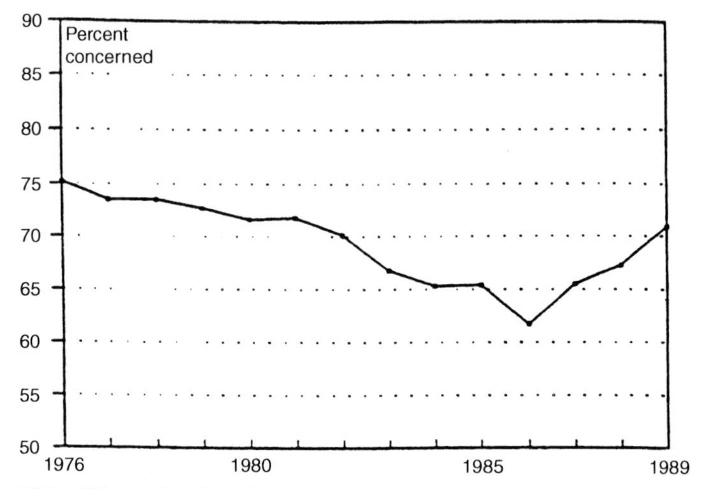

Figure 12.8. High school seniors' concern about emphasis on profit making, 1976–89.

The movement of this series is consistent with the hypothesis of a growing negative impact of scandals on attitudes toward business in the period when plans for majors or careers in business turned down sharply.

Two additional pieces of evidence supporting the idea of an upsurge in antibusiness sentiment among the young may be noted. The first relates to high school seniors' concerns about undue emphasis on profit making. These concerns diminished from the 1970s into the 1980s, as one might expect if making money had become an increasingly acceptable goal (Figure 12.8).[9] After 1986, however, these concerns rise abruptly, a year before the shift in attitudes toward money making. The timing of this reversal is consistent with the "scandal hypothesis."

Second, if the succession of scandals starting in the mid-1980s had an increasingly adverse effect on attitudes toward business, then one might expect such an effect to have occurred not only among high school seniors and college freshmen but among college undergraduates at more advanced levels as well. As a result, among those who started as business majors, some might have had second thoughts and switched out of

[9] The question asked is as follows: "How much do you agree or disagree with... the following statement... ? In the United States we put too much emphasis on making profits and not enough on human well-being" (Bachman et al. 1988, 95). The data in Figure 12.8 are the sum of the response categories "agree" and "mostly agree."

business. An indication of such switching is apparent in the growing disparity between the share of graduates receiving a bachelor's degree in business and the proportion of freshmen planning to major in business four years earlier. From 1976 through 1987, the business share of graduates was almost identical with the proportion of freshmen planning to major in business four years earlier (Figure 12.2). In 1988, however, there is a shortfall of 1.9 percentage points; in 1989, 2.5 percentage points; and in 1990, 3.2 percentage points. As a result, the rise in freshmen business majors from 1983 to 1986 fails to translate into an increasing share of business graduates from 1987 through 1990. Moreover, the more recent the graduating class, and thus the more time to switch plans after the scandals erupted, the greater the shortfall has been.

SUMMARY AND IMPLICATIONS

This analysis suggests that preferences as well as prices played a part in the rise and fall of business enrollments. In this respect, the analysis assimilates the empirical study of occupational choice to that on college major, where preference influences are more frequently recognized. The overall increase in business enrollments appears to have been driven in important part by a marked shift in life goals of the young – a notable upsurge in the importance of making money. Microlevel evidence supports this link between interest in money making and choice of a business major, which is a link probably due to the relatively modest ability requirements for business study compared with other relatively high-income fields such as engineering, law, and medicine. Relative returns to business drifted downward over time, which is a movement consistent with an expansion in relative supply due to preference change rather than with a differential growth in demand.

Contrary to what some have argued, there is little evidence that increased interest in money making among young people is due to a worsening of labor market conditions for college graduates or for the young generally. The increased interest in making money is not associated with greater insecurity among the young about their economic future or worsened job or income expectations. This is demonstrated by survey data probing feelings of insecurity about both one's personal future and the economy in general and also on the nature of one's work experience and long-term job plans. Indeed, at the same time that interest in money making rises, young people express greater confidence about themselves and their job outlook.

The reason for the increase in young people's interest in making money appears to be a growing concern about money among older adults, which was transmitted to the young through contacts at home, in school, and other institutions of socialization. Evidence of a shift in older adults' attitudes is provided by time series data on their satisfaction with their financial situation. Starting in the latter part of the 1960s and continuing into the early 1980s, the dissatisfaction of adults with their financial situation trended sharply upward. This increased concern about money among older adults leads the growth in importance of money making as a life goal among the young by about five years, which is consistent with the notion that the link from older adults to the young is via a gradual socialization process.

In contrast to the situation for young people, the rise in older adults' concerns about their financial situation does appear to reflect macroeconomic developments directly – first, the rising rate of inflation in the latter part of the 1960s and then, in the 1970s and early 1980s, rising unemployment that added to inflation concerns. Macroeconomic conditions thus turn out to be linked to changes in the behavior of the young, not directly and concurrently but indirectly and with a lag, by shaping their preferences in the course of their socialization experience.

Although relative starting salaries by field may not be the best measure of relative lifetime income, it is possible that changes in relative starting salaries may be viewed by young people as signaling changes in relative life cycle income. Indeed, changes in relative starting salaries in engineering and teaching move together with major and career plans in those fields in a manner consistent with this view, but relative starting salaries in business move in a manner consistent with a supply-side effect due to preference change.

After 1987, emphasis on money making among the young leveled off and declined slightly. Plans for a business career, however, turned down much more than would have been expected from the change in life goals. Other plausible explanations of the shift away from business, such as relative price movements or changing employment opportunities, also cannot account for the decline in business career plans. Rather, the decline in those planning a business career appears to be due to an exogenous shock to preferences caused by a rising distaste for business connected with the succession of widely publicized Wall Street scandals. Evidence in support of this hypothesis is provided by three pieces of evidence: time series data on business scandals, survey data indicating an adverse turn in young people's attitudes toward profit making, and a growing defection from business study by those already in college.

If correct, the present results suggest that empirical study of occupational choice needs to take account of nonmarket influences as well as market forces, which is a conclusion similar to that reached in several microlevel studies of choice of major. It seems likely that, among young people reaching adulthood, both preferences and judgments of abilities are affected by their experience while growing up and that surveys of the young may capture these developments empirically. The interplay between interests and abilities, on the one hand, and market forces, on the other, in shaping the pattern of occupational choice offers an attractive opportunity for further inquiry.

Such work might also give more empirical content to recent theoretical work in economics. The last few decades have seen the emergence of a small but increasingly rich economics literature on values and preferences (McPherson 1983). An analytical literature in economics has also developed, like that in sociology, linking family background with the opportunities of children in which there is explicit recognition that children absorb values through membership in a family culture (Becker 1991, 179). Both strands of economic inquiry, however, have been almost entirely theoretical and qualitative. Little attention has been paid to the empirical implementation of the concept of values or the mechanisms by which values are transmitted. To the extent empirical inquiry has been attempted, it has typically been confined to a single point in time and has assumed preferences to be stable over time. One suspects that, before preferences are accorded more equal treatment in economics, theory must be linked with data in a way that demonstrates the importance for behavior of changing preferences over time. This chapter is a start on such an effort.

Epilogue

The world today is in the midst of an unprecedented transformation in the human condition – in material living levels, health and life expectancy, literacy and education, the roles of women and men, and political governance. Viewing human development in this broad sense, I believe there is little support for the simplistic view so popular today in policy-making circles that free markets are the key to solving the world's problems. Free markets in the right institutional context may be conducive to economic growth. But the great advances in life expectancy and universal schooling have principally required governmental initiatives (see Chapters 4, 6, 7).

This is not to say that government can do no wrong. After World War II, demographers pushed to the fore the specter of a catastrophic "population explosion" in less developed countries, using this to promote governmental family planning programs. How much harm was done to how many people to "stop the population explosion at any cost" we will probably never know. But the record of governmental coercion in populous nations like India, Indonesia, and China is well established, if not well publicized (Easterlin 1985, 117–19; Gwatkin 1979; Hull and Hull 1997; Warwick 1982; Wolf 1986). If there had been more awareness of the importance of mortality reduction in creating pressures for limiting family size and the voluntary response of parents everywhere to such pressures (see Chapters 8, 9), a fair amount of human suffering might have been avoided.

Human development is not a simple matter of free markets, individual action, or governmental initiative. A balanced view, I suggest, is that human improvement is a multifaceted phenomenon and that each dimension involves its own set of causes and policies appropriate thereto. This view, I believe, is more consistent with historical experience and social science.

The transformation in the human condition has been driven, at bottom, by breakthroughs in knowledge applicable to problems of everyday life. The onset of rapid economic growth occurred with the emergence of a steam-powered, mechanized factory technology at the start of the nineteenth century. Rapid economic growth in the twentieth century was fueled by another industrial revolution based on a new electrical power–internal combustion engine technology. Rapid life expectancy improvement began in the middle and latter part of the nineteenth century with the sanitation movement and breakthroughs in immunization and was followed in the 1930s and 1940s by the discovery and development of antibiotics to cure infectious diseases. The sequence of these developments corresponds roughly to that in the evolution of natural science knowledge from the sixteenth to nineteenth centuries: mechanics, chemistry, electricity, and biology. Similarly, in the social sciences, as systematic knowledge of the economic system grew from the nineteenth century onward, institutions and policies were gradually devised to deal with social ills such as mass unemployment and rapid inflation.

Progress in the natural sciences continues and will continue to transform the conditions of life. We are today in the midst of a third computer-based industrial revolution and on the brink of a new biogenetic-based breakthrough in health and life expectancy (OECD 1998, 1999). The potential for human development advances at an unabated rate. But whether that potential will be realized depends ultimately on the state of social science – on our ability to deal intelligently with shifts in the international balance of political power engendered by economic growth, to cope with the threat of worldwide terrorism, and to deal with ethnic, religious, and other cultural divisions.

Is social science up to the task? I do not know, but I am troubled by the increasing division of labor in the social sciences. Recently, I've been looking at some research by psychologists. I have benefited considerably from this work but have been struck, too, by the fact that psychology, like every other social science discipline, has its own tunnel-vision – theoretical, methodological, and empirical – and goes its way oblivious to relevant work in other fields. The concerns voiced in this book about economics apply equally to psychology.

The world's leading problems today are not problems of psychology alone, of economics, or any other single social science discipline. Nor are they likely to be solved by assembling a team of disciplinary specialists, each of whom has trouble penetrating the protective walls erected by other disciplines. Rather, the solutions to today's problems require multidisciplinary training and research in economics *and* psychology, in economics *and* political science, and so on. But interdisciplinary programs at colleges and universities have not fared well. This has been true in my personal experience at the University of Pennsylvania with an interdisciplinary economic history program (between the economics and history departments) – now defunct – and an interdisciplinary demography program (between economics and sociology). It is true, too, of my current experience at the University of Southern California, where an interdisciplinary program combining economics, political science, and international relations is on the brink of extinction.

We are left, then, with this basic dilemma. When one looks at the world's problems, the trend in needs is toward multidisciplinary scholars. But the trend in supply is toward disciplinary specialists. Whether this worrisome gap can be bridged remains an open question.

Bibliography

Abel-Smith, Brian, 1960. *A History of the Nursing Profession*. London: Heinemann.

Abel-Smith, Brian, 1964. *The Hospitals, 1880–1948: A Study in Social Administration in England and Wales*. Cambridge, MA: Harvard University Press.

Abramovitz, M., 1959. "The Welfare Interpretation of Secular Trends in National Income and Product." In Moses Abramovitz eds., *The Allocation of Economic Resources: Essays in Honor of Bernard Francis Haley*. Stanford, CA: Stanford University Press.

Abramovitz, M., 1961. "The Nature and Significance of Kuznets Cycles." *Economic Development and Cultural Change*, vol. IX(3) 225–248.

Abramovitz, M., 1964. *Evidences of Long Swings in Aggregate Construction since the Civil War*. New York: National Bureau of Economic Research.

Abramovitz, M., 1968. "The Passing of the Kuznets Cycle." *Economica* 35, 349–367.

Abramovitz, M., 1989. *Thinking about Growth: And Other Essays on Economic Growth and Welfare*. New York: Cambridge University Press.

Ackerknecht, Erwin H., 1968. *A Short History of Medicine*. New York: The Ronald Press Company, revised printing, 1955.

Adkins, Douglas L., 1975. *The Great American Degree Machine*. Berkeley, CA: Carnegie Commission on Higher Education.

Ahlburg, Dennis A., 1983. "Good Times, Bad Times: A Study of the Future Path of U.S. Fertility." *Social Biology* 30:1, 17–23.

Ahlburg, Dennis A. and Morton Owen Schapiro, 1984. "Socioeconomic Ramifications of Changing Cohort Size: An Analysis and Forecast of U.S. Postwar Suicide Rates by Age and Sex." *Demography* 21:1, 97–108.

Anderson, C. Arnold and Mary Jean Bowman, eds., 1965. *Education and Economic Development*. Chicago: Aldine.

Anderson, C. Arnold and Mary Jean Bowman, 1976. "Education and Economic Modernization in Historical Perspective." In Lawrence Stone, ed., *Schooling and Society*. Baltimore, 3–19.

Arriaga, Eduardo E. and Kingsley Davis, 1969. "The Pattern of Mortality Change in Latin America." *Demography* 6:3 (August), 223–242.

Arrow, Kenneth J., 1963. "Uncertainty and the Welfare Economics of Medical Care." *The American Economic Review* LIII:5 (December), 941–973.

Arrow, Kenneth J., 1969. "Classification Notes on the Production and Transmission of Technological Knowledge." *American Economic Review: Papers and Proceedings* 52 (May), 29–35.

Astin, Alexander W., 1977. *Four Critical Years*. San Francisco: Jossey–Bass.

Astin, Alexander W., 1985a. *Achieving Educational Excellence*. San Francisco: Jossey–Bass.

Astin, Alexander W., 1985b. "The Changing American College Student." In Elizabeth H. Locke, ed., *Prospectus for Change: American Private Higher Education*. Charlotte, NC: Duke Endowment, 27–46.

Astin, Alexander W., Kenneth C. Green, and William S. Korn, 1987. *The American Freshman: Twenty Year Trends, 1966–1985*. Los Angeles: University of California, Los Angeles, Higher Education Research Institute.

Astin, Alexander W., William S. Korn, and Ellyne R. Berz, 1990. *The American Freshman: National Norms for Fall 1990*. Los Angeles: University of California, Los Angeles, Higher Education Research Institute.

Azrael, Jeremy R., 1965. "Soviet Union." In James S. Coleman, ed., *Education and Political Development*. Princeton, NJ: Princeton University Press, 233–271.

Bachman, Jerald G., Lloyd D. Johnston, and Patrick M. O'Malley, 1980a, 1980b, 1981, 1984, 1985, 1987a, 1991. *Monitoring the Future: Questionnaire Responses from the Nation's High School Seniors* (volumes for even numbered years 1976 to 1988). Ann Arbor, MI: Survey Research Center, Institute for Social Research.

Bachman, Jerald G., Lloyd D. Johnston, and Patrick M. O'Malley, 1987b. *Monitoring the Future: Questionnaire Responses from the Nation's High School Seniors*. Ann Arbor, MI: Survey Research Center, Institute for Social Research.

Bachman, Jerald G., Lloyd D. Johnston, and Patrick M. O'Malley, 1988. *Monitoring the Future: Questionnaire Responses from the Nation's High School Seniors*. Ann Arbor, MI: University of Michigan, Institute for Social Research.

Bachman, Jerald G., Patrick O'Malley, and Jerome Johnston, 1978. *Adolescence to Adulthood – Change and Stability in the Lives of Young Men*, Ann Arbor, MI: Institute for Social Research.

Baldry, Peter, 1976. *The Battle against Bacteria*, Cambridge: Cambridge University Press.

Balfour, M. C., R. F. Evans, F. W. Notestein, and I. B. Taeuber, 1950. *Public Health and Demography in the Far East*. New York: Rockefeller Foundation.

Bancroft, Gertrude, 1958. *The American Labor Force*. New York: John Wiley and Sons.

Banks, J. A., 1954. *Prosperity and Parenthood*. London: Routledge.

Banks, Arthur S., 1971. *Cross-Polity Time Series Data*. Cambridge, MA: The MIT Press.

Banks, Arthur S., 1992, updated 1995. *Cross-National Time Series Data Archive*. Binghamton, NY: Center for Social Analysis.

Barclay, George W., 1954. *Colonial Development and Population in Taiwan*. Princeton, NJ: Princeton University Press.

Barr, Nicholas, 1992. "Economic Theory and the Welfare State: A Survey and Interpretation," *Journal of Economic Literature* XXX (June), 741–803.

Bash, Wendell H., 1955. "Differential Fertility in Madison County, New York." *The Milbank Memorial Fund Quarterly* 33 (April), 161–182.

Bash, Wendell H., 1963. "Changing Birth Rates in Developing America: New York, 1840–1875." *The Milbank Memorial Fund Quarterly* 41 (April), 161–182.

Bateman, Fred and James D. Foust, 1974. "A Sample of Rural Households Selected from the 1860 Manuscript Censuses." *Agricultural History* 48 (January), 75–93

Becker, Gary S., 1960. "An Economic Analysis of Fertility." In Universities-National Bureau Committee for Economic Research, *Demographic and Economic Change in Developed Countries*. Princeton, NJ: Princeton University Press.

Becker, Gary S., 1965. "A Theory of the Allocation of Time." *Economic Journal* 71:299 (September), 493–517.

Becker, Gary S., 1991. *A Treatise on the Family*, Cambridge, MA: Harvard University Press.

Beeson, Paul B., 1980. "Changes in Medical Therapy during the Past Half Century." *Medicine* 59:2, 79–99.

Behm, Hugo and Arodys Robles Soto, 1991. "Costa Rica." In United Nations, *Child Mortality in Developing Countries*. New York: United Nations.

Behrman, Jere R. and Anil B. Deolalikar, 1988. "Health and Nutrition." In H. Chenery and T. N. Srinivasan, eds., *Handbook of Development Economics*, I. Amsterdam: Elsevier Science Publishers, 631–711.

Bell, Edward B., 1975. "Comment." *Industrial and Labor Relations Review* 28:2 (January), 282–284.

Bellah, Robert N., 1957. *Tokugawa Religion*. Glencoe, IL: Free Press.

Ben-David, Joseph, 1971. *The Scientist's Role in Society*. Chicago: University of Chicago Press.

Ben-Porath, Yoram, 1974. "Notes on the Micro-Economics of Fertility." *International Social Science Journal* 26:2, 302–314.

Ben-Porath, Yoram, 1975. "First Generation Effects on Second Generation Fertility." *Demography* 12 (August), 397–405.

Berger, Mark C., 1988. "Predicted Future Earnings and Choice of College Major." *Industrial and Labor Relations Review* 41, 418–429.

Bertrand, Marianne and Sandhil Mullainathan, 2001. "Do People Mean What They Say? Implications for Subjective Survey Data." *American Economic Review* 91:2 (May), 67–72.

Bhargava, Alok, ed., 1997. "Analysis of Data on Health." *Journal of Econometrics*, special issue 77:1, 1–296.

Bhuyia, Abbas, Kim Streatfield, and Paul Meyer, 1990. "Mother's Hygienic Awareness, Behavior, and Knowledge of Major Diseases in Matlab, Bangladesh." In John Caldwell, Sally Findley, Pat Caldwell, Gigi Santow, Wendy Cosford, Jennifer Braid, and Daphne Broers-Freeman, eds., *What We Know about the Health Transition: The Cultural, Social, and Behavioral Determinants of Health*, Proceedings of an International Workshop, Canberra, Australia May 1989. Canberra, Australia: Health Transition Centre, Australian National University, Vol. 1, 462–477.

Biraben, J. N., 1991. "Pasteur, Pasteurization, and Medicine." In R. Schofield, D. Reher, and A. Bideau, eds., *The Decline of Mortality in Europe*. Oxford: Clarendon Press.

Bobadilla, J.-L., P. Cowley, P. Musgrove, and H. Saxenian, 1994. "Design, Content and Financing of an Essential National Package of Health Services." *Bulletin of the World Health Organization* 72:4, 653–662.

Bobadilla, José Luis, Julio Frenk, Rafael Lozano, Tomas Frejka, and Claudio Stern, 1993. "The Epidemiologic Transition and Health Priorities." In Dean T. Jamison, W. Henry Mosley, Anthony R. Measham, and José Luis Bobadilla, eds., *Disease Control Priorities in Developing Countries*. Oxford: Oxford University Press, 51–63.

Boerma, J. Ties and George Stroh, 1993. "Using Survey Data to Assess Neonetal Tetanus Mortality Levels and Trends in Developing Countries." *Demography* 30:3 (August), 459–475.

Bogue, Allan G. 1994. *From Prairie to Cornbelt*, Ames, IA: Iowa State University Press 51, 185, 193, 266.

Boskin, Michael J., 1974. "A Conditional Logit Model of Occupational Choice." *Journal of Political Economy* 82:2, Pt. 1 (March/April), 389–398.

Böttcher, Helmuth, 1964. *Wonder Drugs: A History of Antibiotics*. Philadelphia: J. B. Lippincott Company.

Bourgeois-Pichat, Jean, 1967. "Social and Biological Determinants of Human Fertility in Nonindustrial Societies." *Proceedings of the American Philosophical Society* 3:3 (June), 160–163.

Bowles, Samuel and Herbert Gintis, 1976. *Schooling in Capitalist America*. New York: Basic Books.

Bowman, Mary Jean and C. Arnold Anderson, 1977. "Concerning the Role of Education in Development." *Economic Development and Cultural Change: Essays in Honor of Bert F. Hoselitz* 25, Supplement, 428–448.

Briggs, Asa, 1985. *The Collected Essays of Asa Briggs*, 2 vols. Urbana and Chicago: The University of Illinois Press.

Brown, John C., 1988. "Coping with Crisis? The Diffusion of Waterworks in Late Nineteenth-Century German Towns." *The Journal of Economic History* XLVIII:2 (June), 307–318.

Brumfitt, W. and J. M. T. Hamilton-Miller, 1988. "The Changing Face of Chemotherapy." *Postgraduate Medical Journal* 64, 552–558.

Bulatao, Rodolfo A., 1993. "Mortality by Cause, 1970 to 2015." In James N. Gribble and Samuel H. Preston, eds., *The Epidemiological Transition*. Washington, DC: National Academy Press.

Bulatao, Rodolfo A. and Ronald D. Lee, eds., 1983. *Determinants of Fertility in Developing Countries*, 2 volumes. New York: Academic Press.

Bumpass, Larry and Charles F. Westoff, 1970. "The 'Perfect Contraceptive' Population." *Science* 169:18 (September), 1177–1182.

Burns, Arthur F., 1934. Production Trends in the United States Since 1870. New York: National Bureau of Economic Research.

Burns, Arthur F., 1948. *The Cumulation of Economic Knowledge*. Annual Report 28. New York: National Bureau of Economic Research.

Burns, E. Bradford, 1970. *A History of Brazil*, New York: Columbia University Press.

Butz, William P. and M. P. Ward, 1977. *The Emergence of Countercyclical U.S. Fertility*. Santa Monica, CA: The Rand Corporation.

Cain, Louis P., 1977. "An Economic History of Urban Location and Sanitation." *Research in Economic History* 2, 337–389.

Cain, Louis P. and Elyce J. Rotella, 1990. *Urbanization, Sanitation, and Mortality in the Progressive Era, 1899–1929*. Chicago: Loyola University Press.

Cairncross, Sandy, 1989. "Water Supply and Sanitation: An Agenda for Research." *Journal of Tropical Medicine and Hygiene* 92, 301–314.

Caldwell, John C., 1986. "Routes to Low Mortality in Poor Countries." *Population and Development Review* 12:2 (June), 171–220.

Caldwell, John, Sally Findley, Pat Caldwell, Gigi Santow, Wendy Cosford, Jennifer Braid, and Daphne Broers-Freeman, 1988, eds., *What We Know about the Health Transition: The Cultural, Social, and Behavioural Determinants of Health*, 2 vols. Canberra, Australia: Australian National University Health Transition Centre.

Caldwell, John, Sally Findley, Pat Caldwell, Gigi Santow, Wendy Cosford, Jennifer Braid, and Daphne Broers-Freeman, eds., 1990. *What We Know about the Health Transition: The Cultural, Social, and Behavioral Determinants of Health*, 2 vols. Proceedings of an International Workshop, Canberra, Australia, May 1989. Canberra, Australia: Health Transition Centre, Australian National University.

Cameron, Rondo, 1975. "The Diffusion of Technology as a Problem in Economic History." *Economic Geography* 51 (July), 217–230.

Cantril, Hadley, 1965. *The Pattern of Human Concerns*. New Brunswick, NJ: Rutgers University Press.

Carnoy, Martin, 1974. *Education as Cultural Imperialism*. New York: D. McKay Co.

Carnoy, Martin, 1977. "Education and Economic Development: The First Generation." *Economic Development and Cultural Change: Essays in Honor of Bert F. Hoselitz* 25, Supplement, 428–448.

Caselli, Graziella, 1991. "Health Transition and Cause-Specific Mortality." In R. Schofield, D. Reher, and A. Bideau, eds., *The Decline of Mortality in Europe*. Oxford: Clarendon Press.

Castañeda, Tarsicio, 1985. "Determinantes del Descenso de la Mortalidad Infantil en Chile: 1975–1982." *Cuadernos de Economía* 22:66 (Agosto), 195–214.

Castañeda, Tarsicio, 1992. *Combating Poverty*. San Francisco: ICS Press.

Cebula, Richard J. and Jerry Lopes, 1982. "Determination of Student Choice of Undergraduate Major Field." *American Educational Research Journal* 19:2 (Summer), 303–312.

Chadwick, Edwin [1842] (1965). *The Sanitary Condition of the Labouring Population of Great Britain*, M. W. Flinn, ed. Edinburgh: Edinburgh University Press.

Chen, Lincoln C., Arthur Kleinman, and Norma C. Ware, eds., 1994. *Health and Social Change in International Perspective*. Cambridge, MA: Harvard University Press.

Chen, N., V. Paolo, and Z. Hania, 1998. "What Do We Know about Recent Trends in Urbanization?" In R. E. Bilsborrow, ed., *Migration, Urbanization, and Development: New Directions and Issues*. Norwell, MA: Kluwer Academic, 59–88.

Chetley, Andrew, 1990. *A Healthy Business? World Health and the Pharmaceutical Industry*. London: Zed Books Ltd.

Citizens' Association of New York, 1866. *Report of the Council of Hygiene and Public Health of the Citizens' Association of New York, Upon the Sanitary Condition of the City*, 2nd ed. New York: D. Appleton and Company.

Clark, Terry Nichols and Michael Rempel, eds., 1997. *Citizen Politics in Post-Industrial Societies*. Boulder, CO: Westview Press.

Cleland, J. G. and J. K. van Ginneken, 1988. "Maternal Education and Child Survival in Developing Countries: The Search for Pathways of Influence." *Social Science Medicine* 27, 1357–1368.

Coale, Ansley J., 1969. "The Decline of Fertility in Europe from the French Revolution to World War II." In S. J. Behrman, Leslie Corsa, Jr., and Ronald Freedman eds., *Fertility and Family Planning: A World View*. Ann Arbor: University of Michigan Press.

Coale, Ansley J. and James Trussell, 1974a. "A New Method of Estimating Standard Fertility Measures from Incomplete Data." *Population Index* 40: 2 (April), 182–210.

Coale, Ansley J. and T. James Trussell, 1974b. "Model Fertility Schedules: Variations in the Age Structure of Childbearing in Human Populations." Population Index 40:2 (April), 185–258.

Coale, Ansley J. and T. James Trussell, 1975. "A New Method of Estimating Standard Fertility Measures from Incomplete Data." *Population Index* 41, 182–210.

Coleman, James S., ed., 1965. *Education and Political Development*. Princeton, NJ: Princeton University Press.

Commission on Health Research for Development, 1990. *Health Research, Essential Link to Equity in Development*. Oxford: Oxford University Press.

Condran, Gretchen A. and Eileen M. Crimmins-Gardner, 1978. "Public Health Measures and Mortality in U.S. Cities in the Late Nineteenth Century." *Human Ecology* 6 (March), 27–54.

Condran, Gretchen A., Henry Williams, and Rose A. Cheney, 1984. "The Decline in Mortality in Philadelphia from 1870 to 1930: The Role of Municipal Services." *The Pennsylvania Magazine of History and Biography*, Medical

Philadelphia Issue, Philadelphia: Historical Society of Pennsylvania 108, 153–177.

Connell, Michael L., 1991. *Starting Salary Offers: An Historical Perspective*. Bethlehem, PA: College Placement Council.

Converse, Philip E., Jean D. Dotson, Wendy J. Hoag, and William H. McGee III, 1980. *American Social Attitudes Data Sourcebook 1947–1978*. Cambridge, MA: Harvard University Press.

Cox, W. Michael and Richard Alm, 1999. *Myths of Rich and Poor: Why We're Better Off Than We Think*. New York: Basic Books.

Cutright, Phillip, 1972. "The Teenage Sexual Revolution and the Myth of an Abstinent Past." *Family Planning Perspectives* 4:1 (January), 24–31.

Cutts, F. T., L. C. Rodrigues, S. Colombo, and S. Bennett, 1989. "Evaluation of Factors Influencing Vaccine Uptake in Mozambique." *International Journal of Epidemiology* 18:2, 427–433.

Danhof, Clarence H., 1969. *Change in Agriculture: The Northern United States, 1820–1870*. Cambridge: Cambridge University Press.

Darity, William, Jr., and Arthur H. Goldsmith, 1996. "Social Psychology, Unemployment and Macroeconomics." *Journal of Economic Perspectives* 10:1 (Winter), 121–140.

David, P. A., 1993. "Knowledge, Property, and the System Dynamics of Technological Change." In *Proceedings of the World Bank Annual Conference on Development Economics 1992*. Washington, DC: The World Bank.

Davis, James C., 1975. *A Venetian Family and Its Fortune 1500–1900*. Philadelphia: American Philosophical Society.

Davis, Kingsley, 1951. *The Population of India and Pakistan*. Princeton, NJ: Princeton University Press.

Davis, Kingsley, 1963. "Theory of Challenge and Response in Modern Demographic History." *Population Index* (October) vol 29(4) 345–366.

Davis, Kingsley and Judith Blake, 1956. "Social Structure and Fertility." *Economic Development and Cultural Change* 4:3 (April), 211–235.

Davis, Lance E., Richard A. Easterlin, and William N. Parker, eds., 1972. *American Economic Growth: An Economist's History of the United States*. New York: Harper-Row, chap. xi.

De Ferranti, David, 1985. *Paying for Health Services in Developing Countries: An Overview*. World Bank Staff Working Paper 721. Washington, DC: World Bank.

Dey, Eric L., Alexander W. Astin, and William S. Korn, 1991. *The American Freshmen: Twenty-Five Year Trends, 1966–1990*. Los Angeles: University of California, Los Angeles, Higher Education Research Institute.

Diamond, Jared, 1998. *Guns, Germs, and Steel*. New York: W.W. Norton and Company.

Diaz-Briquets, Sergio, 1981. "Determinants of Mortality Transition in Developing Countries before and after the Second World War: Some Evidence from Cuba." *Population Studies* 35:3 (November), 399–411.

Diaz-Briquets, Sergio, 1983. *The Health Revolution in Cuba*. Austin: University of Texas Press.

Dixon, Bernard, 1978. *Beyond the Magic Bullet*. New York: Harper & Row.

Doan, Bui-Dang-Ha, 1974. "World Trends in Medical Manpower, 1950–1970." In World Health Organization, *World Health Statistics Report* 27:2, 84–108.

Dominitz, Jeff and Charles F. Manski, 1999. "The Several Cultures of Research on Subjective Expectations." In James P. Smith and Robert J. Willis, eds., *Wealth, Work, and Health: Innovations in Measurement in the Social Sciences. Essays in Honor of F. Thomas Juster*. Ann Arbor, MI: The University of Michigan Press, 15–33.

Dow, C., 1998. "The Importance of Banks, the Quality of Credit, and the International Financial Order: Reflections on the Present Crisis in South East Asia." *Banco Nazionale del Lavoro Quarterly Review* LI:207 (December), 371–386.

Dreeben, Robert, 1968. *On What Is Learned in School*. Reading, MA: Addison Wesley.

Drèze, Jean and Amartya Sen, 1989. *Hunger and Public Action*, Oxford: Clarendon Press.

Drummond, J. C. and Anne Wilbraham, 1939. *The Englishman's Food*. London: Jonathan Cape.

Duesenberry, James S., 1949. *Income, Saving, and the Theory of Consumer Behavior*. Cambridge, MA.: Harvard University Press.

Duffy, John, 1992. *The Sanitarians*, Urbana and Chicago: University of Illinois Press.

Durand, John D., 1948. *The Labor Force in the United States, 1890–1960*. New York: Social Science Research Council.

Durand, John D., 1960. "Comment." In R. A. Easterlin, ed., *Population and Economic Change in Developing Countries*. University of Chicago Press, Chicago, 341–347.

Durkheim, Emile, 1951. *Suicide, A Study in Sociology*. New York: Free Press.

Dyson, Tim and Mike Murphy, 1985. "The Onset of Fertility Transition." *Population and Development Review* 11:3 (September), 399–440.

Easterlin, Richard A., 1968a. Economic Growth: An Overview. *International Encyclopedia of the Social Sciences* IV, New York: Macmillan, 395–408.

Easterlin, Richard A., 1968b. *Population, Labor Force, and Long Swings in Economic Growth: The American Experience*. New York: Columbia University Press.

Easterlin, Richard A., 1969. "Towards a Socio-Economic Theory of Fertility: A Survey of Recent Research on Economic Factors in American Fertility." In S. J. Behrman, Leslie Corsa, Jr., and Ronald Freedman eds., *Fertility and Family Planning: A World View*. Ann Arbor, MI: University of Michigan Press.

Easterlin, Richard A., 1973. "Relative Economic Status and the American Fertility Swing." In Eleanor Sheldon, ed., *Family Economic Behavior: Problems and Prospects*. Philadelphia: J. B. Lippincott Company.

Easterlin, Richard A., 1974. "Does Economic Growth Improve the Human Lot?" In Paul A. David and Melvin W. Reder, eds., *Nations and Households in Economic Growth: Essays in Honor of Moses Abramovitz*. New York: Academic Press, Inc.

Easterlin, Richard A., 1976. "Factors in the Decline of Farm Family Fertility in the United States: Some Preliminary Results." *Journal of American History* LXIII:3 (December), 600–614.

Easterlin, Richard A., 1977. "Population Issues in American Economic History: A Survey and Critique." In Robert E. Gallman, ed., *Recent Developments in the Study of Business and Economic History: Essays in Honor of Herman E. Krooss*. Greenwich, CT: Johnson Associates, 131–158.

Easterlin, Richard A., 1978. "The Economics and Sociology of Fertility: A Synthesis." In Charles Tilly, ed., *Historical Studies of Changing Fertility*. Princeton, NJ: Princeton University Press, 57–133.

Easterlin, Richard A., 1980, 1987. *Birth and Fortune: The Impact of Numbers on Personal Welfare*, 1st ed., New York: Basic Books; 2nd ed., Chicago: University of Chicago Press, 1987.

Easterlin, Richard A., 1983. "Modernization and Fertility: A Critical Essay." In R. A. Bulatao and R. D. Lee, eds., *Determinants of Fertility in Developing Countries*, 2. New York: Academic Press, 562–586.

Easterlin, Richard A., 1985. "Review of 'World Development Report 1984.'" *Population and Development Review* 11 (1 March): 113–119.

Easterlin, Richard A., 1986. "Economic Preconceptions and Demographic Research: A Comment." *Population and Development Review* 12:3 (September), 517–528.

Easterlin, Richard A., 1995. "Will Raising the Incomes of All Increase the Happiness of All?" *Journal of Economic Behavior and Organization* 27:1 (June), 35–48.

Easterlin, Richard A., 1996. *Growth Triumphant: The Twenty-First Century in Historical Perspective*. Ann Arbor, MI: University of Michigan Press.

Easterlin, Richard A., 1999a. "How Beneficent Is the Market? A Look at the Modern History of Mortality." *European Review of Economic History*, 3:3 (December), 257–294.

Easterlin, Richard A., 1999b. "Twentieth Century American Population Growth." In Stanley Engerman and R. E. Gallman, eds., *The Cambridge Economic History of the United States, Vol. III. The Twentieth Century*. New York: Cambridge University Press.

Easterlin, Richard A., 2000. "The Worldwide Standard of Living since 1800." *Journal of Economic Perspectives* 14:1 (Winter), 7–26.

Easterlin, Richard A., 2001. "Income and Happiness: Towards a Unified Theory." *The Economic Journal* 111:473 (July), 465–484.

Easterlin, Richard A., ed., 2002. *Happiness in Economics*. Northampton, MA: Edward Elgar Publishing, Inc.

Easterlin, Richard A. and Eileen M. Crimmins, 1985. *The Fertility Revolution: A Supply-Demand Analysis*. Chicago: University of Chicago Press.

Easterlin, Richard A. and Eileen M. Crimmins, 1991. "Private Materialism, Personal Self-Fulfillment, Family Life, and Public Interest: The Nature, Effects, and Causes of Recent Changes in the Values of American Youth." *Public Opinion Quarterly* 55, 499–533.

Easterlin, Richard A., Gretchen A. Condran, and George Alter, 1978. "Farms and Farm Families in Old and New Areas: The Northern States in 1860."

In Tamara Hareven and Maris Vinovskis, eds., *Family and Population in Nineteenth-Century America*. Princeton, NJ: Princeton University Press, 22–84.

Easterlin, Richard A., Robert A. Pollak, and Michael L. Wachter, 1980. "Toward a More General Economic Model of Fertility Determination: Endogenous Preferences and Natural Fertility." In Richard A. Easterlin, ed., *Population and Economic Change in Developing Countries*. Chicago: University of Chicago Press for NBER, 81–140.

Ehrenberg, Ronald G., 1991. "Decisions to Undertake and Complete Doctoral Study and Choices of Sector of Employment." In Charles T. Clotfelter, Ronald G. Ehrenberg, Malcolm Getz, and John J. Siegfried eds., *Economic Challenges in Higher Education*. Chicago: University of Chicago Press for National Bureau of Economic Research.

Ellis, David M., 1946. *Landlords and Farmers in the Hudson-Mohawk Region: 1790–1850*. Ithaca, NY: Cornell University Press.

Engerman, Stanley L., 1997. "The Standard of Living Debate in International Perspective: Measures and Indicators." In Richard H. Steckel and Roderick Floud, eds., *Health and Welfare During Industrialization*. Chicago: University of Chicago Press, 17–45.

Esrey, S. A., J. B. Potash, L. Roberts, and C. Shiff, 1991. "Effects of Improved Water Supply and Sanitation on Ascariasis, Diarrhoea, Dracunculiasis, Hookworm Infection, Schistosomiasis, and Trachoma." *Bulletin of the World Health Organization* 69:5, 609–621.

Etō, Shinkichi, 1980. "Asianism and the Duality of Japanese Colonialism, 1879–1945." In L. Blussé, H. L. Wesseling, and G. D. Winius, eds., *History and Underdevelopment*. Leiden, The Netherlands: Leiden Centre for the History of European Expansion.

Evans, Richard J., 1987. *Death in Hamburg*. Oxford: Clarendon Press.

Ewbank, D. C. and Preston, S. H., 1990. "Personal Health Behaviour and the Decline Infant and Child Mortality: The United States, 1900–1930. In John C. Caldwell, ed., *What We Know about Health Transition*. Canberra, Australia: University of Canberra Press, 116–147.

Falaris, Evangelos M., 1984. "A Model of Occupational Choice." *Research in Population Economics* 5, 289–307.

Farmayan, Hafez Farman 1968. "The Forces of Modernization in Nineteenth Century Iran: An Historical Survey." In William R. Polk and Richard L. Chambers, eds., *Beginnings of Modernization in the Middle East*. Chicago: University of Chicago Press.

Feachem, Richard G. and Dean T. Jamison, 1991. *Disease and Mortality in Sub-Saharan Africa*. New York: Oxford University Press.

Feachem, Richard G., Wendy J. Graham, and Ian M. Timaeus, 1989. "Identifying Health Problems and Health Research Priorities in Developing Countries." *Journal of Tropical Medicine and Hygiene* 92, 133–191.

Fenner, F., D. A. Henderson, and I. Arita, 1988. *Smallpox and Its Eradication*. Geneva: World Health Organization.

Field, Alexander James, 1979. "Economic and Demographic Determinants of

Educational Commitment: Massachusetts, 1955." *The Journal of Economic History* 39 (June), 439–457.

Fiorito, Jack and Robert C. Dauffenbach, 1982. "Market and Nonmarket Influences on Curriculum Choice by College Students." *Industrial and Labor Relations Review* 36:1 (October), 88–101.

Flinn, M. W., 1965. "Introduction." In E. M. Chadwick, ed., *Report on the Sanitary Condition of the Labouring Population of Great Britain*. Edinburgh: Edinburgh University Press.

Flora, Peter, 1973. "Historical Processes of Social Mobilization: Urbanization and Literacy, 1850–1965." In Shmuel N. Eisenstadt and Stein Rokkan, eds., *Building States and Nations*, Vol. I. Beverly Hills, CA: Sage Publications, 230–237.

Fogel, Robert W., 1993. "New Sources and New Techniques for the Study of Secular Trends in Nutritional Status, Health, Mortality, and the Process of Aging." *Historical Methods* 26:1 (Winter), 5–43.

Fogel, Robert W., 1997. "Economic and Social Structure for an Aging Population." *Philosophical Transactions of the Royal Society of London* 352, 1905–1917.

Fogel, Walter and Daniel J. B. Mitchell, 1973. "Higher Education Decision-Making and the Labor Market." In M. S. Gordon ed., *Higher Education and the Labor Market*. New York: McGraw-Hill, 454–502.

Form, William, 1979. "Comparative Industrial Sociology and the Convergence Hypothesis. *Annual Review of Sociology* 5, 1–25.

Forster, Colin and G. S. L. Tucker, 1972. *Economic Opportunity and White American Fertility Ratios, 1800–1860*. New Haven: Yale University Press.

Foster, Philip, 1965. *Education and Social Change in Ghana*. Chicago: University of Chicago Press.

Freedman, Ronald and J. Y. Takeshita, 1969. *Family Planning in Taiwan: An Experiment in Social Change*. Princeton, NJ: Princeton University Press.

Freeman, Richard B., 1971. *The Market for College-Trained Manpower*. Cambridge, MA: Harvard University Press.

Freeman, Richard B., 1975. "Overinvestment in College Training." *The Journal of Human Resources* X:3 (Summer), 287–311.

Freeman, Richard B., 1976. *The Over-Educated American*, New York: Academic Press.

Freeman, Richard B., 1980. "Employment Opportunities in the Doctorate Manpower Market." *Industrial and Labor Relations Review* 33:2 (January), 185–196.

Frey, Bruno S. and Alois Stutzer, 2002. "What Can Economists Learn from Happiness Research?" *Journal of Economic Literature* XL:2 (June), 402–435.

Friedlander, Dov, 1969. "Demographic Responses and Population Change." *Demography* 6 (November), 359–381.

Frisch, Rose E., 1974. "Demographic Implications of the Biological Determinants of Female Fertility." *Social Biology* 22 (Spring), 17–22.

Frisch, Rose E., 2002. *Female Fertility and the Body Fat Connection*. Chicago: University of Chicago Press.

Fuchs, Victor, 1983. *How We Live*. Cambridge, MA: Harvard University Press.

Furnham, Adrian and Barrie Stacey, 1991. *Young People's Understanding of Society*, London and New York: Routledge.

Gagan, David P., 1981. *Hopeful Travelers*. Toronto: University of Toronto Press.

Gambetta, Diego, 1987. *Were They Pushed or Did They Jump? Individual Decision Mechanisms in Education*. Cambridge. Cambridge University Press.

Gariepy, Thomas P., 1994. "The Introduction and Acceptance of Listerian Antisepsis in the United States." *The Journal of the History of Medicine and Allied Sciences* 49, 167–206.

Gilliand, Pierre and René Galland, 1977. "Outline on International Comparison of Public Health, Based on Data Collected by the World Health Organization." *World Health Statistics Report* 30:2, 227–242.

Glaeser, Edward L., 1998. "Are Cities Dying?" *Journal of Economic Perspectives* 12:2 (Spring), 139–160.

Goldsmith, Raymond W., 1952. "The Growth of Reproducible Wealth." In International Association for Income and Wealth, *Income and Wealth*, Series II. Cambridge, England: Bowes and Bowes, 1952.

Gordon, Margaret S., 1973. *Higher Education and the Labor Market*. New York: McGraw-Hill.

Goubert, Jean-Pierre, 1989. *The Conquest of Water*, Andrew Wilson, trans. Cambridge: Polity Press.

Grabill, Wilson H., Clyde V. Kiser, and P.K. Whelpton, 1958. *The Fertility of American Women*. New York: John Wiley.

Graff, Harvey J., 1979.*The Literacy Myth*. New York: Academic Press.

Grajdanzev, Andrew J., 1944. *Modern Korea*. New York: John Day Co.

Gray, R. H., 1974. "The Decline of Mortality in Ceylon and the Demographic Effects of Malaria Control." *Population Studies* 28:2 (July), 205–229.

Greven, Philip J., Jr., 1970. *Four Generations: Population, Land and Family in Colonial Andover, Massachusetts*. Ithaca, NY: Cornell University Press.

Gribble, James N. and Samuel H. Preston, eds., 1993. *The Epidemiological Transition*. Washington, DC: National Academy Press.

Griscom, John H. [1845] (1970). *The Sanitary Condition of the Laboring Class of New York*. New York: Arno & The New York Times. Originally published 1845, New York: Harper & Brothers.

Gurr, Ted Robert, Keith Jaggers, and Will H. Moore, 1991. "The Transformation of the Western State: The Growth of Democracy, Autocracy, and State Power since 1800." In Alex Inkeles, ed., *On Measuring Democracy: Its Consequences and Concomitants*. New Brunswick, NJ: Transaction Publishers, 69–104.

Gwatkin, Davidson R., 1979. "Political Will and Family Planning: The Implications of India's Emergency Experience." *Population and Development Review* 5:1 (March), 29–59.

Hagen, Everett E., 1962. *On the Theory of Social Change*, Homewood, IL: Dorsey Press.

Haines, Anna J., 1933. "Nursing." In Edwin R. A. Seligman ed., *Encyclopaedia of the Social Sciences*, Vol. 11. New York: Macmillan Co.

Haines, Michael R., Roger C. Avery, and Michael A. Strong, 1983. "Differentials in Infant and Child Mortality and Their Change Over Time: Guatemala, 1959–1973." *Demography* 20:4 (November), 607–621.
Hall, A. Rupert, 1967. "Scientific Method and the Progress of Techniques." In E. E. Rich and C. H. Wilson, eds., *The Cambridge Economic History of Europe* Vol. IV. Cambridge: Cambridge University Press, 96–154.
Halstead, Scott B., Julia A. Walsh, and Kenneth S. Warren, 1985. *Good Health at Low Cost*, Proceedings of conference held at Bellagio Conference Center, Bellagio, Italy. New York: The Rockefeller Foundation.
Hanlon, John J., Fred B. Rogers, and George Rosen, 1960. "A Bookshelf on the History and Philosophy of Public Health." *Journal of Public Health* 50:4 (April), 445–458.
Hanlon, P., P. Byass, M. Yamuah, R. Hayes, S. Bennett, and B. H. M'Boge, 1988. "Factors Influencing Vaccination Compliance in Peri-Urban Gambian Children." *Journal of Tropical Medicine and Hygiene* 91, 29–33.
Hans, Nicholas, 1964. *History of Russian Educational Policy, 1701–1917*. London: P. S. King and Son.
Harbison, Frederick and Charles A. Myers, 1964. *Education, Manpower, and Economic Growth*. New York: McGraw-Hill.
Harris, Marvin, 1968. *The Rise of Anthropological Theory*. New York: Thomas Y. Crowell.
Harrod, Roy F., 1982. *The Life of John Maynard Keynes*. New York: W.W. Norton.
Henderson, William O., 1972. *Britain and Industrial Europe*, 3d ed. Leicester: Leicester University Press.
Hickman, Bert, G., 1960. *Growth and Stability in the Postwar Economy*. Washington, DC:
Higgs, Robert, 1979. "Cycles and Trends of Mortality in 18 Large American Cities, 1871–1900." *Explorations in Economic History* 16, 381–408.
Hobcraft, John, 1993. "Women's Education, Child Welfare and Child Survival: A Review of the Evidence." *Health Transition Review* 3:2, 159–175.
Hohenberg, Paul M. and Lynn Hollen Lees, 1985. *The Making of Urban Europe 1000–1950*. Cambridge, MA: Harvard University Press.
Hudson, Robert P., 1983. *Disease and Its Control*. Westport, CT: Greenwood Press.
Hull, Terence H. and Valerie J. Hull, 1977. "The Relation of Economic Class and Fertility: An Analysis of Some Indonesian Data." *Population Studies* 31:1, 43–57.
Hull, Terence H. and Valerie J. Hull, 1997. "Politics, Culture and Fertility: Transitions in Indonesia." In Gavin W. Jones, Robert M. Douglas, John C. Caldwell, and Rennie M. D'Souza, eds., *The Continuing Demographic Transition*. Oxford: Oxford University Press, 383–421.
Hutchinson, Edward P. 1956. *Immigrants and Their Children, 1850–1950*. New York: John Wiley.
Inglehart, Ronald, 1977. *The Silent Revolution: Changing Values and Political Styles among Western Publics*. Princeton, NJ: Princeton University Press.

Inglehart, Ronald, 1988. "The Renaissance of Political Culture." *American Political Science Review* 82:4 (December), 1203–1230.
Inglehart, Ronald, 1997. *Modernization and Postmodernization*. Princeton, NJ: Princeton University Press.
Inkeles, Alex, 1973. "The School as a Context for Modernization," *International Journal of Comparative Sociology* 14:3–4 (Sep.–Dec.), 163–179.
Inkeles, Alex and David H. Smith, 1974. *Becoming Modern*. Cambridge MA: Harvard University Press.
Institute of Medicine, Division of Health Care Services, Committee for the Study of the Future of Public Health. 1988. *The Future of Public Health*. Washington, DC: National Academy Press.
Isard, W., 1942a. "A Neglected Cycle: The Transport-building Cycle." *Review of Economic Statistics* XXIV:4 (November), 149–158.
Isard, W., 1942b. "Transport Development and Building Cycles." *Quarterly Journal of Economics* LVI (November), 90–110.
Jaggers, Keith and Ted Robert Gurr, 1996. *Polity III: Regime Change and Political Authority, 1800–1994* (computer file). 2d ICPSR version. Boulder, CO: Keith Jaggers/College Park, MD: Ted Robert Gurr (producers), 1995. Ann Arbor, MI: Interuniversity Consortium for Political and Social Research (distributor).
Jamison, Dean T., W. Henry Mosley, Anthony R. Measham, and José-Luis Bobadilla, eds., 1993. *Disease Control Priorities in Developing Countries*. New York: Oxford University Press.
Jannetta, Ann Bowman and Samuel H. Preston, 1991. "Two Centuries of Mortality Change in Central Japan: The Evidence from a Temple Death Register." *Population Studies* 45, 417–436.
Jejeebhoy, Shireen J., 1979. "The Transition from Natural to Controlled Fertility in Taiwan." Ph.D. diss., University of Pennsylvania; published in part as "The Transition from Natural to Controlled Fertility in Taiwan: A Cross-Sectional Analysis of Demand and Supply Factors." *Studies in Family Planning* 9:8, 206–211.
Jejeebhoy, Shireen J., 1995. *Women's Education, Autonomy, and Reproductive Behaviour: Experience from Developing Countries*. Oxford: Clarendon Press.
Johansson, S., Ryan and Carl Mosk, 1987. "Exposure, Resistance and Life Expectancy: Disease and Death during the Economic Development of Japan, 1900–1960." *Population Studies* 41, 207–235.
Juster, F. Thomas and Frank P. Stafford, 1985. *Time, Goods, and Well-Being*. Ann Arbor: Survey Research Center, Institute for Social Research, The University of Michigan.
Kahneman, Daniel, Ed Diener, and Norbert Schwarz, eds., 1999. *Well-Being: The Foundations of Hedonic Psychology*, New York: Russell Sage.
Katona, George, 1960. *The Powerful Consumer: Psychological Studies of the American Economy*. New York: McGraw-Hill Book Company, Inc.
Katz, Michael B. 1971. *Class, Bureaucracy, and Schools*, New York: Praeger.

Kazamias, Andreas M., 1966. *Education and the Quest for Modernity in Turkey*, Chicago: University of Chicago Press.

Kearns, Gerry, 1988. "Private Property and Public Health Reform in England 1830–70." *Social Science Medicine* 26, 187–199.

Kelley, A. C. and J. G. Williamson, 1987. "What Drives City Growth in the Developing World?" In G.S. Tolley and V. Thomas, eds., *The Economics of Urbanization and Urban Policies in Developing Countries*. Washington, DC: The World Bank, 32–45.

Kennedy, Paul, 1987. *The Rise and Fall of the Great Powers*. New York: Random House.

Keynes, John Maynard, 1932. *Essays in Persuasion*. New York: Harcourt-Brace.

Kimura, M., 1993. "Standards of Living in Colonial Korea: Did the Masses Become Worse Off or Better Off under Japanese Rule?" *Journal of Economic History* 53, 629–652.

Kirk, Dudley, 1946. *Europe's Population in the Interwar Years*. Geneva: League of Nations.

Kirk, Dudley, 1971. "A New Demographic Transition." In National Academy of Sciences, *Rapid Population Growth*. Baltimore: The Johns Hopkins Press, 123–147.

Klamer, Arjo and David Colander, 1990. *The Making of an Economist*. Boulder, CO: Westview Press.

Kline, S. J. and N. Rosenberg, 1986. An Overview of Innovation. In R. Landau and N. Rosenberg, eds., *The Positive Sum Strategy: Harnessing Technology for Economic Growth*. Washington, DC: National Academy Press.

Koch, James V., 1972. "Student Choice of Undergraduate Major Field of Study and Private Internal Rates of Return." *Industrial and Labor Relations Review* 26:1 (October), 680–685.

Koch, James V., 1975. "Reply." *Industrial and Labor Relations Review* 28:2 (January), 286–287.

Koford, Kenneth J. and Jeffrey B. Miller, 1991. *Social Norms and Economic Institutions*. Ann Arbor, MI: University of Michigan Press.

Krugman, Paul, 1998. "Space: The Final Frontier." *Journal of Economic Perspectives* 12:2 (Spring), 161–174.

Kunitz, S. J., 1987. "Explanations and Ideologies of Mortality Patterns." *Population and Development Review* 13, 379–408.

Kuznets, Simon, 1930. *Secular Movements in Production and Prices*. New York: Houghton-Mifflin.

Kuznets, Simon, 1947. "Economic Growth: Measurement." *Journal of Economic History* VII, Supplement, 10–34.

Kuznets, Simon, 1948a. "National Income: A New Version." *Review of Economics and Statistics* 30, 151–197.

Kuznets, Simon, 1948b. "On the Valuation of Social Income – Reflections on Professor Hicks' Article." *Economica* 15, 1–16 and 116–131.

Kuznets, Simon, 1949. "Suggestions for an Inquiry into the Economic Growth of Nations." In Universities – National Bureau Committee for Economic

Research. *Problems in the Study of Economic Growth*, No. 1 (mimeographed), 3–20.

Kuznets, Simon, 1955. "Toward a Theory of Economic Growth." In Robert Lekachman, ed., *National Policy for Economic Welfare at Home and Abroad.* New York: Doubleday, 12–77.

Kuznets, Simon, 1958. "Long Swings in the Growth of Population and in Related Economic Variables." *Proceedings of the American Philosophical Society* 102:25–52.

Kuznets, Simon, 1961. *Capital in the American Economy: Its Formation and Financing*. Princeton, NJ: Princeton University Press.

Kuznets, Simon, 1966. *Modern Economic Growth: Rate, Structure, and Spread.* New Haven, CT: Yale University Press.

Kuznets, Simon and Dorothy S. Thomas, eds., 1957, 1960, 1964. *Population Redistribution and Economic Growth, United States, 1870–1950*, Vols. I, II, and III. Philadelphia: American Philosophical Society.

Landes, David S., 1969. *The Unbound Prometheus: Technological Change and Industrial Development in Western Europe from 1750 to the Present*. Cambridge: Cambridge University Press.

Landy, David, ed., 1977. *Culture, Disease, and Healing*. New York: Macmillan Publishing Co. Inc.

Lappé, Marc, 1982. *Germs That Won't Die: Medical Consequences of the Misuse of Antibiotics*. New York: Anchor Press/Doubleday.

Lebergott, Stanley, 1964. *Manpower in Economic Growth: The American Record since 1800*. New York: McGraw-Hill p. 539.

Lee, Ronald, 1978. "Models of Preindustrial Population Dynamics with Applications to England." In Charles Tilly, ed., *Historical Studies of Changing Fertility*. Princeton, NJ: Princeton University Press, 155–207.

Leet, Don R., 1975. "Human Fertility and Agricultural Opportunities in Ohio Counties: From Frontier to Maturity, 1810–1860." In David C. Klingaman and Richard K. Vedder eds., *The Old Northwest: Essays in Nineteenth Century Economic History*, Athens, OH: Ohio University Press.

Leibenstein, Harvey, 1957. *Economic Backwardness and Economic Growth.* New York: John Wiley.

Leibenstein, Harvey, 1974a. "The Economic Theory of Fertility Decline." *Quarterly Journal of Economics* (Fall), 1–31.

Leibenstein, Harvey, 1974b. "An Interpretation of the Economic Theory of Fertility: Promising Path or Blind Alley?" *Journal of Economic Literature* 12:2 (June), 457–479.

Levy, Frank, 1985. "Happiness, Affluence and Altruism in the Postwar Period." In Martin David and Timothy Smeeding, eds., *Horizontal Equity, Uncertainty and Economic Well-Being*. Chicago: University of Chicago Press for the National Bureau of Economic Research, 7–29.

Lewin, Shira, 1996. "Economics and Psychology: Lessons for Our Own Day from the Early Twentieth Century." *Journal of Economic Literature* XXXIV:3 (September), 1293–1323.

Lindberg, David C., 1992. *The Beginnings of Western Science*. Chicago: University of Chicago Press.
Lindert, Peter, 1978. *Fertility and Scarcity in America*. Princeton, NJ: Princeton University Press.
Lipset, Seymour Martin, 1960. *Political Man. The Social Bases of Politics*. Garden City, NY: Doubleday.
Lockridge, Kenneth, 1968. "Land, Population and the Evolution of New England Society, 1630–1790." *Past and Present* 39 (April), 62–80.
Lunn, Peter G., 1991. "Nutrition, Immunity, and Infection." In Schofield, R. and D. Reher, eds., *The Decline of Mortality in Europe*. Oxford: Clarendon Press, 131–145.
Macunovich, Diane J., 2002. *Birth Quake: The Baby Boom and Its Aftershocks*. Chicago: University of Chicago Press.
Maddison, Angus, 1995. *Monitoring the World Economy 1820–1992*. Paris: Development Centre of the Organisation for Economic Co-operation and Development.
Maddison, Angus, 1998. *Chinese Economic Performance in the Long Run*. Paris: Development Centre of the Organisation for Economic Co-Operation and Development.
Mandle, Jay R., 1973. *The Plantation Economy*. Philadelphia: Temple University Press.
Marcus, Alan I., 1979. "Disease Prevention in America: From a Local to a National Outlook, 1880–1910." *Bulletin of the History of Medicine* 53:2 (Summer).
Maslow, Abraham H., 1954. *Motivation and Personality*. New York: Harper.
Mason, K. O., J. L. Czajka, and S. Arber, 1976. "Change in Women's Sex-role Attitudes, 1964–1974." *American Sociological Review* 41:573–596.
Mata, Leonardo and Luis Rosero, 1988. *National Health and Social Development in Costa Rica: A Case Study of Intersectoral Action*, Technical Paper No. 13. Washington, DC: World Health Organization, Pan American Health Organization.
Mayhew, Henry [1851] (1958). *Mayhew's London*. London: Spring Books.
McClelland, David C., 1966. "Does Education Accelerate Economic Growth?" *Economic Development and Cultural Change* 14 (April), 257–278.
McCloskey, Donald N., 1983. "The Rhetoric of Economics." *Journal of Economic Literature* 21:2 (June), 481–517.
McCloskey, Donald N., 1994. "Statics, Dynamics, and Persuasion: Why Economists Have Not Explained the Industrial Revolution." In R. Floud and D. McCloskey, eds., *The New Economic History of Britain, 1700 to the Present*, 2d ed, Vol. 1. Cambridge: Cambridge University Press.
McKeown, T., 1976. *The Modern Rise of Population*. New York: Academic Press.
McNall, Neil Adams, 1952. *An Agricultural History of the Genesee Valley 1790–1860*. Philadelphia: University of Pennsylvania Press.
McNeill, W. H., 1976. *Plagues and Peoples*. New York: Doubleday.

McPherson, Michael S., 1983. "Want Formation, Morality and Some 'Interpretive' Aspects of Economic Inquiry." In Norma Haan, Robert N. Bellah, Paul Rabinow, and William M. Sullivan, eds., *Social Science as Moral Inquiry*. New York: Columbia University Press.

Mecham, J. Lloyd, 1934. *Church and State in Latin America*. Chapal Hill, NC: University of North Carolina Press.

Meegama, Srinivasa A., 1981. "The Decline in Mortality in Sri Lanka in Historical Perspective." In International Union for the Scientific Study of Population, *International Population Conference, Manila, 1981*. Liege, Belgium: IUSSP.

Meeker, E., 1970. "The Economics of Improving Health, 1850–1915." Ph.D. dissertation, University of Washington.

Mercer, Alex, 1990. *Disease, Mortality and Population in Transition*, Leicester: Leicester University Press.

Merrick, Thomas W., 1978. "Fertility and Land Availability in Rural Brazil." *Demography* 15:3, 321–336.

Mill, John Stuart [1850] (1965). *Principles of Political Economy*. Toronto: University of Toronto Press.

Mochizuki, M. M., 1998. "The East Asian Economic Crisis: Security Implications." *Brookings Review* 16:3 (Summer), 30–32.

Modigliani, F., 1949. "Fluctuations in the Saving-Income Ratio: A Problem in Economic Forecasting." In Conference on Research in Income and Wealth, *Studies in Income and Wealth*, Vol. 11. New York: National Bureau of Economic Research, 371–443.

Mohrman, Kathryn, 1987. "Unintended Consequences of Federal Student Aid Policies." *The Brookings Review* (Fall), 24–30.

Mokyr, Joel, 1990. *The Lever of Riches*. New York: Oxford University Press.

Mokyr, Joel, 2000. "Why 'More Work for Mother?' Knowledge and Household Behavior, 1870–1945." *Journal of Economic History* 60:1 (March), 1–41.

Mokyr, Joel and Rebecca Stein, 1997. "Science, Health, and Household Technology: The Effect of the Pasteur Revolution on Consumer Demand." In Timothy F. Bresnahan and Robert J. Gordon, eds., *The Economics of New Goods*. Chicago: University of Chicago Press, 143–200.

Morris, Richard B., 1959. *Studies in the History of American Law*. Philadelphia:

Mosk, Carl and S. Ryan Johansson, 1986. "Income and Mortality: Evidence from Modern Japan." *Population and Development Review* 12:3, 415–440.

Mosley, W. Henry and Lincoln C. Chen, eds., 1984. "Child Survival: Strategies for Research." *Population and Development Review* 10, Special Supplement.

Mowery, D.C. and N. Rosenberg, 1989. *Technology and the Pursuit of Economic Growth*. Cambridge: Cambridge University Press.

Muller, Mike, 1982. *The Health of Nations*. London: Faber and Faber.

Musgrove, Philip, 1996. *Public and Private Roles in Health*, World Bank Discussion Paper No. 339. Washington, DC: The World Bank.

Musson, A. E., 1972. *Science, Technology and Economic Growth in the Eighteenth Century*. London: Methuen & Co. Ltd.

Nathanson, Constance A., 1996. "Disease Prevention as Social Change: Toward a Theory of Public Health." *Population and Development Review* 22:4 (December), 609–637.

National Bureau of Economic Research, various dates. *NBER Reporter*, Cambridge, MA: National Bureau of Economic Research.

National Research Council, 1993. *Demographic Effects of Economic Reversals in sub-Saharan Africa*. Washington, DC: National Research Council, Committee on Population.

Nelson, R. R., 1973. "Recent Exercises in Growth Accounting: New Understanding or Dead End?" *American Economic Review*, 63:462–468.

Nerlove, Marc, 1974. "Household and Economy: Toward a New Theory of Population and Economic Growth," *Journal of Political Economy*. 82:2, Pt. 2 (March/April), S200–S218.

Newman, P., 1965. *Malaria Eradication and Population Growth: With Special Reference to Ceylon and British Guiana*. Research Series No. 10, Bureau of Public Health Economics, School of Public Health. Ann Arbor, MI: University of Michigan.

North, Douglass C., 1990. *Institutions, Institutional Change and Economic Performance*. Cambridge: Cambridge University Press.

O'Connell, Martin, 1975. "The Effect of Changing Age Distributions on Fertility and Suicide in Developed Countries." Unpublished Ph.D. dissertation. Philadelphia: Department of Sociology, University of Pennsylvania.

Ohkawa, Kazushi and Henry Rosovsky, 1965. "A Century of Japanese Economic Growth." In William W. Lockwood, ed., *The State and Economic Enterprise in Japan*. Princeton, NJ: Princeton University Press.

Okun, Bernard, 1958. *Trends in Birth Rates in the United States Since 1870* Baltimore: John Hopkins University Press.

Olusanya, P. O., 1969. "Modernization and the Level of Fertility in Western Nigeria." International Union for the Scientific Study of Population, *International Population Conference* (London) 1, 812–824.

Omran, Abdel R., 1971. "The Epidemiologic Transition: A Theory of the Epidemiology of Population Change." *The Milbank Memorial Fund Quarterly* XLIX:4, P. 1 (October), 509–538.

Oppenheimer, Valerie K., 1970. *The Female Labor Force in the United States: Demographic and Economic Factors Governing Its Growth and Changing Composition*. Population Monograph Series No. 5. Berkeley, CA: University of California.

Organization for Economic Cooperation and Development (OECD), 1968. *Reviews of National Science Policy, United States*. Paris: OECD.

Organization for Economic Cooperation and Development (OECD), 1998. *Twenty-First Century Technologies*. Paris: OECD.

Organization for Economic Cooperation and Development (OECD), 1999. *The Future of the Global Economy*. Paris: OECD.

Over, M., R. P. Ellis, J. H. Huber, and O. Solon, 1992. "The Consequences of Adult Health." In R. G. A., Feachem, T. Kjellstron, C. J. L. Murray, M. Over, and M. A. Phillips, eds., *The Health of Adults in the Developing World*. New York: Oxford University Press, 161–207.

Parish, H. J., 1965. *A History of Immunization*, Edinburgh: E. & S. Livingstone.
Parker, S., 1998. "Out of the Ashes? Southeast Asia's Struggle through Crisis." *Brookings Review* 16:3 (Summer), 18–21.
Parker, William N. 1961. "Economic Development in Historical Perspective." *Economic Development and Cultural Change* 10 (October), 644–661
Parker, William N., 1984. *Europe, America, and the Wider World, Volume I: Europe and the World Economy*. Cambridge: Cambridge University Press.
Passin, Herbert, 1965. *Society and Education in Japan*. New York: Bureau of Publications, Teachers College, Columbia University.
Paul, Benjamin D., ed., 1955. *Health, Culture and Community*. New York: Russell Sage Foundation.
Pebley, Anne, Elena Hurtado, and Noreen Goldman, 1996. "Beliefs about Children's Illness among Rural Guatemalan Women." Labor and Population Program, Working Paper Series 96–11, Santa Monica, CA: Rand Corporation.
Pernia, E. M., 1998. "Population Distribution in Asia: A Region of Contrasts." In United Nations Department of Economic and Social Affairs Population Division, *Population Distribution and Migration*. New York: United Nations, 102–116.
Perrenoud, A., 1991. "The Attenuation of Mortality Crises and the Decline of Mortality." In R. Schofield, D. Reher, and A. Bideau, eds., *The Decline of Mortality in Europe*. Oxford: Clarendon Press, 18–37.
Phelps, Charles E., 1992. *Health Economics*. New York: Harper Collins.
Piachaud, David, 1979. "The Diffusion of Medical Techniques to Less Developed Countries." *International Journal of Health Services* 9:4, 629–643.
Pigou, A. C., 1932. *The Economics of Welfare*. London: Macmillan.
Plotkin, Stanley A. and Edward A. Mortimer, Jr., 1988. *Vaccines*. Philadelphia: W. B. Saunders Company.
Polachek, Solomon Williams, 1978. "Sex Differences in College Major." *Industrial and Labor Relations Review* 31:4 (July), 498–508.
Pollak, Robert A. and Michael L. Wachter, 1975. "The Relevance of the Household Production Function and Its Implications for the Allocation of Time." *Journal of Political Economy* 83 (April), 255–277.
Porter, Theodore M., 1986. *The Rise of Statistical Thinking 1820–1900*. Princeton, NJ: Princeton University Press.
Portney, Paul R., 2000. "Environmental Problems and Policy: 2000–2050." *Journal of Economic Perspectives* 14:1 (Winter), 199–206.
Preston, S. H., 1975. "The Changing Relation between Mortality and Level of Economic Development." *Population Studies* 29:213–248.
Preston, Samuel H., 1980. "Causes and Consequences of Mortality Declines in Less Developed Countries in the Twentieth Century." In R. A. Easterlin, ed., *Population and Economic Change in Developing Countries*. Chicago: University of Chicago Press, 289–341.
Preston, Samuel H. and Michael R. Haines, 1991. *Fatal Years: Child Mortality in Late Nineteenth-Century America*, Princeton, NJ: Princeton University Press.
Preston, Samuel H. and J. McDonald, 1979. "The Incidence of Divorce within

Cohorts of American Marriages Contracted since the Civil War." *Demography* 16:1 (February), 1–25.

Preston, Samuel H., Michael R. Haines, and Elsie Pamuk, 1981. "Effects of Industrialization and Urbanization on Mortality in Developed Countries." In International Union for the Scientific Study of Population, *International Population Conference Manila 1981*. Liege, Belgium: IUSSP.

Preston, Samuel H. and E. van de Walle, 1978. "Urban French Mortality in the Nineteenth Century." *Population Studies* 32, 275–297.

Pritchett, Lant and Lawrence H. Summers, 1996. "Wealthier Is Healthier." *Journal of Human Resources* XXXI:4, 841–868.

Rainoff, T. J., 1929. "Wave-like Fluctuations of Creative Productivity in the Development of West-European Physics in Eighteenth and Nineteenth Centuries." *Isis* XII:287–319.

Rainwater, Lee, 1994. "Family Equivalence as a Social Construction." In O. Ekert-Jaffe, ed., *Standards of Living and Families: Observation and Analysis*. Montrouge, France: John Libbey Eurotext, 23–39.

Reddy, H. and K. N. M. Raju, 1977. *Changes over a Generation in Fertility Levels and Values in Karnataka*, Population Center of Bangalore Occasional Papers, Ser. 2. Bangalore: India Population Project.

Reder, Melvin W., 1999. *Economics: The Culture of a Controversial Science*. Chicago: University of Chicago Press.

Reuschemeyer, Dietrich and Theda Skocpol, eds., 1996. *States, Social Knowledge, and the Origins of Modern Social Policies*. New York: Russell Sage Foundation.

Roberts, G. W., 1969. "Fertility in Some Caribbean Countries." International Union for the Scientific Study of Population, *International Population Conference* (London) 1, 695–711.

Robinson, Warren C. and David E. Horlacher, 1971. "Population Growth and Economic Welfare," *Reports on Population/Family Planning* 6 (February) 1–39.

Rodrik, Dani, 1996. "Understanding Economic Policy Reform," *Journal of Economic Literature* XXXIV (March), 9–41.

Roemer, Milton I., 1993. *National Health Systems of the World, Vol. 2, The Issues*. New York: Oxford University Press.

Rogers, Naomi, 1989. "Germs with Legs: Flies, Disease, and the New Public Health." *Bulletin of History and Medicine* 63:4 (Winter), 599–617.

Roper Organization, 1989. *The Public Pulse*, Vol. 4. New York: Roper Organization.

Roper Starch Organization, 1979. *Roper Reports 79–1*, Storrs, CT: University of Connecticut, The Roper Center.

Roper Starch Organization, 1995. *Roper Reports 95–1*, Storrs, CT: University of Connecticut, The Roper Center.

Rosen, George, 1958. *A History of Public Health*, New York: MD Publications Inc.

Rosen, George, 1968. "Public Health." In *International Encyclopedia of the Social Sciences*, Vol. 13. New York: Macmillan, 164–170.

Rosenberg, Charles E., 1979. "The Therapeutic Revolution: Medicine, Meaning, and Social Change in Nineteenth-Century America." In Morris J. Vogel and Charles E. Rosenberg, eds., *The Therapeutic Revolution*. Philadelphia: University of Pennsylvania Press, 3–25.

Rosenberg, Charles E., 1987. *The Care of Strangers*. New York: Basic Books.

Rosenberg, Morris, 1979. *Conceiving the Self*. New York: Basic Books.

Rosenberg, Nathan, 1970. "Economic Development and the Transfer of Technology: Some Historical Perspectives." *Technology and Culture* 11 (October), 555.

Rosenberg, Nathan, 1976. *Perspectives on Technology*. New York: M. E. Sharpe.

Rosenkranz, Barbara Gutmann, 1972. *Public Health and the State*. Cambridge, MA: Harvard University Press.

Rosenzweig, Mark R. and T. Paul Schultz, 1985. "The Demand for and the Supply of Births: Fertility and Its Life Cycle Consequences." *American Economic Review* 75:5 (December), 992–1015.

Ross, Myron H., 1975. "Comment." *Industrial and Labor Relations Review* 28:2 (January), 285–286.

Roth, Gabriel, 1987. *The Private Provision of Public Services in Developing Countries*. New York: Oxford University Press.

Samuelson, Paul A., 1992. "My Life Philosophy: Policy Credos and Working Ways." In Michael Szenberg, ed., *Eminent Economists: Their Life Philosophies*. Cambridge: Cambridge University Press, 236–247.

Sandiford, P., J. Cassel, M. Montenegro, and G. Sanchez, 1995. "The Impact of Women's Literacy on Child Health and Its Interaction with Access to Health Services." *Population Studies* XLIX (March), 5–17.

Sarkar, N., 1957. *The Demography of Ceylon*. Colombo Ceylon: Government Press.

Sawyer, Diana Oya, 1981. "Effects of Industrialization and Urbanization on Mortality in the Developing Countries: The Case of Brazil." International Union for the Scientific Study of Population, *International Population Conference Manila 1981*. Liege, Belgium: International Union for the Scientific Study of Population.

Saxonhouse, Gary, 1974. "A Tale of Japanese Technological Diffusion in the Meiji Period." *The Journal of Economic History* 34 (March), 149–165.

Schairer, Reinhold, 1927. *Die Studenten im internationalen Kulturleben: Beitrage zur Frage des Studiums in fremdem Lande*. Munster in Westfalen: Aschenolorff.

Schapiro, Morton Owen, 1986. *Filling up America: An Economic Demographic Model of Population Growth and Distribution in the Nineteenth Century United States*, Vol. 8, Industrial Development and the Social Fabric Series. Greenwich, CT: JAI Press, Inc.

Schapiro, Morton Owen and Dennis A. Ahlburg, 1986. "Why Crime Is Down." *American Demographics* 8:10 (October), 56–58.

Schofield, R., D. Reher, and A. Bideau, 1991. *The Decline of Mortality in Europe*. Oxford: Clarendon Press.

Schön, L., 1998. "Industrial Crises in a Model of Long Cycles: Sweden in an International Perspective." In T. Myllyntaus, ed., *Economic Crises and Restructuring in History: Experiences of Small Countries*. St. Katharinen: Scripta Meruturae Verlag.

Schön, L., 2000. "Electricity, Technological Change, and Productivity in Swedish Industry, 1890–1990." *European Review of Economic History* 4, P. 2 (August), 175–194.

Schultz, T. Paul, 1973. "A Preliminary Survey of Economic Analyses of Fertility." *The American Economic Review* 63:2 (May), 71–78.

Schultz, T. Paul, 1981. *Economics of Population*. Reading, MA: Addison-Wesley.

Schultz, Theodore W., ed., 1973. "The Value of Children: An Economic Perspective." *Journal of Political Economy* 81:2, Pt. 2 (March/April), S2–S13.

Schultz, Theodore W., 1974. "The High Value of Human Time: Population Equilibrium," *Journal of Political Economy* 82:2, Pt. 2 (March/April), S2–S10.

Sen, Amartya, 1994. "Economic Regress, Concepts and Features." *Proceedings of the World Bank Annual Conference on Development Economics*, Washington, DC: The World Bank.

Shattuck, Lemuel et al. [1850] (1948). *Report of the Sanitary Commission of Massachusetts 1850*, Cambridge: Harvard University Press.

Shorter, Edward, John Knodel, and Etienne van de Walle, 1971. "The Decline of Non-Marital Fertility in Europe, 1880–1940." *Population Studies* 25:3 (November), 375–393.

Simon, Julian L., 1968. "The Effect of Income on the Suicide Rate: A Paradox Resolved." *American Journal of Sociology* 74:302–303.

Simon, Julian L., 1969. "The Effect of Income on Fertility." *Population Studies*, 23:327–341.

Simon, Julian L., 1975. "Response to Barnes's Comment." *American Journal of Sociology* 80:1460–1462.

Simon, Julian L., 1996. *The Ultimate Resource 2*. Princeton, NJ: Princeton University Press.

Simon, Sir John, 1890. *English Sanitary Institutions*, London: Cassell & Co.; New York: Johnson Reprint Co.

Siow, Aloysius, 1984. "Occupational Choice under Uncertainty." *Econometrica* 52:3 (May), 631–645.

Smith, Daniel S., 1972. "The Demographic History of Colonial New England." *The Journal of Economic History* 32 (March), 165–183.

Smith, Stephen, 1911. *The City That Was*. New York: Frank Allaben.

Solow, R., 1957. "Technical Change and the Aggregate Production Function." *Review of Economics and Statistics* 39:312–20.

Spencer, Daniel Lloyd, 1970. *The Technological Gap in Perspective*. New York: Spartan Books.

Spengler, Joseph J., 1930. *The Fecundity of Native and Foreign-Born Women in New England*. The Brookings Institution Pamphlet Series, Vol. II:1 (June 30).

Spengler, Joseph J., 1968. *France Faces Depopulation*, 2d ed. New York: Greenwood Press.

Spillman, W. J., 1919. "The Agricultural Ladder." *American Economic Review* 9 (March 1919), 170–179.

Srinivasan K. and S. J. Jejeebhoy, 1981."Changes in Natural Fertility in India, 1959–1972." In K. Srinivasan and S. Mukerji, eds., *Dynamics of Population and Family Welfare*. Bombay: Himalaya Publishing House.

Srinivasan, K., H. Reddy, and K. N. M. Raju, 1978. "One Generation to the Next: Changes in Fertility, Family Size Preferences, and Family Planning in an Indian State between 1951 and 1975." *Studies in Family Planning* 9:10–11, 258–71.

Starr, Paul, 1982. *The Social Transformation of American Medicine*. New York: Basic Books Inc.

Steckel, Richard H., 1995. "Stature and the Standard of Living." *Journal of Economic Literature* XXXIII (December), 1903–1940.

Steckel, Richard H. and Roderick Floud, eds., 1997. *Health and Welfare during Industrialization*. Chicago: University of Chicago Press.

Stone, Lawrence, 1976. "Introduction." In Lawrence Stone, ed., *Schooling and Society*. Baltimore: Johns Hopkins University Press pp. xi–xvii.

Stouffer, Samuel A. et al., 1949. *The American Soldier: Adjustment during Wartime Life*, Vol. 1. Princeton, NJ: Princeton University Press.

Strassman, W. Paul, 1959. *Risk and Technological Innovation*, Ithaca, NY: Cornell University Press.

Strauss, John and Duncan Thomas, 1995. "Human Resources: Empirical Modeling of Household and Family Decisions." In J. Behrman and T.N. Srinivasan, eds., *Handbook of Development Economics*, Vol. III, 1885–2023.

Strumpel, Burkhard, James N. Morgan, and Ernest Zahn, eds., 1972. *Human Behavior in Economic Affairs*. San Francisco: Jossey-Bass.

Stys, W., 1957. "The Influence of Economic Conditions on the Fertility of Peasant Women." *Population Studies* 2 (November), 136–148.

Summers, Robert and Alan Heston, 1991. "The Penn World Tables (Mark 5): An Expanded Set of International Comparisons, 1982–88." *Quarterly Journal of Economics* 106:2, 327–368.

Sundin, Jan, 1995. "Culture, Class, and Infant Mortality during the Swedish Mortality Transition, 1750–1850." *Social Science History* 19:1, 117–145.

Svennilson, Ingvar, 1964. "Technical Assistance: The Transfer of Industrial Know-how to Non-Industrialized Countries." In Kenneth Berill, ed., *Economic Development with Special Reference to East Asia*. New York: St. Martin's Press.

Sydenstricker, Edgar, 1932. "A Study of the Fertility of Native White Women in a Rural Area of Western New York." *The Milbank Memorial Fund Quarterly* 10 (January), 17–32.

Szreter, Simon, 1988. "The Importance of Social Intervention in Britain's Mortality Decline c. 1850–1914: A Re-Interpretation of the Role of Public Health," *The Society for the Social History of Medicine* 1:1–38.

Szreter, Simon, 1997. "The Politics of Public Health in Nineteenth Century Britain," *Population and Development Review* 23:4 (December), 693–728.

Tabbarah, Riad B., 1971. "Toward a Theory of Demographic Development." *Economic Development and Cultural Change* 19:2 (January), 257–277.
Taeuber, Conrad and Irene B. Taeuber, 1958. *The Changing Population of the United States*. New York: John Wiley.
Taeuber, Irene B., 1958. *The Population of Japan*. Princeton, NJ: Princeton University Press.
Taeuber, Irene B., 1962. "Asian Populations: The Critical Decades." In Committee on the Judiciary, *Study of Population and Immigration Problems*. Washington, DC: U.S. Government Printing Office.
Tarver, James D., 1952. "Intra-family Farm Succession Practices." *Rural Sociology* 17 (September), 266–271.
Teece, David J., 1976. *The Multinational Corporation and the Resource Cost of International Technology Transfer*. Cambridge, MA: Ballinger Publishing Co.
Thomas, Lewis, 1983. *The Youngest Science*, NewYork: The Viking Press.
Thompson, Warren S., 1959. *Population and Progress in the Far East*. Chicago: University of Chicago Press.
Throop, Adrian, 1992. "Consumer Sentiment: Its Causes and Effects." *Economic Review*, Federal Reserve Bank of San Francisco 1, 35–59.
Thut, I. N. and Don Adams, 1964. *Educational Patterns in Contemporary Societies*. New York: McGraw-Hill.
Tietze, Christopher, 1972. "Teenage Sexual Revolution," *Family Planning Perspectives* 4:2 (April), 6.
Tolaro, K. and A. Tolaro, 1993. *Foundations in Microbiology*. Dubuque, IA: William C. Brown Communications.
Tomes, Nancy, 1990. "The Private Side of Public Health: Sanitary Science, Domestic Hygiene, and the Germ Theory, 1870–1900," *Bulletin of History and Medicine* 64:4 (Winter), 509–539.
Tuge, Hideomi, ed., 1961. *Historical Development of Science and Technology in Japan*. Tokyo: Kokusai Bianka Shinko kai.
UNESCO, 1957. *World Illiteracy at Mid-Century*. Paris: United Nations Educational, Scientific and Cultural Organization.
UNESCO, 1994. *Statistical Yearbook 1994*. New York: United Nations.
United Nations, 1952. *Preliminary Report on the World Social Situation*. New York: United Nations.
United Nations, 1957. *Report on the World Social Situation*. New York: United Nations.
United Nations, 1961. *Report on the World Social Situation*. New York: United Nations.
United Nations, 1962. *Demographic Aspects of Manpower*. New York: United Nations.
United Nations, 1963a. *1963 Report on the World Social Situation*. New York: United Nations.
United Nations, 1963b. *Population Bulletin of the United Nations*, No. 6. New York: United Nations.
United Nations, 1973. *The Determinants and Consequences of Population Trends*. New York: United Nations.

United Nations, 1977. *Population Bulletin No. 8–1976*. New York: United Nations.

United Nations, 1982. *Levels and Trends of Mortality since 1950*. New York: United Nations.

United Nations, 1985. *Socio-Economic Differentials in Child Mortality in Developing Countries*. Population Study 97. New York: United Nations.

United Nations, 1991. *Child Mortality in Developing Countries*. New York: United Nations.

United Nations, 1992. *Child Mortality since the 1960s*. New York: United Nations.

United Nations, 1993. *World Population Prospects: The 1992 Revision*. New York: United Nations.

United Nations, 1995. *Demographic Indicators 1950–2050 (The 1994 Revision)*. New York: United Nations.

United Nations Department of Economic and Social Affairs, 1961. *The Mysore Population Study*. New York: United Nations.

United Nations Department of Economics and Social Affairs, 1998. *World Population Prospects: The 1998 Revision*, Vol. I, Comprehensive Tables. New York: United Nations.

United Nations Department of Economic and Social Affairs Population Division, 1998. *World Urbanization Prospects: The 1996 Revision*. New York: United Nations.

United Nations Development Program, 1995. *Human Development Report 1995*. New York: United Nations.

Vallin, J., 1991. "Mortality in Europe from 1720 to 1914: Long-Term Trends and Changes in Patterns by Age and Sex." In R. Schofield, D. Reher, and A. Bideau, eds., *The Decline of Mortality in Europe*. Oxford: Clarendon Press, 38–67.

van de Kaa, Dirk, 1999. "Europe and Its Population: The Long View." In Dirk van de Kaa, Henri Leridon, Giuseppe Gesano, and Marck Okólski, eds., *European Populations: The Long View*. Boston, MA: Kluwer, 1–49.

Van Landingham, Mark and Charles Hirschman, 2001. "Population Pressure and Fertility in Pre-transition Thailand." *Population Studies*, 55: 233–248.

Vatikiotis, P. J., 1969. *The Modern History of Egypt*. London: Weiden and Nicolson.

Veenhoven, Ruut, 1993. *Bibliography of Happiness*. Rotterdam, The Netherlands: Erasmus University.

Vogel, Morris J., 1980. *The Invention of the Modern Hospital*. Chicago: University of Chicago Press.

Wachter, Michael L., 1972. "A Labor Supply Model for Secondary Workers." *Review of Economics and Statistics* 54:141–151.

Wachter, Michael L., 1976. "The Changing Cyclical Responsiveness of Wage Inflation." *Brookings Papers on Economic Activity* 1:115–167.

Wachter, Michael L., 1977. "Intermediate Swings in Labor Force Participation." *Brookings Papers on Economic Activity* 2:545–576.

Wainright, Milton, 1990. *Miracle Cure: The Story of Penicillin and the Golden Age of Antibiotics*. Cambridge, MA: Basil Blackwell.

Ware, Helen, 1984. "Effects of Maternal Education, Women's Roles, and Child Care on Child Mortality." In W. Henry Mosley and Lincoln C. Chen, eds., *Child Survival: Strategies for Research, Population and Development Review* 10, Special Supplement, 191–214.

Warner, John Harley, 1986. *The Therapeutic Perspective: Medical Practice, Knowledge, and Identity in America, 1820–1855*. Cambridge, MA: Harvard University Press.

Warwick, Donald P., 1982. *Bitter Pills: Population Policies and Their Implementation in Eight Developing Countries*. Cambridge: Cambridge University Press.

Weiss, Mitchell G., 1988. "Cultural Models of Diarrheal Illness: Conceptual Framework and Review." *Social Science Medicine* 27:1, 5–16.

Wells, Robert V., 1971a. "Demographic Change and the Life Cycle of American Families." *Journal of Interdisciplinary History* 2 (Autumn), 273–282.

Wells, Robert V., 1971b. "Family Size and Fertility Control in Eighteenth Century America: A Study of Quaker Families." *Population Studies* 25 (March), 73–82.

Wells, Robert V., 1995. "The Mortality Transition in Schenectady, New York, 1880–1930," *Social Science History* 19:3, 399–423.

Williams, Alan, 1987. "Public Health." In John, Eatwell Murray Milgate, and Peter Newman, eds., *The New Palgrave: A Dictionary of Economics*. New York: The Stockton Press, 3, 1066–1068.

Williamson, J. G., 1964. *American Growth and the Balance of Payments, 1820–1913*. Chapel Hill, NC: University of North Carolina Press.

Williamson, Jeffrey G., 1981. "Urban Disamenities, Dark Satanic Mills, and the British Standard of Living Debate." *Journal of Economic History* XLI:1, 75–83.

Williamson, Jeffrey G., 1982. "Was the Industrial Revolution Worth It? Disamenities and Death in 19th Century British Towns." *Explorations in Economic History* 19, 221–245.

Winslow, C.-E. A., 1931. "Communicable Diseases, Control of." In E. R. A. Seligman, ed., *Encyclopaedia of the Social Sciences* Vol. IV. New York: The MacMillan Co.

Winslow, C.-E. A., 1943. *The Conquest of Epidemic Disease*. Princeton, NJ: Princeton University Press.

Winslow, C.-E. A., 1951. *The Cost of Sickness and the Price of Health*, Geneva: World Health Organization.

Wohl, Anthony S., 1983. *Endangered Lives, Public Health in Victorian Britain*. Cambridge, MA: Harvard University Press.

Wolf, Arthur P., 1986. "The Preeminent Role of Government Intervention in China's Family Revolution." *Population and Development Review* 12:1, 101–116.

Woodruff, W., 1967. *Impact of Western Man*. New York: St. Martin's Press.

Woods, Robert, 1985. "The Effects of Population Redistribution on the Level of Mortality in Nineteenth-Century England and Wales." *Journal of Economic History* XLV:3, 645–651.

Woods, R. and J. Woodward, eds., 1984. *Urban Disease and Mortality in Nineteenth-Century England*. New York: St. Martin's Press.

World Almanac and Book of Facts, 1993. New York: Newspaper Enterprise Association.

World Bank, 1980. *World Development Report*, Chap. 5. Washington, DC: World Bank.

World Bank, 1989. *Sub-Saharan Africa: From Crisis to Sustainable Growth, A Long-Term Perspective Study*. Washington, DC: World Bank.

World Bank, 1992. *World Development Report 1992: Development and the Environment*. New York: Oxford University Press.

World Bank, 1994a. *Social Indicators of Development: 1994*. Washington, DC: World Bank.

World Bank, 1994b. *World Development Report 1994: Infrastructure for Development*. Oxford: Oxford University Press.

World Bank, 1999. *World Development Report 1998/99. Knowledge for Development*. New York: Oxford University Press.

World Health Organization, 1980. *World Health Statistics 1980*. Geneva: World Health Organization.

World Health Organization, 1991. *The Public/Private Mix in National Health Systems and the Role of Ministries of Health*, Report, Hacienda Cocoyoc, State of Morelos, Mexico, July 22–26. Geneva: World Health Organization.

World Health Organization, 1992. *Global Health Situation and Projections, Estimates*. Geneva: World Health Organization, Division of Epidemiological Surveillance and Health Situation and Trend Assessment.

World Health Organization, 1994. *World Health Statistics 1993*. Geneva: World Health Organization.

Wrigley, E. A., 1969. *Population and History*. New York: McGraw-Hill.

Wrigley, E. A. and R.S. Schofield, 1981. *The Population History of England 1541–1871*. Cambridge, MA: Harvard University Press.

Yasuba, Yasukichi, 1962. *Birth Rates of the White Population in the United States, 1800–1860*. Baltimore: Johns Hopkins University Press, 70–72.

Yasuba, Yasukichi, 1987. "The Tokugawa Legacy." *Economic Studies Quarterly* 38:4 (December), 290–308.

Zabalza, A., 1979. "The Determinants of Teacher Supply," *Review of Economic Studies* XLVI :1, No. 142 (January), 131–147.

Zarkin, Gary A., 1985. "Occupational Choice: An Application to the Market for Public School Teachers." *The Quarterly Journal of Economics* C:2 (March), 409–446.

Index

Bold-Face Indicates Tables or Figures